Global Britain and Neo-colonialism in Africa

"In this book, Africa's development is the subject matter once again and the usual suspect, Great Britain, is unashamedly at the centre of it again. With an exceptionally in-depth examination of key geopolitical issues such as trade, aid, development finance and security, Langan uncovers how the same old colonial interventions and political rhetoric with racist undertones are being refashioned to perpetuate an emergent Empire 2.0. The usage of Nkrumah's critique of global coloniality particularly elevates the theoretical and material relevance of the book beyond the UK and Brexit. It is a must read for anyone seeking a critical understanding of the continuities of the colonial machinery that perpetuates plunder, exploitation and domination through trade deals and economic partnerships masquerading as 'fair', 'pro-poor' or 'mutually beneficial'."

—Dr Nathan Andrews, *McMaster University*

"This book is an exceptional intellectual contribution to the political economy of UK-Africa relations. Through the lens of neo-colonialism and global coloniality, the text revitalises the conventional debates on the logic of the UK's interests in Africa, amidst the reality of Brexit and the resurgence of the 'new scramble' for Africa. Mark Langan interrogates the 'celebrated' conversations around Global Britain and British exceptionalism and locates these within the context of contemporary Africa-UK relations."

—Adeoye O. Akinola, *Head of Research and Teaching, Institute for Pan-African Thought and Conversation, University of Johannesburg, South Africa*

"Mark Langan offers a powerful critique of post-Brexit Britain's trade relations with African nations. It sheds light on the neo-colonial nature of these of relations, but also highlights the ability of Africans to resist the 'Global Britain' project. Whether you're a scholar, policymaker or concerned global citizen, this book is an essential reading for understanding Britain's contemporary interactions with Africa."

—Mehdi Boussebaa, *Professor of International Business, University of Glasgow, and Co-Editor-in-Chief of Critical Perspectives on International Business*

Mark Langan

Global Britain and Neo-colonialism in Africa

Brexit, 'Development' and Coloniality

Mark Langan
King's College London
London, UK

ISBN 978-3-031-42481-6   ISBN 978-3-031-42482-3 (eBook)
https://doi.org/10.1007/978-3-031-42482-3

© The Editor(s) (if applicable) and The Author(s), under exclusive license to Springer Nature Switzerland AG 2023

This work is subject to copyright. All rights are solely and exclusively licensed by the Publisher, whether the whole or part of the material is concerned, specifically the rights of translation, reprinting, reuse of illustrations, recitation, broadcasting, reproduction on microfilms or in any other physical way, and transmission or information storage and retrieval, electronic adaptation, computer software, or by similar or dissimilar methodology now known or hereafter developed.
The use of general descriptive names, registered names, trademarks, service marks, etc. in this publication does not imply, even in the absence of a specific statement, that such names are exempt from the relevant protective laws and regulations and therefore free for general use.
The publisher, the authors, and the editors are safe to assume that the advice and information in this book are believed to be true and accurate at the date of publication. Neither the publisher nor the authors or the editors give a warranty, expressed or implied, with respect to the material contained herein or for any errors or omissions that may have been made. The publisher remains neutral with regard to jurisdictional claims in published maps and institutional affiliations.

This Palgrave Macmillan imprint is published by the registered company Springer Nature Switzerland AG
The registered company address is: Gewerbestrasse 11, 6330 Cham, Switzerland

Paper in this product is recyclable.

For Luis Filipe Lopes Costa

Acknowledgements

Special thanks to Luis Costa and to my parents, Michelle and Charles Langan, for your encouragement and support. Thank you also to Katharine Wright, Nuno Costa, Antonio Costa, Richard Neilson, Jamie Ellis and John Narayan.

Contents

1 Global Britain and 'Empire 2.0' in Africa: Critical Perspectives on UK Imperial Impulses — 1
2 Africa and the Commonwealth: UK Imperial Imaginaries — 31
3 Global Britain and Africa-UK Trade Relations — 61
4 Global Britain and UK Aid Policy Towards Africa — 93
5 Global Britain and Development Finance in Africa — 123
6 UK Corporate Interests and Neo-colonialism in Africa — 155
7 UK Security Interests and Neo-colonialism in Africa — 189
8 Contesting Global Britain: Considering African Agency — 223

Index — 247

Acronyms

AAAP	Africa Adaptation Acceleration Programme
ACP	African, Caribbean and Pacific
AfCFTA	African Continental Free Trade Area
AfDB	African Development Bank
AfT	Aid for Trade
AGOA	African Growth and Opportunity Act
AJTPZ	Jeunes Tchadiens de la Zone Petroliere
ANC	African National Congress
ATPU	Anti-Terrorism Police Unit
ATT	Arms Trade Treaty
AU	African Union
BATUK	British Army Training Unit Kenya
BII	British International Investment
BP	British Petroleum
BRI	Belt and Road Initiative
CAAT	Campaign Against the Arms Trade
CAP	Common Agricultural Policy
CARIFORUM	Caribbean Forum
CBC	Commonwealth Business Council
CDC	Commonwealth Development Corporation
CHOGM	Commonwealth Heads of Government Meeting
CSR	Corporate Social Responsibility
DAC	Development Assistance Committee
DBT	Department for Business and Trade
DCFTAs	Deep and Comprehensive Free Trade Agreement
DCTS	Developing Countries Trading Scheme

DDA	Doha Development Round
DFI	Development Finance Institution
DfID	Department for International Development
DFQF	Duty Free and Quota Free
DG	Directorate General
DIT	Department for International Trade
DRC	Democratic Republic of the Congo
EAW	European Arrest Warrant
EBA	Everything But Arms
ECB	European Central Bank
ECOWAS	Economic Community of West African States
EDF	European Development Fund
EEC	European Economic Community
EIAs	Environmental Impact Assessments
EIB	European Investment Bank
EMFTA	Euro-Mediterranean Free Trade Area
ENP	European Neighbourhood Policy
EPAs	Economic Partnership Agreements
ESA	Eastern and Southern Africa
ESG	Economic, Social and Governance
EU	European Union
FCDO	Foreign, Commonwealth and Development Office
FCO	Foreign and Commonwealth Office
FDI	Foreign Direct Investment
FRN	Federal Republic of Nigeria
FTAs	Free Trade Agreements
G2G	Government-to-Government
GATT	General Agreement on Tariffs and Trade
GFC	Global Financial Crisis
GNI	Gross National Income
GNP	Gross National Product
GSP	Generalised Scheme of Preferences
HIPC	Highly Indebted Poor Countries Initiative
HLPPs	High Level Prosperity Partnerships
ICAI	Independent Commission for Aid Impact
ICC	International Criminal Court
ICF	Investment Climate Facility
IDC	International Development Committee
IFC	International Finance Corporation
IMF	International Monetary Fund
IOCs	International Oil Companies
IRDC	International Relations and Defence Committee
ITC	International Trade Committee

LDCs	Least Developed Countries
LNG	Liquid Natural Gas
MDGs	Millennium Development Goals
MEP	Member of the European Parliament
MNCs	Multinational Corporations
NAFSN	New Alliance for Food Security and Nutrition
NAFTA	North Atlantic Free Trade Agreement
NAO	National Audit Office
NATO	North Atlantic Treaty Organisation
NCA	National Crime Agency
NCP	National Contact Point
NDICI	Neighbourhood Development and International Cooperation
NEPAD	New Partnership for African Development
NGOs	Non-Governmental Organisations
NHS	National Health Service
NTC	National Transitional Council
ODA	Official Development Assistance
OECD	Organisation for Economic Co-operation and Development's
PF	Patriotic Front
PILC	Public Interest Law Centre
PMCs	Private Military Companies
PNRD	Passenger Named Records Database
PP	Prosperity Party
PSA	Production Sharing Agreement
PSD	Private Sector Development
RAID	Rights and Accountability in Development
RECs	Regional Economic Communities
SACU	Southern African Customs Union
SACUM	Southern African Customs Union plus Mozambique
SAGCOT	Southern Agricultural Growth Corridor
SAPs	Structural Adjustment Programmes
SARS	Special Anti-Robbery Squad
SDGs	Sustainable Development Goals
SFO	Serious Fraud Office
TPA	Trade Partnership Agreement
TPLF	Tigray People's Liberation Front
UDI	Unilateral Declaration of Independence
UK	United Kingdom
UK-AIS	UK-African Investment Summit
UKEF	UK Export Finance
UKGT	UK Global Tariff
UKIP	UK Independence Party
UN	United Nations

UNGC	United Nations Global Compact
UNHCR	UN High Commissioner for Refugees
UPND	United Party for National Development
USA	United States of America
WMD	Weapons of Mass Destruction
WPS	Women, Peace and Security
WTO	World Trade Organisation
WW2	World War Two

CHAPTER 1

Global Britain and 'Empire 2.0' in Africa: Critical Perspectives on UK Imperial Impulses

Introduction

The United Kingdom's (UK) decision to leave the European Union (EU) in 2016 has been heralded as Britain's launch of 'Empire 2.0' in Africa. Adopting this term, UK civil servants disparaged the imperial nostalgia of the government in its attempts to realise a 'Global Britain' project based upon the deepening of Commonwealth linkages with Africa (Leroux, 2017). Meanwhile, the UK's pursuit of enhanced global influence in African countries in the Brexit era has also been viewed as part of a 'new scramble' for the continent's resources amid geopolitical competition with the EU, China, Russia and other global actors (Mailafia, 2020). Interestingly in terms of EU fragmentation, however, the creation of the European Economic Community (EEC) in 1957 was met with scepticism by African leaderships. They feared that the pan-European project would amount to a form of collective colonialism. Kwame Nkrumah (1965), the first President of Ghana, was particularly concerned about the implications of the European supranational endeavour for African liberation struggles. Nkrumah feared that the coming together of the European powers—including colonial states such as France and Belgium—would enable the EEC to stall independence movements via the 'Association' of African economies to the newly established European common market (cited in Obeng, 1979a: 51). Or else, upon the achievement of independence, African states would be subjected to forms of EEC neo-colonialism that

© The Author(s), under exclusive license to Springer Nature Switzerland AG 2023
M. Langan, *Global Britain and Neo-colonialism in Africa*, https://doi.org/10.1007/978-3-031-42482-3_1

would suffocate sovereignty and herald what Tanzania's Nyerere labelled an era of 'flag-independence' only (cited in Mwakikagile, 2010: 269).

Brexit and the launch of a 'Global Britain' project by UK politicians are thus interesting to consider in terms of the imperial legacy. The referendum result was analysed within both British and foreign media as a symptom of imperial romanticism combined to working-class disenfranchisement—as well as UK elites' recourse to populism (Saunders, 2020). This has been accompanied by a scholarly literature that assesses the contours of the Brexit result in terms of a British 'postcolonial melancholia', imperial nostalgia following World War Two (WW2) and juridical decolonisation (Calhoun, 2017; Koegler et al., 2020; Narayan & Sealey-Huggins, 2017; Thackeray & Toye, 2019; Tronicke, 2020). As part of this imperial hangover, Brexiteer political elites are understood to have viewed UK acquiescence to the demands of the EU Commission as the ultimate humiliation amid the former's shrinking global status (McLeod, 2020: 610). Brexit thus sought to reassert British exceptionalism and 'grandeur' on the world stage. Meanwhile, scholars have also assessed the referendum result in terms of rising forms of exclusionary nationalism that fuel anti-immigration sentiment within post-industrial towns in England (McLeod, 2020; Wellings, 2021). This literature draws attention to exclusionary forms of English nationalism and how a 'Take Back Control' rhetoric deployed by Leave campaigners appealed to a sense of disenfranchisement and a lost sense of community in English towns and rural locales. Calhoun (2017) provides some convincing assessment in this vein, pointing to a regressive form of English populism that simultaneously denigrated London, multiculturalism and (neoliberal) globalisation.

Interestingly, however, Saunders (2020) claims that the legacy of Empire not only shaped the discourse of Brexiteer politicians and Brexit itself but, crucially, also infused the worldviews of UK elites who wished to remain within the European project—notably politicians associated with New Labour. While Brexiteer discourse surrounding the need for the UK to forge a global future outside of the EU as part of 'Global Britain' did draw upon the colonial lineages of British Empire, so too, Saunders argues (2020), did Remainer discourse about Britain finding a global leadership role at the heart of the European enterprise. Saunders (2020) states here that the desire of elites including Tony Blair and Gordon Brown to 'lead Europe' had an imperial pedigree. In this sense, certain Remain politicians wished to regain British global influence by participating in, and spearheading, the 'collective colonialism' of the European project (c.f.

Nkrumah, 1965). The shadow of the British Empire, in this reading, falls not only upon the Leave camp but also upon the Remain coalition. And when considering the foreign policy legacy of the Blair premiership, it is difficult to deny the imperial logic at the heart of New Labour's vision of British leadership within the EU. Note Blair's attempt to gain French and German approval for the illegal invasion of Iraq in 2003 (Serfarty, 2008). Or the record of New Labour architect, Peter Mandelson, during his time as the EU Commissioner for Trade—and his vigorous pursuit of unfair EU free trade deals in Africa (Goodison, 2005; Hurt et al., 2013). In relation to both episodes, the argument levied by Saunders (2020) gains credence.

Accordingly, this text examines the imperial logic of Brexit in terms of competing (neo)colonialisms between the UK and the EU (amid other actors) as part of the 'new scramble' for the continent (Carmody, 2016). It assesses Westminster elites' Global Britain project—focused on gaining prosperity and geopolitical influence on the world stage—by examining their engagement with African states. In this task, it engages Nkrumah (1965) on neo-colonialism, as well as more recent decolonial scholarship focused upon the critique of global coloniality (Fakasin, 2021; Grosfoguel, 2002; Mignolo, 2007; Ndlovu-Gatsheni, 2014, 2015; Quijano, 2000, 2007). It concurs with Nkrumah that the European project has pursued a form of neo-colonial relations with African countries since 1957. Nevertheless, it examines the UK's decision to Leave the EU in terms of a narcissistic British exceptionalism (Buettner, 2019; Koegler et al., 2020). In this discussion, the book draws attention to an exclusionary form of English nationalism that denigrates racialised minorities at home, while seeking to dominate and exploit former British colonies abroad (Gilroy, 2004). It also draws attention to how Brexiteer populism and ethnic nationalism find political parallels within the EU member states. It finds that imperial impulses drive forward the foreign policies of UK and EU elites as politicians seek to satiate domestic populations' desire for access to cheap commodities, lucrative markets and the 'recovery' of a perceived lost global influence through interventions in Africa.

The first half of the book is structured as follows. This first chapter explores critical perspectives on Brexit and the imperial impulses behind the British decision to leave the EU. It engages the scholarship that points to nostalgia for Empire and an English imperial romanticism that fuelled the Leave campaign. It notes debates surrounding the EU's own imperial lineage and the complicity of New Labour figures therein. Thereafter, it highlights the ongoing utility of Nkrumah's (1965) concept of neo-colonialism for making sense of UK and EU diplomatic and economic policies towards African countries. It does this in the context of an influential decolonial scholarship on global coloniality, especially the seminal contributions of Ndlovu-Gatsheni (2015) on coloniality within Africa. Chapter 2 reflects on the history of UK relations with Africa since juridical decolonisation, with a focus on the discourse of 'the Commonwealth'. It explores UK elites' appeals to the Commonwealth in terms of their own ontological security and in terms of satiating domestic desire for global relevance. It also highlights Brexiteer pledges that a decision to leave the EU would have positive consequences in terms of fairer trade and aid linkages to Commonwealth countries in Africa. Chapter 3 assesses the pursuit of 'Global Britain' through the UK's trade with African countries. It highlights the UK's historical role within the EU in pushing for liberalised free trade deals with the African continent. It explains how 'cut and paste' Brexit deals have since followed the parameters of the EU's own Economic Partnership Agreements (EPA Monitoring, 2018). Britain is seen to be in (neo)colonial competition with the EU-27 for access to lucrative African markets via such trade deals. Chapter 4 examines UK aid-giving to African states in the Brexit era. It provides historical context by exploring New Labour attempts to brand the UK as an ethical actor in Africa and to project soft power influence in the continent via the Department for International Development (DfID). It then explores the current usages of UK aid in the pursuit of Brexit trade deals, the pursuit of UK commercial advantage via 'Aid for Trade' and populist appeals against migration.

The second half of the book continues this interrogation of British neo-colonialism in Africa. Chapter 5 examines the role of UK development finance in Africa. It explores the activities of the Commonwealth Development Corporation (CDC)—now renamed British International Investment (BII)—and how this body's role has been reinterpreted in relation to a Global Britain strategy. The activities of CDC/BII are understood in terms of UK competition (and possibly in collaboration) with the EU's Global Gateway scheme, and with China's Belt and Road Initiative (BRI), for African resources. Chapter 6 assesses Britain's corporate interests in the continent in relation to oil, minerals and land. It explores how the Global Britain project impacts their pursuit, notably in terms of the enhanced role of UK Export Finance (UKEF). It juxtaposes the propoor private sector development (PSD) language of UK politicians with the material consequences of UK investments in terms of alleged human rights violations and environmental degradation. Chapter 7 examines the UK's security interests in Africa, with emphasis upon UK elites' securitisation of migration, as well as British sale of arms to African governments with dubious human rights records. Chapter 8 concludes the book by reflecting on the utility of the concept of neo-colonialism in conjunction with recent work on global coloniality. It reflects on how African civil society groups and governments can contest 'Global Britain'. Namely that they can capitalise on the fragility of the British state and contest its interventions in the continent.

Brexit and Imperial Impulses at the Heart of 'Global Britain'

The UK's decision to leave the EU has been the subject of intense debate and interpretation since 2016. A combination of public dissatisfaction with domestic issues including austerity politics and migration—alongside a desire to radically reshape UK external affairs, notably the relationship with Brussels and the Commonwealth—assisted the victory of Brexiteer elites. Accordingly, there has been an influential scholarship assessing how a regressive brand of right-wing populism impacted upon the decision of predominantly English voters to leave the European project (Calhoun, 2017). This has been examined in terms of a British, or more accurately, an English nationalism that denigrates racialised minorities at home, while seeking to recover a lost sense of imperial grandeur abroad—with a predatory eye towards nations once subjugated under British Empire (Saunders, 2020). Perhaps most memorably here, Westminster civil servants labelled Brexiteer ministers' Global Britain strategy as an imperial adventure under the moniker Empire 2.0. With this term, civil servants both ridiculed the UK government's emphasis upon non-European markets for salvaging British prosperity in the economic aftermath of Brexit, while raising alarm as to the potentially exploitative nature of UK policy in the 'Global South' (Narayan & Sealey-Huggins, 2017; Thackeray & Thorpe, 2019).

Moreover, there has been scholarly focus on the psychological and discursive legacies of Empire upon British political imaginaries in relation to both Europe and the Commonwealth—and how these shaped the decision to exit the EU. For instance, Bhambra (2017) assesses how anti-immigration sentiments and resentment towards racialised minorities are rooted in imperial legacies. She notes that populist appeals against immigration during the referendum had an imperial pedigree:

> The rancour that marks the Brexit debate seems to stem more from the loss of this privileged position [of Empire], based as it is on white elites and a working class offered the opportunity to see themselves as better than the darker subjects of empire – hierarchies of class and caste if you will, embodied in the hierarchies of race. Austerity has simply provided the fertile ground for its re-emergence and expression. (2017: 92)

Her interpretation is corroborated by a series of authors. Koegler et al. (2020), for instance, explain the referendum outcome in terms of a colonial nostalgia combined to a form of narcissistic victimhood articulated by Brexiteer elites against the EU and migrants. They explain that this is a similar pattern to right-wing populism in other European societies in which the coloniser presents itself as the victim. Wellings (2021), meanwhile, points to the imperial nostalgia articulated by political figures such as former Prime Minister Boris Johnson in relation to the Brexit vote. This is also explored by Buettner (2019: 53) who points to certain commonalities—but also certain departures—in terms of British imperial nostalgia from its continental counterparts in EU member states themselves:

> Imperial legacies… are far from an exclusively British phenomenon, being irrevocably woven into the fabric of many of the EU's 'small nations' whose global histories greatly exceed their current confines. Where Britain is unique in post-colonial Europe is in the way common perceptions of its imperial past have fed political fantasies of global alternatives to continental associations to the extent that they have become construed as incompatible with European loyalties.

With echoes of Nkrumah (1965), certain EU member states are seen to pursue their (neo)colonial agendas through the functions of the supranational European project in terms of a collective colonialism. A narcissistic British exceptionalism, however, propels Brexiteer elites on the right of the Conservative Party (and beyond) to seek to exert global influence alone. Macejka (2021) and Drayton (cited in Ascherson, 2019) describe Brexiteers as viewing Britain as an 'exceptional nation' and explain their use of 'Global Britain' as a 'providential idea'. Ascherson (2019), meanwhile, explains UK elites' worldview in terms of an English romanticism towards Empire which he contrasts with a form of denialism in Scotland. Scottish voters sought to remain within the EU in 2016, while Scottish nationalism has sometimes sought to represent the guilt of the imperial past as belonging to England alone. A left-of-centre Scottish nationalism in this sense has forged a pro-European identity while downplaying, or attributing to England, the imperial past. Virdee and McGeever (2018) also draw distinctions between English and Scottish nationalisms. They view the English variety as often building upon white working-class resentment towards racialised minorities, owing in large part to the defeat of more progressive forms of solidarity in England in the 1980s under Prime Minister Margaret Thatcher. Related to this, they make clear that the concept of Global Britain now pursued by Brexiteer politicians is inevitably linked to 'Empire 1.0', in terms of the imaginaries of Westminster elites.

Perhaps most interestingly, however, Saunders (2020: 1143) has argued that it is inaccurate to depict Brexiteer politicians as being uniquely influenced by 'imperial modes of thought'. He points to how Remainer politicians, largely those associated with the New Labour project, sought British global power via leadership of European institutions. He argues that their ambition to utilise the EU to project global influence also had an 'imperial pedigree'. And he notes the appeals of Gordon Brown during the 2016 referendum to the need for the UK's leadership of Europe. Moreover, New Labour's external agenda in the 2000s corroborates much of Saunders' (2020) analysis. Tony Blair as Prime Minister invoked the need for Britain to project global influence through leadership within the European project (Kassim, 2008). Blair's aggressive foreign policy towards Iraq, for example, was accompanied by his attempts to win European support for the 'coalition of the willing'. Rallying eastern and central European states to the UK and US position on Iraq caused a fault-line within Europe, with President Jacques Chirac of France reportedly telling then EU candidate countries that they had 'missed an opportunity to shut up' on the Iraq question (Smith, 2003).

In keeping with Saunders' (2020) critique, UK power projection also found resonance in the New Labour years in terms of Peter Mandelson's position as the EU Commissioner for Trade. Mandelson was accused of shouting 'neo-colonial style' at African officials amid their reluctance to acquiesce to EU free trade deals—Economic Partnership Agreements

(EPAs) (Monbiot, 2008). Seeking to project British commercial interests in Africa—and that of the wider EU as part of what Nkrumah defined as collective colonialism—Mandelson acted according to a (neo)colonial trade agenda (Langan, 2018). Saunders' claims also appear valid in the case of Conservative Remainers such as David Cameron. Cameron, who paved the path to Brexit, followed Blair's example—rallying European allies within the North Atlantic Treaty Organisation (NATO) to launch regime change in Libya (Weir, 2011). Saunders' (2020) emphasis upon Remainer politicians as having also been impacted by 'imperial modes of thought' therefore finds much credence in an evaluation of the pathologies of New Labour—and of the outlook of Conservative Remainers such as David Cameron.

Related to New Labour politicians' pursuit of British 'grandeur' via EU institutions, recent remarks by President Emmanuel Macron of France and the EU's High Representative for Foreign Affairs, Josep Borrell, also betray an imperial logic within the European project itself. Macron derided calls for an African Marshall Plan on the basis that such an economic package would be insufficient for poverty reduction given that Africans allegedly suffered from what he defined as 'a civilisational problem' (Narayan & Sealey-Huggins, 2017). Macron blamed Africans for having 'seven or eight children' for the failures of 'development'. This correlates to what decolonial scholar, Grosfoguel (2002: 213), has identified as the 'new racism':

> The new racism contends that the failure of colonial/ized groups is not due to inferior genes or inferior IQ (although is still a pervasive and popular perception) but rather to cultural habits and/or an inferior culture. This emphasis on culture over genes is what characterized the new cultural racisms dividing the world between groups with a superior culture and an inferior or inadequate culture. This new racism has been legitimized by academic approaches that portray the high poverty among people of color both in the core and in the periphery in terms of their traditional, inadequate, underdeveloped, and cultural values.

Racist imaginaries continue to pervade the upper echelons of the EU member states. Even in the case of Macron—a self-styled progressive politician—racialised portrays of African citizenries are apparently deemed legitimate in discussions of 'development'. In the French Parliament, meanwhile, a member of the far-right National Rally interrupted the speech of a black parliamentarian by shouting 'go back to Africa' (Francis & Noack, 2022). Racialaised discourse at the heart of Europe was further underscored by High Representative Josep Borrell who explained that Europe was a well-cultivated 'garden' endangered by the surrounding 'jungle'. He called upon European 'gardeners' to go out into the 'jungle' to cultivate it, and to prevent it from overcoming the walls of Europe (Bishara, 2022). Despite outcries that his language had explicitly racist overtones in the context of debates surrounding migration, Borrell insisted that his remarks had been misinterpreted. It is clear, therefore, that had Britain voted to remain within the EU, then the influence of Empire would not have dissipated in terms of British politics. Rather the imperial impulses at the heart, the British establishment would have found expression in joint enterprise within a collective European (neo)colonialism, as predicted by Nkrumah.

This is not to say, however, that the imperial impulses within Brexiteer and Remainer discourse are identical within the British polity. As noted earlier, the Brexiteer discourse of Britain going 'global' outside of the EU has been married to regressive nationalist sentiment mobilised against racialised ethnic minorities at home. While it is true that Remainer centrist politicians have demonstrated an imperial ethos in their expression of the need for the UK to lead Europe, nevertheless, they largely have not engaged in such sustained and vociferous racist rhetoric within UK domestic politics. Nevertheless, there are exceptions here—notably the then Home Secretary Theresa May's notorious 'Go Home' vans in 2013 amid the unfolding Windrush Scandal (Grayson, 2013). Brexiteer politicians, however, have more regularly engaged in highly racialised language in their approach to UK domestic politics. Perhaps most notably, former Prime Minister Johnson had been heavily criticised for his racialised mockery of veiled Muslim women in the UK (The New Statesman, 2019). His racialised mockery of black Commonwealth citizens also drew heavy criticism (Forrest, 2019).

Interestingly here, there has been recent debate with the appointment of Rishi Sunak to the office of Prime Minister that the Conservative Party—and perhaps the UK itself—has reached a post-racial phase (Thakur, 2022). The fact that leading Conservatives from ethnic minority backgrounds supported Brexit (such as Suella Braverman and Priti Patel) is also seen as a balm against negative images of the Conservative Party and of the Brexit project (cf. Alexander-Collier, 2021). The claim to have reached a post-racial politics within the Conservative Party, however, has been widely discredited by an array of academic and media commentators (see for instance Andrews, 2022; Deshpande, 2022; Mishra, 2022; Rima et al., 2023; Suroor, 2022). These authors point to how ethnic minority elites in the Conservative Party pursue domestic policy agendas that disproportionately victimise ethnic minority working-class families and migrants. Accordingly, the Conservative Party is seen to have co-opted certain elite politicians from ethnic minority communities on the understanding that these individuals then articulate and implement racialised policy agendas. Outcry at the populist language of the then Home Secretary, Suella Braverman, in her depiction of a migrant 'invasion' of Britain—and her failure to apologise to a Holocaust survivor for engaging in dangerous discourse—is but one example of how ethnic minority political elites at the heart of the UK establishment do not necessarily mitigate against white supremacism or ethnic nationalism (Hubbard, 2022; Salter, 2023). On the contrary, some such politicians may feed into a dangerous form of exclusionary English nationalism for party-political success and personal career advancement. This is evidenced by the rhetoric of Suella Braverman amid her policy desire to send 'illegal' refugees and human trafficking victims from the UK to Rwanda as part of a highly controversial migration deal (Rankin, 2023).

The Brexit project's combination of its 'going global' discourse to ethnic nationalism at home bodes ill for countries in the Commonwealth and the wider 'Global South'. This negative outlook not only holds true in the current situation of a Conservative government dominated by Brexiteer politicians. But it holds equally true in the eventuality of a (New) Labour government under Sir Keir Starmer. The Leader of the Opposition has actively co-opted the rhetoric of the Brexit campaign in relation to being tough on migration and 'taking back control' (Hayward, 2023; Stacey & Crerar, 2023). Starmer has also spoken of the need to enhance Britain's influence overseas, endorsing the ideal of Global Britain (Hansard, 2020). His Labour Party (2023) insists that 'as we leave the European Union, keeping Britain global is one of our country's most urgent tasks'. The imperial prerogative of New Labour under Tony Blair is well and present within the Starmer shadow cabinet. In this context, it is necessary to now consider conceptual frameworks that can interrogate UK involvement in Africa and unpack the implications of the Global Britain project for African citizenries. Accordingly, the chapter turns to an assessment of the resonance of Nkrumah's writings—and his political speeches—on neo-colonialism. It also engages more recent decolonial scholarship that critiques global coloniality in terms of 'North–South' power asymmetries.

Nkrumah, Neo-Colonialism and Global Coloniality

Nkrumah's writings and speeches on neo-colonialism remain key resources for making sense of problems facing legally independent African countries in an international realm marked by 'North–South' power asymmetries and foreign interventions. Confronted by the realities of the Cold War in the 1960s—and the desire of European nations to maintain their 'sphere of influence' in Africa—Nkrumah (1965) warned that the attainment of legal independence and statehood would not in of and itself secure well-being in African societies. In his seminal texts *'Africa Must Unite'* (1963) and *'Neo-Colonialism: The Last Stage of Imperialism'* (1965)—explored in detail in Langan (2018)—Nkrumah laid out his premise regarding the economic and political dominance of Western nations over newly independent African states. He warned that European governments would seek to maintain colonial forms of trade and economic exploitation in relation to the African continent. To achieve such aims, European states would utilise aid monies to subvert African politicians and to make them dependent upon their benefactors (Nkrumah, 1965: ix, xv). This would breed African officials' acquiescence to the preferences of European aid-givers, not least in terms of the signing of unequal trade pacts that would allow Europeans unfettered access to African markets while closing down opportunities for domestic diversification away from colonial import/export models (Nkrumah, 1963: 182–183). Nkrumah also warned that—in addition to aid—foreign powers would engage in military support to regimes that acquiesced to foreign interests. Foreign entities, meanwhile, would destabilise and demonise African leaderships that sought to gain a truer measure of economic and political sovereignty (Nkrumah, 1965: xi). Nkrumah himself was overthrown in a coup d'etat supported by the United States of America (USA) in the aftermath of the publication of his 1965 treatise condemning Euro-American elites' power projection and neo-colonialism (Botwe-Asamoah, 2005: 173).

To overcome neo-colonialism—the situation in which African states enjoyed a form of legal independence but remained politically and economically subordinate to external/Western governments—Nkrumah

(1963: 170) advocated for the immediate unification of the African continent within a pan-African federal model. He argued that isolated individual African states—or even limited regional formations in Western/Eastern Africa—would be unable to guard against foreign predations. Only with the economies of scale made possible by continental union, would a united Africa be able to industrialise and diversify away from colonial patterns of dependency (ibid). Certain forms of foreign investment would be welcomed in this endeavour of building a common African market, but only if subdued and directed within economic plans authored by an African executive (Nkrumah, 1965: 9). Foreign aid, meanwhile, would eventually become redundant as a united Africa enjoyed the fruits of growth and industrialisation that economies of scale within a federal union had enabled (*ibid*). In this context, Nkrumah viewed with great suspicion the efforts of European politicians such as Charles de Gaulle in promoting limited regionalisms that would act as barriers to continental unity (cited in Obeng, 1979a: 210). Moreover, he viewed the endeavour of the EEC to forge a trade and aid 'Association' agreement with former colonies as an attempt to perpetuate dependency, and to divide and rule African countries. He saw that Associated African countries would enjoy preferential tariff access to Europe, while non-Associated countries that sought to mitigate against European economic and political influence would be discriminated against via high tariff walls (Nkrumah, 1965: 19). Nkrumah in this vein condemned what he perceived as the collective colonialism of the European project and noted that Europeans themselves sought to unite on a continental basis while cynically denying the same political logic to the African situation (cited in Obeng, 1979a: 51–53).

Nkrumah's work retains currency and resonates with current realities facing African societies. His intellectual contribution sits comfortably with an increasingly influential decolonial scholarship that has sought to understand and assess the impact of 'global coloniality' upon Africa and the wider 'Global South'. This decolonial literature—in large part deriving from Latin American scholarship—has sought to understand how colonialism shaped the emergence of the modern capitalist world system dating back to the sixteenth century and the era of the European 'discoveries'. It emphasises that the racial, political, economic and epistemic hierarchies that were established during colonialism did not simply disappear when countries in Africa, Asia and Latin America gained a legal form of independence (Patnaik and Patnaik, 2015). Instead, multiple hierarchies and inequalities remained intact as part of what decolonial scholars refer to as the condition of coloniality/modernity—and as the situation currently facing nations in the Global South known as 'global coloniality' (ibid).

The concept of global coloniality in an African context is best explained by Ndlovu-Gatsheni (2014, 2015) through his engagement with the seminal works of key scholars within the decolonial field, notably Quijano (2000), Grosfoguel (2002) and Mignolo (2007). Ndlovu-Gatsheni (2013, 2014, 2015, 2021) explains that there are three core elements or 'matrices of power' comprising global coloniality as a system of domination and exploitation confronting countries in Africa. First, there is the 'coloniality of power'—which in Ndolvu-Gatsheni's (2014: 190) own formulation largely refers to the material power structures and institutions which promote Western hegemony over countries in Africa, Asia and Latin America. This includes the Bretton Woods institutions such as the International Monetary Fund (IMF), World Bank and World Trade Organisation (WTO). The coloniality of power involves these institutions' promotion of global free markets and (neo)liberal policy prescriptions antithetical to African economic sovereignty. It also includes donor-recipient relations and the usages of material aid monies in the swaying of local officials towards Western economic and political interests.

Second, Ndlovu-Gatsheni (2014: 199) points to the 'coloniality of knowledge' in which the West continues to insist upon its epistemic supremacy and to devalue alternative cultures and knowledge systems emanating from Africa and the wider 'Global South'. This, as the term suggests, builds upon the legacy of colonial administration and the ways in which colonial regimes appropriated certain forms of knowledge (e.g. mining and agricultural techniques). Simultaneously, the colonisers promoted so-called European 'civilisation' as the antidote to what they derided as 'primitive, barbaric and descriptive' African knowledge systems (Afolambi, 2020: 97). Drawing upon de Sousa Santos, Ndolvu-Gatsheni (2021: 52) explains that the West built what the former terms a 'cognitive empire'—which continues to this day in the way that Western ideologies dominate citizenries' mindsets in the 'Global South'. Such Eurocentrism is deemed detrimental to the formation of alternative epistemologies deriving from local culture and lived experiences within the African continent. In this sense, contemporary forms of Western-led globalisation can be seen to anchor the 'coloniality of knowledge' (Chimakonam & Enyimba, 2022: 2).

Third, Ndlovu-Gatsheni (2013: 10) identifies the 'coloniality of being' as the final element of the triangular matrixes of power that constitute global coloniality. This third concept refers to the racialisation of groups in relation to the racial hierarchies constructed by Europeans during the period of formal colonialism. These colonial hierarchies rendered subjugated peoples as 'inferior races', which continues to form the basis for white supremacism as it is expressed today. As Grosfoguel (2002: 213) notes, today there is also a 'new racism' that focuses on perceived cultural dissimilarities between white populations and 'people of colour'. This new racism, nevertheless, similarly draws upon colonial lineages and the racialised dichotomies (for instance, civilisation/barbarism) imagined and articulated by colonial administrations. Global coloniality—comprised of these three forms (coloniality of power, knowledge and being)—persists in a manner that demonstrates the ongoing legacies of Empire even beyond the moment of the juridical 'decolonisation' that took place after WW2.

Ndlovu-Gatsheni's (2015) triangular focus on the coloniality of (i) power, (ii) knowledge and (iii) being bears some parallels to Robert Cox's (1981) critical political economy assessment of Western hegemony within the international realm. Cox's formulation, drawing upon Antonio Gramsci's conception of hegemony as involving both consent and coercion, focused upon the triangular combination of (i) institutions, (ii) ideas and (iii) material resources in cementing Western dominance. Cox argued that Pax Britannica and Pax Americana—and the respective hegemony of the British Empire and USA—could be understood in terms of these three ingredients of power. He explains that the British Empire exerted its dominance on the international stage not only in terms of gunship diplomacy or economic coercion (material resources) but relied upon ideas (of civilisation, Christianity) and institutions (monarchy, navy, parliament) in the imposition of imperial rule. Ideas became key to the longevity and durability of British Empire as elites within the colonies began to psychologically and culturally affiliate themselves to Britain. Salem (2021), meanwhile, has written convincingly of the compatibility of Gramscian insights to a decolonial approach that seeks to liberate societies of the 'Global South' from the 'common sense' of Western knowledge constructs.

Interestingly here, the focus upon ideational power in the exercise of Empire has a long lineage associated with the history of anti-colonial struggles themselves. In relation to debates surrounding the ideational traction of Empire, Frantz Fanon ( ]) in his seminal contribution *The Wretched of the Earth* deconstructed the cultural hegemony cultivated by the colonial powers and the ways in which elite groups within the colonies were subjected to a false consciousness in which they sought to emulate the alleged 'superior' culture of the metropole. Colonial governance in Fanon's understanding was not only made possible by colonial police forces and colonial armies, but also through the cultural and psychological dominance of the coloniser. Similarly, Aimé Césaire (2000, 1950]) explored Western colonisers 'thingification' of the peoples they oppressed in Africa and beyond. Reflecting on the legacies of colonial experiences, he lamented the

> societies drained of their essence, cultures trampled underfoot, institutions undermined, lands confiscated, religions smashed, magnificent artistic creations destroyed, extraordinary possibilities wiped out. They throw facts at my head, statistics, mileages of roads, canals, and railroad tracks.

Nkrumah also reflected on the psychological aspects of colonialism and encouraged the recovery of an African personhood via 'consciencism' in its aftermath (Botwe-Asamoah, 2005: 9).

A focus upon ideational power in relation to the coloniality of knowledge, however, is neatly balanced by consistent focus on material power within the decolonial scholarship. Scholars working within this prism seek not only to dismantle 'cognitive empires' but also to dismantle material sources of domination in an era of global coloniality (Chimakonam & Enyimba, 2022). This is one of the key distinctions between the decolonial school (and its avowedly political agenda to empower formerly colonised peoples in both epistemic *and* material terms) and postcolonial studies that derive inspiration from Michel Foucault. While postcolonial scholars deconstruct key texts to challenge 'Orientalism' and Eurocentrism, nevertheless, this scholarly enterprise has devoted itself more to the critique of language than to the interrogation of material factors—for instance, trade policies, military configurations and security policies—that underpin neo-colonialism today. And additionally, while decolonial scholarship views modernity and coloniality as wholly intertwined, postcolonial scholarship makes a historical demarcation between the formal period of colonialism and modernity. As Ndlovu-Gatsheni (2015) writes:

postcolonial theorists somehow try to decouple modernity and colonialism in the process missing the fact that modernity and coloniality are inextricably intertwined… The postcolonial 'cultural turn' is different from the 'decolonial turn' because the former is located and revolves within a Euro-North American-centric modernist discursive, historical, and structural terrain.

Decolonial scholars' emphasis on the incomplete nature of decolonisation, the contemporary exercise of imperial prerogatives by the West/'Global North' and the prevalence of coloniality/modernity break from the postcolonial scholarship and its literary orientation.

Moreover, the avowedly political project within the decolonial scholarship to challenge global coloniality and the matrixes of power that sustain Western dominance makes this school wholly compatible with Nkrumah's insights on neo-colonialism. Ndolvu-Gatsheni (2015) and Emiljanowicz (2021) in fact draw upon Nkrumah and the concept of neo-colonialism in their critique of global coloniality. They point to the relevance of the concept of neo-colonialism for conceptualising the strategies of Euro-American elites in their attempts to maintain economic and political tutelage in Africa. Both authors do this while emphasising the continuities between the early colonial period and the period following juridical decolonisation in the 1950s and 1960s. And this insight itself—the continuity between early colonialism and the stage of neo-colonialism—is something which Nkrumah also emphasised (cited in Obeng, 1979a, 1979b: 51). While African states might gain outward trappings of sovereignty upon attainment of legal independence, nevertheless (neo)colonial rule was continued in another guise. Co-opted African leaderships within formal institutions of African sovereignty would betray the interests of their domestic populations in the service of an external benefactor (ibid).

However, while Nkrumah's work is key to the dissection of 'Global Britain's' agenda in Africa, and is clearly compatible with the thriving decolonial scholarship, nevertheless there remains a relative lack of thorough engagement with his writings and speeches (notwithstanding some notable exceptions, as above). This is problematic since Nkrumah's approach helps to move beyond Western-centric epistemologies—as well as to challenge the material and institutional structures that perpetuate neo-colonial relations in Africa. Accordingly, the next section explores the concept of neo-colonialism as articulated by Nkrumah in a series of political speeches before, during and after his Presidency in Ghana. While his key books are explored in this author's (Langan, 2018) earlier reflection on neo-colonialism, this chapter emphasises the importance of engaging his spoken text. While his speeches clearly were given in specific historical circumstances—for instance, after the murder of his friend Patrice Lumumba—nevertheless, they retain contemporary resonance given recent interventions and subversions perpetrated by European powers (including Global Britain) in Africa (Williams, 2021: 349). His warnings bear fruit when considering the role of so-called new actors within Africa today too—namely, those powers who now compete with Euro-American elites in what Carmody (2016) terms 'the new scramble'.

Nkrumah's Political Speeches and the Interrogation of Neo-Colonialism

While Nkrumah's dissection of neo-colonialism is best known in terms of his written texts, nevertheless his speeches deserve scholarly attention. His warnings in his remarks to world leaders, students, and other audiences leave a large body of conceptual work concerned with the position of legally independent—but economically subordinate—African states vis-à-vis colonial metropoles and emerging powers within the international system. Surveying 150 speeches by Nkrumah compiled in by Obeng (1979a, 1979b), it becomes clear that the key themes within his written work find equally lucid expression within his oral remarks. The warnings he provides are wholly relevant to the situation of African countries facing 'geopolitical Europe', Global Britain, as well as a myriad of other 'geopolitical' actors, not least Russia. For instance, in his 1963 address to the Conference of African Heads of State and Government, Nkrumah makes clear that the struggle for independence does not end with legal statehood:

> the struggle against colonialism does not end with the attainment of national independence. Independence is only the prelude to a new and more involved struggle for the right to conduct our own economic and social affairs, to construct our society according to our aspirations, unhampered by crushing and humiliating neo-colonialist controls and interference… nothing will be of avail, except the united act of a united Africa. (cited in Obeng, 1979a: 165)

With parallels to the decolonial scholarship, Nkrumah recognises that colonial inequalities do not end upon the attainment of juridical statehood—rather they persist in a newer form. With interesting linkages to Quijano and Latin American decolonial scholars, Nkrumah warns that African countries will fall prey to the neo-colonialism already operating in Latin America should its Heads of State fail to deliver upon unity via a federal Union of African States (ibid).

Nkrumah's awareness that juridical decolonisation did not put an end to colonial power asymmetries—or to imperialism as Nkrumah refers to it—is further expressed within his remarks to the delegates of the Afro-Asian Solidarity Conference, one year before his ousting in the 1966 coup d'etat. With clear overlaps to contemporary decolonial scholarship and its focus upon the 'false' dawn and/or 'false' narrative of decolonisation, Nkrumah warns that economic exploitation, racial inequality and insecurity remain after the achievement of juridical statehood:

> Decolonization, national liberation, the Charter of the United Nations... none of these momentous developments in the modern world have caused imperialism to deviate from its course of economic exploitation, or to desist from undermining the independence of nations to make this exploitation possible. Whenever and wherever we seek the causes of war, we find the answer in economic exploitation, the heart of imperialism. We seek the causes of national and racial oppression, and we find the answer in economic exploitation... we seek the causes of continued undermining of emergent nations, and we find the answer in economic exploitation. (cited in Obeng, 1979b: 450)

With parallels to the concept of global coloniality as the triangular combination of the coloniality of power, the coloniality of knowledge and the coloniality of being within Ndlovu-Gatsheni's (2013, 2014, 2015) work, Nkrumah highlights the ongoing challenges of economic exploitation, oppression of emerging nations and racial hierarchies.

With resonance for the 'cognitive empires' that persist beyond decolonisation, Nkrumah also speaks of the denigration of African cultures by the (neo)colonialists. He explains how cultural hegemony does not disappear upon the attainment of legal statehood and how African scholars must constantly seek to reconstruct their own histories and culture:

African music, dancing and sculpture were labelled "primitive art". They were studied in such a way to reinforce the picture of African society as something grotesque, as a curious, mysterious human backwater, which helped to retard social progress in Africa and to prolong colonial domination over its peoples… [we must] study the history, culture and institutions, languages and arts of Ghana and of Africa… in entire freedom from the propositions and presuppositions of the colonial epoch. (cited in Obeng, 1979a: 274–275)

With parallels to Aimé Césaire's and Frantz Fanon's critique of Western cultural impositions, Nkrumah recognises that imperialism is a symptom of a European civilisational problem—and that European civilisational disintegration is in progress:

Ghana inherited a colonial economy and similar disabilities in most other directions. We cannot rest content, until we have demolished this miserable structure and raised in its place an edifice of economic stability… despite the ideological bankruptcy and moral collapse of a [European] civilization in despair, we must go forward with our planned economic growth to supplant the poverty, ignorance, disease, illiteracy and degradation left in their wake by discredited colonialism and decaying imperialism. (cited in Obeng, 1979a: 32)

Europe was not to be imitated by African elites or governments. Rather, a sovereign African personhood was to be rebuilt in the aftermath of (neo)colonialism and its cultural vandalism.

Moreover, to build economic stability and diverge from colonial patterns of trade, Nkrumah warned against any 'Association' between the EEC and African countries. He warned that a free trade zone between industrialised and non-industrialised countries would only perpetuate colonial forms of trade—and act as a barrier to economic diversification. In similar terms, he viewed the promise of aid under the European Development Fund (EDF) as means to facilitate the acquiescence of African leaderships to what would be disastrous free trade deals with European powers (Langan, 2018). With historical influence upon the formation of the African Continental Free Trade Area (AfCFTA), Nkrumah also argued that a desirable alternative to an economic coalition with the Europeans would be for African countries themselves to form a common market. Within an African common market—overseen by an African federal executive—African societies could realise the economies of scale necessary for full industrialisation. As a result, they would no longer be dependent upon Europe for either manufactured goods or aid money. Nkrumah in his 1962 speech to the Nationalists' Conference of African Freedom Fighters explained as follows:

> There is an alternative to Euro-African association, with its deadly implications for Africa's independence and progress. It is an African Economic Community, in which we can all pool our production and our trade, to the common advantage. It is not difficult to imagine that the neo-colonialists will describe this as a pooling of poverty. It is, however, too simple a distortion of fact. Africa is rich and not poor, as the great wealth that has been taken out of our continent over five centuries of despoilation and extortion very well proves. (cited in Obeng, 1979a: 52)

In clear terms, Nkrumah warned against the collective colonialism of the EEC and its desire to impose unequal trading arrangements. As will be discussed in Chapter 3, this has significant resonance for the critique of Global Britain and the UK's 'cut and paste' trade deals that mirror the EU's Economic Partnership Agreements (EPAs). It also bears resonance in terms of contemporary concerns about the EU's attempts to 'hijack' the AfCFTA by using intra-African liberalisation as a stepping-stone to a continent-to-continent Eurafrican free trade zone (Langan & Price, forthcoming). With a focus on economic exploitation combined to a critique of the cultural hegemony of the (neo)colonialists, Nkrumah aligns to the concerns of the decolonial school to assess the ideational and material elements of (neo)colonialism today.

Importantly, Nkrumah also warned about the danger of divided loyalties and tribalism. Related to his warnings about cultural hegemony, he lamented that certain African leaders felt allegiances to the former coloniser. He reflected that:

> I must admit that I find it strange to watch some of us return willingly to the colonialist fold. This time, they don't even have the excuse of being forced to subject themselves to foreign domination…unhappily for us, colonialism creates in some, intellectual allegiances which are not severed at the moment of independence, but remain to condition loyalties away from Africa towards the metropolis which draws them. (cited in Obeng, 1979a: 51)

Such African leaderships might attach greater priority to forging linkages with Europe, rather than focusing upon—what Nkrumah saw as—the urgent task of immediate African unification. Alongside the cultural pull of Europe, Nkrumah also discerned the 'Machiavellian' hand of Europeans in stirring up tribal tensions within newly formed African polities for their own geopolitical advantage. In the Democratic Republic of the Congo (DRC), Nkrumah highlighted the role of Belgium in fermenting secessionist movements in Katanga and in sabotaging the newly formed state from its infancy:

> The Congo is perhaps one of the most glaring examples of how the neo-colonialists use the most Machiavellian means to continue their imperialist depredations, by turning to their contrivance the ambitions of power-thirsty politicians and tribal divisions. Belgium, as we know, never prepared her colonies for independence… the ground was well set for the interfering tactics of the imperialist and cold war interests that entered Katanga to guard their investments and sever it from the jurisdiction of the central government. (cited in Obeng, 1979a: 63)

In similar terms, Nkrumah viewed European interventions as the source of intra-African tensions in relation to the building of a continental African Union. He viewed emerging frictions between the Casablanca Group of states dedicated towards a federal polity and the Monrovia Group of states geared towards confederal co-operation, as deriving from the influence of de Gaulle. He viewed the building of sub-continental groupings in East, West and South Africa as stumbling blocks to continental unity. He reflected that:

> Regional grouping [other than continental association] of any kind are a serious threat to the unity of Africa. Such groupings have divisive influences which can break the forces of cohesion and unity among us. General de Gaulle knows quite well that if regional federalism, this political commodity of dubious value, can be sold to Africa, the economic future of his Europe will be assured. Only by formenting and nursing regional and sectoral political groupings in Africa can the imperialists and ex-colonial powers be sure of retaining their rapidly waning influence in Africa. (cited in Obeng, 1979a: 210)

Nkrumah therein warned against regional projects that would lead to the 'Balkanization' of Africa and that would allow foreign interests to dominate, and to play off against each other, these divided regional formations.

Despite his objections to the machinations of European elites in African affairs, Nkrumah decried any racial antagonism between Africans and Europeans, rejecting racism in all forms. To the Conference of Afro-Asian Solidarity in 1965, he declared:

> Delegates, we meet as a Conference of Afro-Asian Solidarity. Let no one mistake this as a racial alignment. We are neither racists nor racialists, although we happen to be non-white in overwhelming numbers on these two continents, and although imperialism today operates from countries where the peoples are predominantly white. We are not here because we come from Africa and Asia, but because we belong to that part of the human race whose lands have been colonised… we do not forget that the peoples of Latin America, who suffered the same fate as we… are of European as well as Indian and African origin… [they have not been] excluded from our solidarity. (cited in Obeng, 1979b: 453)

In similar terms, he emphasised that the working class and intelligentsia in Europe at certain historical moments might act as allies for the achievement of a genuine form of African independence, notably in terms of protesting (neo)colonialism:

> There are many people within their [European] countries whose sympathy and moral support we know we have…. We must not overlook the struggle which some sections of the European working class and intelligentsia are bringing out into the open against colonial governments in Africa.., it is possible that our struggles could be joined, on the absolutely clear and accepted understanding that we shall brook no interference with our right to independence. (cited in Obeng, 1979a: 59)

And moreover, even European investors might be welcomed into Africa—if, crucially, their activities were overseen and subordinated to developmentalist economic plans authored by African executives—and that such enterprises played no role in influencing political affairs:

> We welcome foreign investors in a spirit of partnership. They can earn their profits here, provided they leave us with an agreed portion for promoting the welfare and happiness of our people as a whole as against the greedy ambitions of the few. From what we get out of this partnership, we hope

to be able to expand the health services of our people, to feed and house them well, to give them more and better educational institutions and to see to it that they have a rising standard of living.

Nkrumah in his speeches described this economic outlook as 'socialist' while denying that socialism belonged to any one people or continent.

On the question of accepting foreign aid money, however, he again made clear that this represented a threat to the sovereignty of newly independent polities. On the question of aid under the EDF being linked to a trading 'Association' between the EEC and African countries, he explained that while he could understand African leaderships' desire to have aid in order to redress immediate social problems, nevertheless, in the long run its acceptance would close down opportunities for economic advancement:

> I have said that I understand the difficulties of these states which are drawing themselves away from the African community back into that Europe. Faced with the demands of their people for rising standards of living and better social conditions, but charged with an economy that hardly meet the recurrent expenses of administration and maintenance, they are in a dilemma. And standing at their elbows are the neo-colonialist agents, beckoning them back.... [but] the irresistible bait of immediate help will be far outweighed, as they will experience with no great loss of time, by the knots into which their economies will be tied by the Euro-African association. (cited in Obeng, 1979a: 51)

Aid, therefore, for Nkrumah, was part of the material element of neo-colonialism, or what in the more recent decolonial scholarship might be appropriately referred to as the coloniality of power.

Surveying the spoken text of Nkrumah, it is clear that his analysis bears relevance for a critique of Western interventions in Africa today. Nkrumah understood that the achievement of a legal form of independence upon 'decolonisation' was not the end point of African liberation. Instead, he explained how the legacies of colonialism—and their exploitative material, economic, psychological and racial hierarchies—would not dissipate upon the attainment of juridical statehood in Africa. Western powers would utilise cultural hegemony, colonial patterns of trade, aid monies, corporate influence, as well as military intervention and political subterfuge to maintain their dominance. Neo-colonialism in this sense was not a break from colonialism per se, but its continuation in a new guise.

Nkrumah's critique of neo-colonialism is wholly commensurate with the insights of the decolonial scholarship on global coloniality. It is a pity that relatively few scholars within this field—with notable exceptions such as Ndlovu-Gatsheni (2015) and Emiljanowicz (2021)—have systematically engaged Nkrumah for the advancement of debates and movements centred around the dismantling of coloniality in the twenty-first century. Nkrumah's downfall and the West's tarnishing of his reputation may play some part in this historical omission. Yet Nkrumah's work mirrors that of the scholars held up as the 'founding fathers' of the decolonial approach. His focus on the cultural, psychological, economic and epistemic elements of (neo)colonialism provides a rich intellectual inheritance for the current generation of decolonial scholars. Moreover, his clarity of thought and his use of popular language attuned not only to academic debate, but to reception within trade unions, student movements and the wider citizenry, are a boon to a contemporary movement focused upon resistance to global coloniality. This book's critique of Global Britain's interventions in Africa, therefore, engages with both the decolonial literature and Nkrumah.

Conclusion

The Brexit result was fuelled by a regressive English nationalism and what Saunders (2022) terms the 'exceptionalism' of Brexiteer politicians with regard to the need for the UK to 'recover' power on the international stage. The launch of the Global Britain project—and its focus upon gaining influence among Commonwealth states—was underpinned by imperial nostalgia. Nevertheless, it would be inaccurate to deny that Remainer politicians within the UK establishment—notably Tony Blair and David Cameron—were similarly motivated by 'imperial modes of thought' in their championing of British foreign policy prowess via the EU. Blair's push for European support for the illegal invasion of Iraq in 2003, combined to Peter Mandelson's pursuit of premature trade liberalisation in Africa via EU EPAs, underscores that the shadow of Empire falls upon both the Brexit and Remainer camps in terms of Britain's political elites.

In the context of Global Britain's interventions in African countries today, therefore, it is necessary to engage the decolonial scholarship that seeks to understand—and challenge—power asymmetries between states in the 'Global North' and 'Global South'. As the chapter has demonstrated, Ndlovu-Gatsheni's (2013, 2014, 2015) triangular conception of global coloniality is particularly helpful as a framework for assessing Global Britain's trade, aid, financial and security interventions in the African continent. Application of the insights of the decolonial scholarship highlights the continuities of the colonial period and the current period of juridical statehood in Africa, not least in terms of Britain's pursuit of economic dominance via 'cut and paste' EPA free trade deals (EPA Monitoring, 2018). Moreover, the decolonial approach can help to challenge the ideational bases of British influence in Africa, for instance in terms of the concept of 'win–win' free trade itself.

As the chapter has also shown, the critique of Global Britain can benefit from close engagement with Nkrumah. Nkrumah's concept of neo-colonialism emphasises the material, ideational and cultural continuities of European dominance before and after juridical 'decolonisation'. His focus upon Euro-American elites' use of unequal trade deals, aid monies, military interventions and political subterfuge is enlightening in terms of helping to dissect Global Britain's attempted exertion of dominance over states in Africa. The decolonial scholarship, meanwhile, through systematic engagement with Nkrumah could enhance its ability to influence not only academic debates, but to impact upon trade unionists, student activists and other potential contributors to counter-movements against neo-colonialism within Africa. Nkrumah's articulate dissection—and denunciation—of the role of Euro-American politicians and entities in forestalling the attainment of a unified federal Africa can enable the decolonial scholarship to cultivate opposition to contemporary injustices enacted upon African citizenries. Accordingly, the book now turns to the historical assessment of Britain's imperial nostalgia in its post-WW2 relationship with African countries following their attainment of legal independence from the 1950s onwards. It focuses upon UK elites' cultivation of 'Commonwealth' narratives that emphasise the equality of the (neo)colonial 'family' of nations.

Bibliography

Afolabi, O. S. (2020). Globalisation, Decoloniality and the Question of Knowledge Production in Africa. *Journal of Higher Education in Africa/revue De L'enseignement Supérieur En Afrique, 18*(1), 93–110.

Alexandre-Collier, A. (2021). The Post-Referendum Reconfigurations of Conservative Cleavages around Black and Asian Minority Ethnic MPs. *Journal of Contemporary European Studies, 29*(3), 391–404.

Andrews, K. (2022, October 26). Opinion: Do Not Fall for the Symbolism of Rishi Sunak's Premiership. *CNN.* https://edition.cnn.com/2022/10/26/opinions/rishi-sunak-prime-minister-do-not-fall-symbolism-andrews/index.html. Accessed 24 June 2023.

Ascherson, N. (2019). Scotland, Brexit and the Persistence of Empire. In S. Ward & A. Rasch (Eds.), *Embers of Empire in Brexit Britain* (pp. 71–78). Bloomsbury.

Bhambra, G. (2017). Locating Brexit in the Pragmatics of Race, Citizenship and Empire. In W. Outhwaite (Ed.), *Brexit: Sociological Responses* (pp. 91–100). Anthem Press.

Bishara, M. (2022, October 17). Opinion - Josep Borrell as Europe's Racist "Gardener". *Al Jazeera.* https://aje.io/tyw3dv. Accessed 24 June 2023.

Botwe-Asamoah. (2005). *Kwame Nkrumah's Politico-Cultural Thought and Policies: An African-Centred Paradigm for the Second Phase of the African Revolution.* Routledge.

Buettner, E. (2019) 'How Unique is Britain's Empire Complex?' in S. Ward and A. Rasch (Eds.) *Embers of Empire in Brexit Britain* (pp. 37–48). Bloomsbury.

Calhoun, C. (2017). Populism, Nationalism and Brexit. In W. Outhwaite (Ed.), *Brexit: Sociological Responses* (pp. 57–76). Anthem Press.

Carmody, P. (2016). *The New Scramble for Africa.* Polity Press.

Césaire, A. [1950] (2000). *Discourse on Colonialism.* NYU Press.

Chimakonam, J., & Enyimba, M. (2022). Globalisation and the Challenge of Coloniality of Power. *South African Journal of International Affairs, 29*(2), 119–138.

Cox, R. W. (1981). Social Forces, States and World Orders: Beyond International Relations Theory. *Millennium, 10*(2), 126–155.

Deshpande, R. (2022, October 24). It Doesn't Matter if the Prime Minister is Brown. The UK is Still as Racist as Ever. *The Tab.* https://thetab.com/uk/2022/10/24/it-doesnt-matter-if-the-prime-minister-is-brown-the-uk-is-still-as-racist-as-ever-278661. Accessed 24 June 2023.

Emiljanowicz, P. (2021). From Karl Marx to Kwame Nkrumah: Towards a Decolonial Political Economy. In S. J. Ndlovu-Gatsheni & M. Ndlovu (Eds.), *Marxism and Decolonization in the 21st Century: Living Theories and True Ideas* (pp. 68–88). Routledge.

EPA Monitoring. (2018, March 12). The Complications of "Rolling-Over" Current EPAs into "Cut and Paste" Bilateral "UK-Only" Trade Deals. *EPA Monitoring.* https://epamonitoring.net/the-complications-of-rolling-over-current-epas-into-cut-and-paste-bilateral-uk-only-trade-deals/. Accessed 24 June 2023.

Fasakin, A. (2021). The Coloniality of Power in Postcolonial Africa: Experiences from Nigeria. *Third World Quarterly, 42*(5), 902–921.

Fanon, F. [1961] (2005). *The Wretched of the Earth*. Grove Press.

Forrest, A. (2019, June 30). Boris Johnson Says Describing Black People as Having "Watermelon Smiles" Was "Wholly Satirical". *The Independent*. https://www.independent.co.uk/news/uk/politics/boris-johnson-conservative-leadership-latest-racism-watermelon-smiles-satirical-a8981166.html. Accessed 24 June 2023.

Francis, E., & Noack, R. (2022, November 4). French Lawmaker Suspended After "Go Back To Africa" Outburst in Parliament. *Washington Post*.

Gilroy, P. (2004). *Postcolonial Melancholia*. Columbia University Press.

Goodison, P. (2005). The European Union: New Start or New Spin? *Review of African Political Economy, 32*(103), 167–176.

Grayson, J. (2013, August 22). The Shameful "Go Home" Campaign. *Institute of Race Relations*. https://irr.org.uk/article/the-shameful-go-home-campaign/. Accessed 24 June 2023.

Grosfoguel, R. (2002). Colonial Difference, Geopolitics of Knowledge, and Global Coloniality in the Modern/Colonial Capitalist World-System. *Review (fernand Braudel Center), 25*(3), 203–224.

Hansard. (2020). Global Britain. *Hansard*. https://hansard.parliament.uk/commons/2020-06-16/debates/20061637000001/GlobalBritain. Accessed 22 March 2023.

Hayward, F. (2023, March 8). PMQs: Keir Starmer Talks Tough on Migrants. *The New Statesman*. https://www.newstatesman.com/politics/uk-politics/2023/03/pmqs-today-keir-starmer-rishi-sunak-talks-migrants. Accessed 24 June 2023.

Hubbard, P. (2022, November 22). Suella Braverman's Talk of a Refugee "Invasion" is a Dangerous Political Gambit Gone Wrong. *King's College London*. https://www.kcl.ac.uk/suella-bravermans-talk-of-a-refugee-invasion-is-a-dangerous-political-gambit-gone-wrong. Accessed 22 March 2023.

Hurt, S., Lee, D., & Lorenz-Carl, U. (2013). The Argumentative Dimension to the EU-Africa EPAs. *International Negotiation, 18*(1), 67–87.

Kassim, H. (2008). A Bid Too Far? New Labour and UK Leadership of the European Union under Blair. In J. Hayward (Ed.), *Leaderless Europe* (pp. 167–187). Oxford University Press.

Koegler, C., Kumar, P., & Tronicke, M. (2020). The Colonial Remains of Brexit: Empire Nostalgia and Narcissistic Nationalism. *Journal of Postcolonial Writing, 56*(5), 585–592.

The Labour Party. (2023). Britain in the World. *The Labour Party*, Accessed 20 January 2023.

Langan, M. (2018). *Neo-Colonialism and the Poverty of 'Development' in Africa*. Palgrave.

Leroux, M. (2017, March 6). Ministers Aim to Build "Empire 2.0" with African Commonwealth. *The Times*. https://www.thetimes.co.uk/article/ministers-aim-to-build-empire-2-0-with-african-commonwealth-after-brexit-v9bs6f6z9. Accessed 24 June 2023.

Macejka, J. (2021). The Connection Between British Exceptionalism and Brexit. *North Carolina Journal of European Studies, 2*, 54–64.

McLeod, J. (2020). Warning Signs: Postcolonial Writing and the Apprehension of Brexit. *Journal of Postcolonial Writing, 56*(5), 607–620.

Mailafia, O. (2020, January 28). Britain and the New Scramble for Africa. *Vanguard*. https://allafrica.com/stories/202001280550.html. Accessed 24 June 2023.

Mignolo, W. (2007). Delinking. *Cultural Studies, 21*(2–3), 449–514.

Mwakikagile, G. (2010). *Nyerere and Africa: End of an Era*. New Africa Press.

Mishra, P. (2022, October 29). What is Not on Sunak's Agenda? Ending Racism. *Taipei Times*. https://www.taipeitimes.com/News/editorials/archives/2022/10/29/2003787902. Accessed 24 June 2023.

Monbiot, G. (2008, September 8). Protect and Survive. *The Guardian*. https://www.monbiot.com/2008/09/09/protect-and-survive/. Accessed 24 July 2023.

Narayan, J., & Sealey-Huggins, L. (2017). Whatever Happened to the Idea of Imperialism? *Third World Quarterly, 38*(11), 2387–2395.

Ndlovu-Gatsheni, S. J. (2013). *Coloniality of Power in Post-Colonial Africa*. CODESRIA.

Ndlovu-Gatsheni, S. J. (2014). Global Coloniality and the Challenges of Creating African Futures. *Strategic Review for Southern Africa, 36*(2), 181–202.

Ndlovu-Gatsheni, S. J. (2015). *Empire*. Berghahn Books.

Ndlovu-Gatsheni, S. J. (2021). Revisiting Marxism and Decolonisation Through the Legacy of Samir Amin. *Review of African Political Economy, 48*(167), 50–65.

The New Statesman. (2019, June 5). Boris Johnson's Racist Insults, Dog Whistles and Smears. *The New Statesman*. https://www.newstatesman.com/politics/uk-politics/2019/06/boris-johnson-s-racist-insults-dog-whistles-and-slurs. Accessed 24 June 2023.

Nkrumah, K. (1963). *Africa Must Unite*. Panaf Press.

Nkrumah, K. (1965). *Neo-Colonialism: The Last Stage of Imperialism*. Panaf Press.

Obeng, S. (1979a). *Selected Speeches of Kwame Nkrumah* (Vol. 1). Afram Publishers.

Obeng, S. (1979b). *Selected Speeches of Kwame Nkrumah* (Vol. 2). Afram Publishers.

Patnaik, U., & Patnaik, P. (2015, July 1). Imperialism in the Era of Globalization. *Monthly Review*. https://monthlyreview.org/2015/07/01/imperialism-in-the-era-of-globalization/. Accessed 24 July 2023.

Quijano, A. (2000). Coloniality of Power and Eurocentrism in Latin America. *International Sociology, 2*, 215–232.

Quijano, A. (2007). Coloniality and Modernity/Rationality. *Cultural Studies, 21*(2–3), 168–178.

Rankin, J. (2023, March 20). Experts Cast Doubts on Braverman's Hopes of ECHR Rule Change on Rwanda. *The Guardian*. https://www.theguardian.com/politics/2023/mar/20/experts-dispute-uks-claim-of-possible-echr-reforms-on-rwanda. Accessed 24 June 2023.

Rima, S., Bankole, M., & Neema, B. (2023). The 2022 Conservative Leadership Campaign and Post-Racial Gatekeeping. *Race and Class*, accepted/in press. https://eprints.mdx.ac.uk/37525/. Accessed 22 March 2023.

Salem, S. (2021). Gramsci in the Postcolony: Hegemony and Anticolonialism in Nasserist Egypt. *Theory, Culture & Society, 38*(1), 79–99.

Salter, J. (2023, January 17). I Confronted Suella Braverman Because as a Holocaust Survivor I Know What Words of Hate Can Do. *The Guardian*. https://www.theguardian.com/commentisfree/2023/jan/17/confronted-suella-braverman-holocaust-survivor-refugees-home-secretary?CMP=share_btn_tw. Accessed 23 June 2023.

Saunders, R. (2020). Brexit and Empire: "Global Britain" and the Myth of Imperial Nostalgia. *The Journal of Imperial and Commonwealth History, 48*(6), 1140–1174.

Serfaty, S. (2008). *Architects of Delusion: Europe*. University of Pennsylvania Press.

Smith, C. (2003, February 18). Chirac Upsets East Europe by Telling It to "Shut Up" on Iraq. *New York Times*. https://www.nytimes.com/2003/02/18/international/europe/chirac-upsets-east-europe-by-telling-it-to-shut-up-on.html. Accessed 24 June 2023.

Stacey, K., & Crerar, P. (2023, January 5). Starmer Vows to Let Communities "Take Back Control" in Labour's First Term. *The Guardian*. https://www.theguardian.com/politics/2023/jan/05/keir-starmer-vows-to-let-communities-take-back-control-in-labour-first-term?CMP=share_btn_tw. Accessed 24 June 2023.

Suroor, H. (2022, October 27). Why Rishi Sunak's Election Doesn't Make Britain a "Post-Racial" Society. *First Post*.

Thackeray, D., & Toye, R. (2019). Debating Empire 2.0. In S. Ward & A. Rasch (Eds.), *Embers of Empire in Brexit Britain* (pp. 15–24). Bloomsbury.

Thakur, R. (2022, November 5). Rishi is the Face of Post-Racial UK. *The Spectator Australia*. https://www.firstpost.com/opinion-news-expert-views-news-analysis-firstpost-viewpoint/why-rishi-sunaks-election-doesnt-make-britain-a-post-racial-society-11517401.htm. Accessed 24 June 2023.

Tronicke, M. (2020). Imperial Pasts, Dystopian Futures, and the Theatre of Brexit. *Journal of Postcolonial Writing, 56*(5), 662–675.

Virdee, S., & McGeever, B. (2018). Racism, Crisis, Brexit. *Ethnic and Racial Studies, 41*(10), 1802–1819.

Weir, K. (2011, March 9). Cameron Seeking International Backing for Libya Action. *Reuters*.

Wellings, B. (2021). Brexit, Nationalism and Disintegration in the European Union and the United Kingdom. *Journal of Contemporary European Studies, 29*(3), 322–334.

Williams, S. (2021). *White Malice: The CIA and the Covert Recolonization of Africa*. Public Affairs.

CHAPTER 2

Africa and the Commonwealth: UK Imperial Imaginaries

INTRODUCTION

The 2016 vote to leave the EU was underpinned by Leave campaign narratives that appealed to voters' anxieties regarding declining British power and imperial romanticism (Wellings, 2021). One important theme in relation to Leave visions of the UK's power exertion on the world stage was Brexiteer officials' focus upon the Commonwealth. Brexiteer politicians spoke of the benefits that leaving the EU would bring in terms of a reorientation of UK foreign and economic policies away from 'Fortress Europe' and onto the Commonwealth 'family' (Namusoke, 2016; Ølholm Eaton, 2020; Ølholm Eaton & Smith, 2020). A vote in favour of Brexit was presented not as an insular act of turning inward. Instead, it was cast as a positive choice in favour of reasserting a powerful 'global' role for the UK. Brexiteer campaigners also sought to draw normative dividing lines between the apparent values of Britain and the EU. Namely, that British championing of free trade would find expression in terms of the pursuit of mutually advantageous trade deals with Commonwealth states. This was contrasted with the apparent protectionist instincts of trade officials in Brussels, notwithstanding EU free trade agreements with African, Caribbean and Pacific (ACP) countries, for example (Vickers, 2018: 291).

The chapter accordingly examines the ideational significance and imperial imaginaries associated with the concept of the Commonwealth in

British political discourse. It explores how British imperial nostalgia impacts upon UK officials' current attitudes and policy approach towards Commonwealth states. This is especially explored in terms of the launch of 'Empire 2.0' in Africa as part of the Global Britain project. In this discussion, the chapter underscores how British officials' paternalistic and patronising attitudes to Africa permeate their contemporary approach to issues of trade, aid, finance, investment and security. Moreover, UK officials' policy approach in Africa is seen to be influenced by problematic notions of humanitarian moral duty—a 'mission civilisatrice' akin to a twenty-first-century equivalent of the 'White Man's Burden' (cf. Polonksa-Kimunguyi & Kimunguyi, 2017: 327, 343). It is seen to align to the 'new racism' and to illustrate the *coloniality of being* (Grosfoguel, 2002; Ndlovu-Gatsheni, 2015). Namely, that British officials—with clear parallels to EU officials such as Josep Borrell—often operate from the basis of an apparent racialised worldview in their approach to former colonies (Bishara, 2022). The importance of Commonwealth Africa for British officials' ontological security is also underscored. Namely, how it informs elites' sense of self that then informs their behaviour towards other actors within the international realm (Haastrup et al., 2021; Zarakol, 2010).

The chapter is structured as follows. The first section considers British discourse in relation to the Commonwealth after World War Two (WW2) up to the end of the Cold War. It underscores British officials' historical need for the transformation of the Commonwealth away from sole focus upon the 'White Dominions'—Australia, Canada and New Zealand—towards 'new' members in Asia and Africa amid legal 'decolonisation' (Murphy, 2018). It also emphasises the role played by President Kwame Nkrumah of Ghana in the debates surrounding the changing role of the Commonwealth in the 1960s (Obeng, 1979). The second section explores the recent 'rebirth' of the Commonwealth in terms of British politicians' increasing enthusiasm for that organisation from the 1990s onwards. It examines the attitudes of New Labour architects towards Commonwealth links, and in fulfilling a moralist vision of healing the 'scar on the conscience of the world', as Blair described the African continent (Porteous, 2005: 289). This underscores British officials' ontological security in terms of the UK's paternalistic approach towards African countries. The third section assesses the Brexit referendum and the politicisation of the Commonwealth in terms of the Leave campaign's appeal to imperial romanticism and English nationalism. It underscores how campaigners emphasised a British sense of loyalty to a 'family' with Commonwealth nations, and how this was used to defend against accusations of an 'insular' Brexit future. The final section examines British officials' discourse on the Commonwealth in the post-Brexit era. It assesses how the Commonwealth remains key to the Global Britain project, not least in terms of the 'new scramble for Africa' (Leroux, 2017).

British Officials and Conceptions of the Commonwealth in the Post-War Era

The role of the Commonwealth as a (post)imperial 'family' is rooted in the history of British Empire when white settler colonies gained increasing autonomy from London. This was initiated by the granting of 'Dominion' status from 1926 to Canada, Newfoundland, New Zealand, Australia, the Irish Free State and South Africa under the Balfour Declaration (Murray-Evans, 2018: 198). This grouping of white settler societies—minus the Irish Republic which boldly renounced its Commonwealth status in 1949—has become known as the 'old' Commonwealth. This label is used to distinguish from the 'new' Commonwealth—including India, Pakistan, Malaysia and African countries such as Ghana—that gained juridical statehood in the post-war era. As the section on the Brexit referendum will later emphasise, there is still often a discursive distinction made between the so-called White Dominions and other Commonwealth countries based on some Brexiteers' political desire to construct an alliance involving the 'Anglosphere' or 'CANZUK' (Canada, Australia, New Zealand, UK) (Saunders, 2020: 1142).

The Commonwealth underwent major transformation in the post-WW2 era as a war-weary and indebted British state capitulated to the demands of liberation movements in India and Pakistan in 1947 for legal independence—notwithstanding the bloody ordeal of partition apparently stoked by British officials (Von Tunzelmann, 2017). Sri Lanka soon followed suit in 1948. The capitulation of British officials to the post-war demands for independent statehood in the African continent, beginning with Ghana in 1957, cemented this transformation. Many British officials, however, were hostile towards the admission of non-white societies to the 'family' of nations, and the shift of the Commonwealth to a multiracial association. Winston Churchill, for instance, sought to grant Ghana a 'mezzanine' status short of full Commonwealth membership (McIntyre, 2000: 136). On the other hand, the Commonwealth as an informal 'club' was seen as a useful asset by other British officials, such as Lord Home, for maintaining political and economic influence in their sphere of (neo)imperial control (Ovendale, 1995: 462).

As Wilkes explains, however, there was a distinction between politicians on the left and right in UK politics as to how an expanding Commonwealth impacted their sense of self as British actors on the global stage. Wilkes makes clear that 'the right wing of the Conservative Party hoped for a revival of imperial ties so as to make Britain a world power; those on the left saw the Commonwealth of the future as a multiracial family co-operating to combat inequality' (cited in Brysk et al., 2002: 292). For differing reasons therefore, British elites' ontological security—in terms of their self-conceptualisation as influential and relevant foreign policy actors with a global reach—was broadly enhanced by the prospect of an enlarged Commonwealth. In a sense, the existence of the Commonwealth acted as a balm to British 'trauma' surrounding the surrender of the UK state to liberation movements in Africa and Asia:

> [Bringing together states subject to Empire] certainly gave the Commonwealth an important role as a transition organization that simultaneously helped eased the trauma of Britain's lost imperial role (decolonization could then be interpreted as the move from one kind of empire to another more informal one), while also giving former colonies an easy lead into the world of international organizations and inter-state relations. (Ashworth cited in McIntyre et al., 2007: 63)

The Commonwealth as a 'transition organisation' played an important role in buttressing British elites' ontological security that they remained as truly global players on the international stage.

Moreover, India's admission to the Commonwealth in 1947 amid the Cold War was seen by British elites as a bulwark against the expansion of Communism within Asia (Catterall, 2018: 833). By maintaining Commonwealth linkages, British officials could also pursue what Churchill had described in 1948 as the three important circles of UK global influence. As Daddow (2018: 210) explains:

> Churchill's idea was that Britain occupied an exceptional position in world affairs because it operated at the intersection of three great circles of power and influence. The first circle, 'naturally', was the British Commonwealth and Empire... The second circle was 'the English-speaking world in which we, Canada, and the other British Dominions play so important a part'.

This was, in effect, the Anglosphere circle, including countries such as the United States, Australia and New Zealand. The third circle – note the ordering – was 'United Europe'.

By expanding Commonwealth membership beyond the Old Dominions, Britain could seek to maintain global influence even in the face of the emerging conflict between the two superpowers. This tripartite vision of relevance and potent actorness within (i) the Commonwealth, (ii) the English-speaking world and (iii) Europe underscored British officials' ontological security and their sense of Britain's ongoing relevance in global politics as processes of 'decolonisation' unfolded.

However, many British officials saw UK commitment to the Commonwealth—and the UK's possible membership of the European Economic Community (EEC)—as sitting in tension (ibid: 210). In the 1930s, Britain had established a system of imperial preferences where Commonwealth states granted lower tariff entry to one another, to the chagrin of third-party countries including the United States of America (USA) (Láng, 1979: 284). The system of Commonwealth preferences had been put under pressure with the establishment of the General Agreement on Tariffs and Trade (GATT) in October 1947 as part of the outcome of the Bretton Woods conference (Murphy, 2018: 208). The prospect of the UK joining the founding six members of the EEC within a common market sat uneasily with the maintenance of the imperial preferences system. Despite this, however, the first UK application to join the EEC came as early as 1961 (Daddow, 2018: 222). Britain's eventual entry to the EEC in 1973 was seen as a form of 'betrayal' by certain Commonwealth countries who found themselves facing higher tariffs (cf. Murray-Evans, 2016). A sense of impending 'betrayal' was also felt in the 1960s as Britain unsuccessfully sought entry into the European project. This was compounded by African leaders' fears about the neo-colonial logic of EEC trade policies. Writing in the early 1960s, Holmes (1962: 300)—a Canadian diplomat—explained that:

> The European Economic Community is regarded by the Commonwealth states of Africa with disquiet. They see in it a sinister move of the Europeans, under the suspect leadership of France, to reassert their power, to reimpose through the mechanism of the status of "Associated Overseas Territories" their domination over Africa, and to keep them producing cheap raw materials for European industry. Their objections to EEC are

more political than economic and they tend to view British entry into the Market not only as a disaster for their economies but also as an act of betrayal.

Nkrumah (1965: 182–183) especially viewed the EEC as a neo-colonial venture, decrying its intention to use aid money to compel African leaderships to prematurely open their markets. This would perpetuate colonial forms of trade while closing down industrialisation strategies. Upon UK accession to the EEC in the 1970s, however, African Commonwealth countries found themselves in a more favourable tariff position as compared to states such as India and Sri Lanka. Namely, Anglophone African states soon became party to the Lomé Conventions (1975–2000) between Europe and the African, Caribbean and Pacific (ACP) bloc. African countries as part of the ACP group successfully negotiated for lower tariff access to EEC markets, while successfully resisting EEC calls to 'reciprocate' trade liberalisation as part of the Lomé framework (Price & Nunn, 2018).

Despite the UK's early bids for EEC membership, African states did actively engage British officials in the 1960s within Commonwealth meetings. With some overlap with the British political left, African officials sought to build the Commonwealth as a multi-racial association that would promote mutual prosperity and solidarity. Kwame Nkrumah as the first President of Ghana was particularly active in his calls for the establishment of a Commonwealth Secretariat (cited in Obeng, 1979: 411, 457). He believed that its creation would enable the Commonwealth to gain an independent executive able to act in the interests of its full membership, rather than that of the British alone. Related to this, African officials viewed the Commonwealth as an important instrument by which to collectively call upon the UK and the white settler 'dominions' to pay aid monies, and to grant fairer trade to societies still reeling from racialist imperial policies (Holmes, 1962: 300). Nkrumah's own stance here becomes visible across a number of political speeches delivered during his Presidency of Ghana. Speaking in January 1965, for example, he made clear that:

> With regard to the Commonwealth, we have played an active part in its deliberations, and have recently made suggestions for the setting up of a Commonwealth Secretariat which, when implemented, would make

the Commonwealth a more positive force for progress and understanding. (cited in Obeng, 1979: 411)

Earlier, in February 1962, Nkrumah had warned that UK entry into the EEC would have deleterious effects for the trade of Commonwealth members. He explained that this would not only impact 'new' members such as Ghana, but also states such as Canada:

> We regard the Commonwealth as an association of free and independent sovereign states, equal in all respects and bound together by the common desire to work for the good and well being of its members… We are however faced with another problem: the dangers to which we are exposed by the prospect of the European Common Market… we are opposed to any grouping or arrangements which are used as a cloak for perpetuating colonial privileges in Africa. The unpleasant effect on the Commonwealth of Britain joining the European Common Market cannot be over stated. I am glad that in this matter, Canada, like Ghana, is very much alive to the serious issues involved. (cited in Obeng, 1979: 457)

In these terms, Nkrumah (1965) decried UK membership of the EEC since British markets would then favour European states while discriminating against the Commonwealth. EEC officials would then inevitably demand 'reciprocal' free trade involving African countries' dismantling of their tariff walls for them to continue to enjoy the equivalent of Commonwealth trade preferences. Notably, EEC officials under the Yaoundé Conventions signed in 1963 did demand that Francophone African states acquiesce to 'reciprocity' to enjoy low tariff access to the wider EEC (Sakr, 2023). It was only during the Lomé Conventions that EEC members acquiesced to ACP countries' demands for 'non-reciprocity' (Gruhn, 1976). Nkrumah's fears about Europe's neo-colonial demands for premature tariff dismantling in Africa were well founded and remain so in the context of EU free deals explored in Chapter 3.

In the Cold War era, however, British officials found that their political influence and moral suasion within the Commonwealth was quickly undermined by the question of apartheid in South Africa and white minority rule in Rhodesia. The UK Prime Minister Harold MacMillan's 'Wind of Change' speech to the South African parliament in 1960 had acknowledged a new political era in Africa (Hyam, 1998: 172). However, MacMillan's position did not resolve the problem of the existence of racialist regimes in South Africa and Rhodesia. As a result, British officials found themselves regularly criticised by other Commonwealth members for their failure to sufficiently penalise and ostracise white supremacist governments (Murphy, 2011: 271). South Africa announced its departure from the Commonwealth in 1961 due to its unwillingness to redress other members' concerns about its avowedly racist ideology (Hyam, 1998). Rhodesian officials, meanwhile, issued a Unilateral Declaration of Independence (UDI) in 1965 (Taylor, 2000: 60). Harold Wilson's failure to countenance intervention against the white minority regime in Rhodesia after UDI led to much condemnation of Britain within the Commonwealth, despite other Labour figures such as Tony Benn speaking the language of anti-racism (Murphy, 2011: 271).

While Britain did impose some trade sanctions on Rhodesia and South Africa, nevertheless, successive UK governments were condemned for not more forcefully confronting these white supremacist regimes. As a result, from the mid-1960s up until the release of Nelson Mandela in 1990, the UK's participation in the Commonwealth was mired in odium (Taylor, 2000: 60). This was exacerbated by the uncompromising stance of Prime Minister Margaret Thatcher throughout the 1980s on the issue of Mandela's captivity and apartheid (Beswick, 2019: 129). The former head of the British diplomatic service has since confirmed that Thatcher believed that South Africa should be a 'whites-only-state' (*The Independent*, 2018). White supremacist attitudes in Southern Africa—and in London—limited the UK's successful operation within the Commonwealth. As the next section demonstrates, however, the Commonwealth gained a 'revival' in the 1990s as the fall of Thatcher—combined to the fall of the apartheid regime—opened-up new opportunities for Britain's more active promotion of Commonwealth linkages (Murphy, 2011: 273–274).

A Renewed Commitment to the African Commonwealth? From Blair to Brexit

The release of Mandela in 1990—combined to the end of the Cold War—led to a renewal of UK activism within the Commonwealth. The creation of a multi-racial democracy in South Africa removed what had been a large impediment to the UK's successful diplomacy within the grouping. The moral failings of successive UK administrations were partially obscured by celebrations associated with Mandela's release and South Africa's subsequent re-joining of the Commonwealth in 1994. Likewise, the collapse of white minority rule in Rhodesia in 1980—renamed Zimbabwe under President Robert Mugabe—removed another racialist regime, albeit later creating difficulties for Prime Minister Blair in relation to Mugabe's confiscation of white owned farms (McKinnon, 2004: 406). The end of the Cold War, meanwhile, gave renewed impetus to British pressure for democratisation and free market reform in the continent (Taylor, 2000: 65–66). Britain sought to engage African Commonwealth members to promote ostensible British values surrounding democracy and free trade within a series of Commonwealth Heads of Government Meetings (CHOGM). This included the Harare 1991 meeting where Prime Minister John Major found a positive reception from his Commonwealth peers—on the basis that he had replaced Thatcher (Murphy, 2011: 274).

One major turning point in Britain's re-assertion of its diplomatic weight within the Commonwealth was the 1996 publication of a report on the future of the association (Murphy, 2018: 204). The Foreign Affairs Committee in Westminster called upon the UK government to take greater advantage of the investment opportunities present within Asian and African markets (ibid). Soon afterwards, the New Labour government of Tony Blair, elected in May 1997, gave a certain priority to the Commonwealth since the UK was due to host its first CHOGM summit in over twenty years. At the CHOGM Edinburgh summit in 1997, then Foreign Secretary, Robin Cook, emphasised the benefits of greater trade and economic linkages, leading to the creation of the Commonwealth Business Council (CBC) (ibid). The CBC sought to stimulate greater private sector interest in the Commonwealth and to facilitate a networked approach to inter-business linkages. This reflected the New Labour emphasis upon the importance of the private sector for stimulating growth necessary for poverty reduction—a logic followed by Blair's government in both its domestic policy approach (the Third Way) and its stance on international development (the Post-Washington Consensus) (Abrahamsen, 2005; Williams, 2005).

The New Labour governments of Tony Blair and Gordon Brown were both motivated by a moralist humanitarianism in their engagement with the African Commonwealth. This found expression in Blair's condescending characterisation of Africa as the 'scar on the conscience of the world' (Porteous, 2005: 289). Blair's premiership coincided with United Nations (UN) consultations on what became the UN Millennium Development Goals (MDGs). Blair viewed the Commonwealth as an instrument for promoting pro-poor economic development through engagement with Africa (Taylor, 2012: 457; Williams, 2005: 386). Related to this moralist humanitarian instinct, the Blair government established a new Department for International Development (DfID) (Gallagher, 2011). This sought to rectify the 'Realist' foreign policy that the Foreign and Commonwealth Office (FCO) had pursued during the previous eighteen years of Conservative rule vis-à-vis Africa (Polonksa-Kimunguyi & Kimunguyi, 2017: 329). Under Development Secretary, Clare Short, DfID became a symbol of the nominal social democratic attitudes of the Blair government (Gallagher, 2011: 87). Blair's encouragement of Commonwealth ties fitted neatly with the launch of DfID and his government's international development commitments to the UN MDGs. Related to this, the Labour Party as an organisation historically viewed itself as being uninhibited by colonial guilt due to its early anti-imperial stance in the pre-WW2 era. Focusing on the well-being of African Commonwealth countries was thus a useful political strategy for Blair in his attempts to unite 'old' and 'new' Labour elements behind him. Gallagher (2011: 86) notes that development initiatives were able to unite figures such as Jeremy Corbyn—a Labour socialist and later leader of the party—with politicians in the New Labour mould.

Moreover, UK commitment to the Commonwealth and to 'development' soon became central to the Conservative Party, from the leadership of Michael Howard onwards. The party, while in opposition, sought to portray itself as a compassionate political entity that cared for 'the poor' in African Commonwealth members and beyond (Beswick, 2019). Furthermore, Eurosceptic members of the Conservative Party continued to emphasise the need for a foreign policy reorientation away from the EU towards the (post)imperial 'family' (Murray-Evans, 2018). Consequently, a British political consensus was arrived upon wherein commitment to the Commonwealth became central to a sense of ontological security among British policy-makers of both the left and right. Namely, that political elites' understanding of their own British identities and their global clout as UK political actors became intimately linked to notions of humanitarianism and 'family' found through participation in Commonwealth forums. As such, Britain's global role from the 2000s onwards became increasingly related to the future of the Commonwealth, as well as to participation within other international forums such as the G8 (now G7) and the North Atlantic Treaty Organisation (NATO).

Prime Minister Blair's attention to poverty reduction in the Commonwealth, however, was impacted by his growing sense of the need for muscular interventionism, dating back to his government's interventions in Kosovo and Sierra Leone (Porteous, 2005: 288). Infamously, the British state's illegal invasion of Iraq alongside US forces distracted his government's attention away from its erstwhile 'ethical foreign' policy as had been articulated by Robin Cook. Furthermore, not only did the Blair government increasingly focus upon security matters in the sense of the invasion of Muslim societies in Afghanistan and Iraq. But its broader view of international development as an enterprise itself became increasingly 'securitised' (Abrahamsen, 2005). Namely, the rationale behind poverty reduction in Commonwealth Africa became increasingly motivated by British security concerns. For instance, in terms of British support for de-radicalisation strategies in African societies with high proportions of Muslim citizens. As Abrahamsen (2005: 56) explains:

> Through this securitization, dealings and interactions with Africa are gradually shifting from the category of "development/humanitarianism" to a category of "risk/fear/ security," so that today Africa is increasingly mentioned in the context of the "war on terrorism" and the dangers it poses to Britain and the international community. Given Blair's global profile, these issues go beyond UK foreign policy and raise important questions relating to Africa's place within structures of power and global governance.

New Labour's moralist humanitarianism in Africa, therefore, became increasingly connected with a 'Realist' foreign policy desire to prevent radicalisation and social instability in so-called fragile states (Gallagher, 2011).

The defeat of New Labour in 2010, meanwhile, gave rise to the coalition government led by Prime Minister David Cameron and his Deputy, Nick Clegg, of the Liberal Democrats. The Cameron government followed in the footsteps of his mentor, Michael Howard, in promoting UK participation within the Commonwealth as a form of Conservative 'modernisation' (Beswick, 2019:126). Cameron's approach to the Commonwealth also sought to respond to sentiments among his backbenchers, notably in terms of the Eurosceptic wing who championed (neo)colonial linkages with the Commonwealth. Interestingly, Cameron's orientation towards Africa during his premiership was foreshadowed by his 2006 tour of the continent while leader of the opposition:

Cameron visited war-torn Darfur with his Shadow International Development Secretary Andrew Mitchell, and made an unannounced trip to South Africa to meet the former President and iconic leader of the anti-apartheid movement, Nelson Mandela. In doing so he sought to demonstrate his credentials as a potential international statesman, but also took the opportunity to position engagement with Africa as part of Conservative Party modernization. (ibid: 126)

This 2006 tour was followed by Cameron's 2007 visit to Rwanda. Cameron also condemned the failure of previous Conservative governments—notably that of Margaret Thatcher—to sufficiently combat the evils of apartheid South Africa during the Cold War, as part of his attempts to modernise the party (ibid).

Cameron in government, however, followed a 'Realist' approach to African Commonwealth states in both an economic and a security sense. He focused upon forging trade and investment linkages with South Africa and Nigeria as rising economic powers, as well as dealing with 'security threats'. Notably, this was reflected in terms of intervention in South Sudan, Somalia and—disastrously—in Libya with the overthrow of the Gaddafi regime followed by civil war and open-air slave markets (Beswick, 2019: 133; Ramdani, 2019). Reflecting the degree to which humanitarian concerns, however, have become central to British officials' ontological security within Whitehall, Cameron did also pledge to meet the UN target of 0.7% Gross National Income (GNI) spending on overseas development assistance (ODA). As Brown (2019: 139) explains:

> Labour made so much of the running on international development that not only did David Cameron feel compelled to back Labour's pledges on aid spending but his first Secretary of State for International Development, Andrew Mitchell, claimed that international development policy had moved beyond party politics.

This Conservative aid commitment—as well as Cameron's support for the work of DfID—was, however, in the context of a domestic austerity politics that witnessed severe cuts to UK social services. It is perhaps not surprising therefore that UK aid spending on humanitarian projects in Africa became increasingly targeted by right-wing UK media outlets that contrasted the state of the UK's own underfunded social services with British aid-giving (see, for example, Groves, 2014 in *The Daily Mail*). A politics of resentment emerged in which the Conservatives' commitment to the 0.7% aid target became politically contentious in relation to its own voter base. Subsequently, 'aid sceptic' ministers such as Justine Greening and Priti Patel were placed into DfID to satiate Conservative voters' opinion about apparently corrupt usages of British aid (see, for example, Nelson, 2012 on Greening's appointment). This politics of resentment later fed into a wider populist backlash against the Cameron government, which saw UK affiliations with the Commonwealth weaponised in the context of the Brexit referendum.

The Brexit Referendum and Discourse on Africa and the Commonwealth

The second term of the Cameron government was short lived due to his failure in the Brexit referendum in the summer of the following year. Brexiteer campaigners including Michael Gove, Liam Fox, Nigel Farage and Daniel Hannan made regular speeches about the likely benefits of UK withdrawal from the EU in terms of British economic prosperity and foreign policy clout. Several narrative themes were developed in this context, both in terms of addressing domestic controversies such as migration and the condition of the National Health Service (NHS), as well as external matters including UK relations with the Commonwealth. Brexiteer discourse on the Commonwealth was particularly useful in helping to deflect and counter arguments from the Remain campaign that Brexit would reflect a shift to a more xenophobic and insular foreign policy. Pro-Brexit politicians made a series of claims about the positive contribution of a Leave victory to the prosperity and 'family' unity of the Commonwealth as an association of English-speaking nations (Namusoke, 2016).

Interestingly, there was tension in Brexiteer discourse in terms of the supposed 'old' and 'new' Commonwealths, reflecting the historical development of the association in the post-WW2 era. Certain Brexiteer campaigners spoke fondly of the need to develop a CANZUK alliance—namely between UK and the 'old' Dominions—Canada, Australia and New Zealand (Bell & Vucetic, 2019: 369). Others expanded this category to include the USA in terms of the development of an 'Anglosphere' (ibid: 371). This was seen as a solution, in part, to the economic turbulence that even Brexiteer politicians admitted might be forthcoming upon UK withdrawal from the European supranational project. Moreover, Brexit discourse on the topic of the CANZUK and/or Anglosphere alliance emphasised the apparent convergence of norms between the constituent nations—on the rule of law, democracy, free trade and fair play—based upon the common heritage shared between the UK and these white settler societies. In this conceptualisation of the Commonwealth, therefore, emphasis was placed upon the 'old' allies of the UK in North America and Australasia. As Bell and Vucetic (2019: 368) explain, such visions of Anglosphere or CANZUK solidarity were also articulated during the campaign in juxtaposition to the apparent protectionism of the EU, as well as the historical 'betrayal' that UK membership of the EEC allegedly constituted:

> Negatively, the Anglosphere is often pitched as an alternative to European institutions, and especially the EU. Many Anglosphere devotees regard Britain's accession to the European Economic Community (EEC) in 1973 as both a monumental mistake and an act of treachery — a mistake because it ignored the weakness of the European project and treachery, because it spurned the true British 'kith and kin'. Hence, Boris Johnson's criticism that 'we betrayed our relationships with Commonwealth countries such as Australia and New Zealand'.

Brexit was legitimised as a return to 'normalcy' in the sense that it would restore an alliance between English-speaking peoples with shared values while correcting the perceived betrayal of Commonwealth nations allegedly enacted upon UK accession to the EEC in 1973.

This Brexiteer call for CANZUK and Anglosphere associations clearly correlates to a form of 'imperial nostalgia' in which politicians such as Boris Johnson drew upon—and romanticised—the legacies of Empire (Koegler et al., 2020). Brexit in this sense was presented as an opportunity to revive earlier imperial models of co-operation such as the Commonwealth preferences system established in the 1930s. In reality, therefore, Brexiteer claims to be championing ideals of free trade were highly questionable since the ideological foundations of imperial preferences were to be found in the political project of Joseph Chamberlain who advocated for free trade within the Empire, but who simultaneously called for protectionist measures to be imposed upon third-country nations (such as the USA) (Siméon, 2019). Brexiteer discourse in this sense simplified highly complex imperial legacies in the presentation of a 'Leave' vote as a patriotic choice for an English-speaking alliance in opposition to EU membership.

Importantly in relation to the later launch of a Global Britain project, certain Brexiteer discourse also invoked the 'plight' of African countries vis-à-vis the EU. Perhaps most notably, Daniel Hannan, a Conservative Member of the European Parliament (MEP) from 1999 until the UK withdrawal in 2020, criticised the EU for its treatment of African, Caribbean and Pacific (ACP) countries within the Cotonou Partnership Agreement. In a speech to the European Parliament in 2013, he lambasted the EU's aid programme in Africa (Conservative Home, 2013). African politicians with an external revenue stream—namely EU aid money—he explained would neglect their domestic economies and their own citizen-tax payers since they could rely upon EU largesse instead. This, he claimed, accounted in large part for the lack of economic growth within certain authoritarian African states (ibid). Moreover, in an article for the *Financial Times* during the referendum, Hannan (2016) extolled British voters to liberate the UK economy from the protectionist constraints of Brussels that had allegedly prevented Britain from trading freely with countries such as Ethiopia and India. Pointing to the lower costs of international trade due to technological innovation, Hannan (2016) argued that it was time for the UK to return to trading with economies in the 'Global South' such as Ethiopia, India and China:

> The purpose of trade is to swap on the back of differences – to purchase from abroad what you do not produce yourself. I am not sure it made sense for Britain to abandon the Commonwealth, a genuinely diverse global market system – one that brought together agrarian, commodity-based, manufacturing and service-oriented economies – in exchange for membership of a more homogenous bloc of advanced western European states. But whether it made sense or not in the 1970s, it plainly makes no sense now.

Hannan, meanwhile, has spoken in the post-Brexit context of the need for a Global Britain project that forges strong trading links with Africa, as will be discussed more in Chapter 4.

Brexiteers such as James Cleverly, the current Home Secretary within the Conservative government of Rishi Sunak, also spoke during the referendum campaign of the injustices committed upon African countries under the EU's Common Agricultural Policy (CAP). Brexit was presented as an opportunity for an independent UK trade policy that would more fairly treat agricultural commodities emanating from African origins:

> The EU's protectionist attitudes, particularly in food, keeps poor African farmers poor… It loudly promotes free market principles but on a global stage, it spectacularly fails to deliver. Far from levelling the playing field the EU reinforces the structural inequalities that favour big businesses and powerful countries at the expense of developing nations… The Common Agricultural Policy subsidizes continental European farmers to produce food in quantities that we cannot eat. Those heavily subsidised surpluses completely distort African and other markets. They undercut the prices of domestically produced food. They make it impossible for impoverished African farmers to compete, impossible for them to make a sustainable living. (Cleverly cited in Vote Leave, 2016)

Cleverly extolled the benefits of Brexit vis-à-vis the EU's immoral trade and agricultural policies that negatively impacted poorer communities in Africa. He additionally explained that his mother came from Sierra Leone, a Commonwealth nation, and that this underscored his moral objective to deliver fairer trade between the UK and African countries (ibid).

Furthermore, on the issue of migration, Leave campaigners made the case that Brexit would deliver a fairer migration system beneficial to Commonwealth countries in Africa. Nigel Farage himself made this argument. Speaking on breakfast television, the UK Independence Party (UKIP) leader stated that migrants from Africa and India were discriminated against in relation to migrants from EU member states. He claimed that this would be rectified under a post-Brexit points system:

> I believe in the Commonwealth, I believe in our relationship with the Commonwealth is vital, I think we have been stupid to turn our backs on it in favour of UK membership… And the effect of what I'm proposing – a points system, call it the Australia one or whatever you like -actually more black people would qualify to come in under that. (Dathan, 2016)

Juxtaposing European migration and Commonwealth migration, Farage sought to downplay accusations of xenophobia. This of course sat very uneasily with the notorious 'Breaking Point' poster that depicted predominantly non-white migrants as a threat to the UK's stability.

During the Brexit campaign, therefore, Leave campaigners clearly made appeals to a sense of a Commonwealth 'family'. Focusing on 'old' CANZUK ties and 'new' Commonwealth countries, Brexiteer politicians appealed to an imperial romanticism. Commonwealth narratives were also clearly central to Brexiteer elites' own ontological security and in terms of their nationalist foreign policy vision of the UK as a vigorous and empowered global actor. Moreover, Leave discourse about Commonwealth solidarity sought to negate portrayals of Brexit as an isolationist act that would leave Britain adrift. It is important to note, however, that much of this pro-Commonwealth narrative was undermined by the lead Leave campaigner, Boris Johnson, when he blamed US President Barack Obama's 'ancestral dislike of the British empire' for his support for Remain. This remark did much to undermine the Leave campaign's attempts to present itself as having a genuine concern for Commonwealth African nations (Namusoke, 2016: 469). African nations, as did the aforementioned 'Breaking Point' poster. As the next section explains, these events did not, however, prevent politicians such as Johnson from making positive discursive overtures to African Commonwealth countries in the post-Brexit articulation of the Global Britain project.

The Global Britain Project and 'Development' in Commonwealth Africa

With the resignation of David Cameron and the Conservative governments of Theresa May (2016–2019), Boris Johnson (2019–2022), Liz Truss (2022–2022) and Rishi Sunak (2022–to time of writing), Conservative elites' articulation of a post-Brexit Global Britain project has built upon Commonwealth historical narratives. The premiership of Theresa May emphasised that African Commonwealth countries would be a key partner for Britain after the withdrawal from the EU—eventually finalised in 2020 after a four-year transition. Notably, she embarked in 2018 upon her 'dancing' tour of Africa as part of a trade mission to South Africa, Kenya and Nigeria alongside a twenty-nine person business delegation (BBC News, 2018). In her speech in Cape Town, she emphasised that the UK would rely upon African partners for mutual prosperity in the post-Brexit context. Moreover, she expressed that the UK would replicate controversial EU free trade deals—Economic Partnership Agreements (EPAs) to be explored in more detail in Chapter 3. Echoing the securitised 'development' rhetoric of the Blair era, she stated that:

> The challenges facing Africa are not Africa's alone. It is in the world's interest to see that those jobs are created, to tackle the causes and symptoms of extremism and instability, to deal with migration flows and to encourage clean growth...that is why I want to create a new partnership

between the UK and our friends in Africa, one built around our shared prosperity and shared security. (UK Government, 2018)

May's securitised narrative of trade leading to economic development and social stability was also articulated by her then Trade Secretary, Liam Fox. In a speech to Commonwealth trade ministers in 2017, he remarked that:

> I have long believed that free trade is one of the most powerful tools we have to help those in greatest need around the world... The UK remains committed to pursuing free trade. That includes seeking to achieve continuity in our trade and investment relationships with third world countries... It is an unavoidable truth that prosperity, including an open and free trading environment, social stability, political stability and security are part of the same continuum. (UK Government, 2017)

According to Fox, UK trade with Commonwealth Africa would ensure both stability and development, while demonstrating Britain's ongoing global relevance.

The centrality of the Commonwealth—and African countries—to the Global Britain project was repeated by May's successor, Boris Johnson, during his tenure as Prime Minister. Echoing campaign narratives from the Brexit referendum, Johnson argued that the UK would benefit from a trade dividend with Commonwealth countries based on shared norms and language. Writing in *The Telegraph* in June 2022, he explained that emerging markets in British former colonies would provide an opportunity for UK entrepreneurialism and prosperity in relation to its 'sovereign' trade policy:

> All of this creates a unique opportunity for Britain whereby the Commonwealth – and only the Commonwealth – combines vast and rapidly growing markets with a real and quantified trading advantage. That is why we are mobilising the UK's regained sovereignty to sign free trade or economic partnership agreements with as many Commonwealth countries as possible...The Commonwealth's GDP - $13.1 trillion – has risen by a quarter since 2017. Over the next five years, it's forecast to jump by close to another 50 per cent to $19.5 trillion. (Johnson, 2022)

This narrative of win–win co-operation between the UK and emerging markets was repeated on his trip to Rwanda for the Commonwealth

Business Forum that same month where he finished a speech on the benefits of the Commonwealth for economic development in Africa (while comparing the association to 'fertiliser') with the remarks that:

> we in the UK have the technology, the City of London certainly has the finance, the Government that I'm proud to lead has the will, and our wonderful, wonderful Commonwealth, that great institution, has the super fertiliser, to be sprinkled across this extraordinary grouping of countries and above all to help to help you forge a new Africa, sharing your optimism that the people of this continent and every member of the Commonwealth can thrive and prosper from free trade and free enterprise. (UK Government, 2022a)

Within the speech, Johnson also voiced his support for the African Union's (AU) launching of the African Continental Free Trade Area (AfCFTA) and lauded his government's support for its new Secretariat based in Accra, Ghana (ibid).

In similar terms, his successor as Prime Minister, Liz Truss, while serving as Trade Minister and Foreign Secretary, articulated her own strong support for African countries within the Commonwealth as part of the Global Britain project. As part of her leadership campaign to succeed Johnson, Truss wrote for *The Times* extolling the need for a new Commonwealth economic partnership to counter the global influence of China. Coinciding with the UK's hosting of the Commonwealth Games, she stated that:

> Trading more with the Commonwealth isn't just about our economy, it's about countering the threats from malign actors. It is the largest grouping of nations that does not contain Russia or China. It has growing heft on the world stage, making up a third of the global population and about 30 per cent of the votes at the United Nations, with a combined GDP of more than £16 trillion. The Commonwealth can be a geopolitical powerhouse of the future, with an increasingly vital role to play in a more uncertain and febrile world. (cited in Zeffman, 2022)

With parallels to the securitisation of Africa under Blair, Truss articulated the need for Commonwealth solidarity in face of the emergence of China as a global superpower. In relation to Africa, she also made clear—in a speech to the UK-Africa Investment Summit (UK-AIS) in 2020—that

British business understood the opportunities to be acted upon within emerging markets:

> The UK has overtaken the US and is now the second largest G7 investor in the African continent. And why is that? It is because all of us here in the UK see the massive opportunities available. And what we know is that as the UK leaves the European Union, only a few days away, there are huge opportunities around the world. 90% of GDP growth is outside the EU. And the continent of Africa is one of the largest opportunities there is. In Africa there are 8 of the world's 15 largest growing economies. By 2030, 5 cities will have more than 10 million people. Kinshasa and Cairo will be in the global top 10. (UK Government, 2020)

Referencing the UK's imminent departure from the EU in that 2020 speech, she also repeated Brexit campaign themes relating to the need to pivot from Europe to emerging economies in the 'Global South'. This was despite that Truss herself had campaigned for Remain.

Her successor as Prime Minister, Rishi Sunak, has continued his predecessors' emphasis on the importance of the Commonwealth and of African states for Global Britain. Ahead of the second UK-AIS due in April 2024, Sunak emphasised the importance of African relationships to the UK economy:

> To grow the UK's economy, create opportunities for growth and bolster our economic security, we must deepen our ties with partners across the world. This summit will ensure we are able to harness the potential of our relationships across Africa and grow our economies together, making them stronger, resilient, and innovative. (UK Government, 2023a)

Sunak's then Foreign Secretary, James Cleverly, also re-emphasised Britain's commitment to the continent. A UK government (2023a) press release explained that:

> The Foreign Secretary committed last December to focusing on partnerships of the future with countries whose economies, populations and ultimately influence globally are growing. He sees countries in Africa as central to this and is seeking to build on our partnerships across the continent on the basis of respect, mutual benefit, common interests, and, most importantly, by listening to African countries' perspectives.

This emphasis on 'listening' to African countries coincided with Cleverly's earlier statement that 'as Foreign Secretary of a former imperial power, I know that in the past we succumbed to the temptation of will and appetite' (UK Government, 2022b). Cleverly presented his foreign policy approach as being historically informed and sensitive to the need for an equal relationship between the UK and African states. His successor as Foreign Secretary, Lord David Cameron of Chipping Norton, meanwhile, has already proved his own discursive commitment to Africa as Prime Minister. Endorsing the need for Britain to remain 'global' in his foreword to the UK government (2023b) White Paper on International Development published in November 2023, Lord Cameron is likely to focus upon Africa-UK linkages in the lead up to the second UK-AIS summit in April 2024.

It is clear from the above survey of elite politicians' statements on Africa and the Commonwealth in the post-Brexit period that the continent remains key to the ontological security of British policy-makers. By emphasising the humanitarian instincts of Global Britain, these politicians present the Global Britain project of extending trade and investment linkages as being part of the creation of pro-poor markets. In this sense, British engagement with African markets is not deemed to be motivated by pure self-interest as part of geopolitical competition vis-à-vis a 'new scramble for Africa'. Instead, Britain is seen to act upon moral values concerned with fair-dealing in the international economy. For instance, Britain is seen to be willing to allow competitive agricultural producers in African contexts to access British consumers without the protectionist equivalent of the CAP.

Interestingly, there appears to be consistency between the statements of Conservative and New Labour politicians not only in terms of focus upon humanitarian endeavours in Africa, but upon the security rationale behind these interventions. UK politicians regularly speak of the benefits of prosperity for stabilising otherwise 'dangerous' societies. This is also part of British politicians' ontological security and draws upon imperial notions of a 'civilised' Britain bringing stability and peace to 'barbarian' lands (Polonksa-Kimunguyi & Kimunguyi, 2017: 326). Many British politicians surveyed above act from a deep-seated sense of paternalism and fear regarding the potential dangers of an 'untamed' African continent. Blair's rhetoric in the post-9/11 context is perhaps the most glaring example of such paternalistic sentiments. More recent statements by politicians such as Theresa May, Liam Fox and Liz Truss, however, demonstrate that this strand of thinking remains present within Whitehall and within the Conservative Party. This is combined to the fact that New Labour architects—Peter Mandelson and Tony Blair in particular—are apparently mentoring the potential next Prime Minister in the form of Sir Keir Starmer. A securitised approach to Africa is not something that appears to be dissipating in the British political context.

Moreover, this securitised and paternalistic form of British 'humanitarianism' wholly lends itself to neo-colonial interventions in the African continent. UK elites' ontological security is rooted in their sense of a superior British or Anglosphere culture rooted in the ostensible values of democracy, fair play, free trade, the rule of law and a 'civilising' British mode of conduct. Not only does imperial romanticism motivate certain elite politicians—notably Johnson—but a deeper sense of cultural supremacy is readily apparent in the speeches of key UK political figures in the ways in which they talk about exporting not merely British commodities to Africa, but also British 'values'. The neo-colonial logic of such thinking is all too apparent and becomes readily visible in the subsequent chapters' discussion of UK trade, aid, security, corporate and investment policies. While Brexiteer politicians talked boldly of regaining Britain's 'sovereignty' in the international system, nevertheless, they endorse policy agendas that denude sovereignty in African country contexts. A system of 'global coloniality' is not dismantled by British interventions in Africa but is sustained and fortified by them.

Moreover, the concept of the coloniality of knowledge is particularly helpful in assessing the implications of British official discourse for African states (Ndlovu-Gatsheni, 2013, 2014, 2015). The concept underscores how British political elites—Prime Ministers, Foreign Secretaries and Trade Ministers—impose British knowledge constructs of free trade and 'pro-poor' economic growth upon African 'partners'. Liam Fox, for example, as Trade Minister spoke against the apparent false promises of 'protectionism' for developing economies while lauding the teachings of Adam Smith on the advantages of the free market (UK Government, 2016). This domineering political discourse from UK government elites—when combined to material forms of power such as British aid money and trade arrangements—has potentially transformative effects in the sense of closing-down alternative developmentalist policy avenues in African states. This of course depends upon African officials' responses to British power exertion, with Nkrumah's drive for an African Common Market being one example of a successful manoeuvre by African elites to restrain external influence (discussed in more detail in the concluding chapter).

Conclusion

British imperial imaginaries of the Commonwealth have been key to British political elites' ontological security in the post-war era. The expansion of the Commonwealth beyond the 'White Dominions' to include the 'new' members in Asia and Africa contributed to British elites' sense of security and prosperity within the wider international realm as 'decolonisation' unfolded. During the Cold War, the presence of the Commonwealth was key to British politicians' sense of their, and their country's, relevance in global affairs amid superpower competition between the USA and the Soviet Union. By maintaining (post)imperial linkages with Africa, Britain could be seen to maintain influence over a large swathe of countries in the 'Global South'. Moreover, certain Conservative politicians viewed UK admission to the EEC as sitting in tension with British commitment to the Commonwealth 'family', which later influenced the Brexit referendum in terms of Brexiteer narratives of a 'betrayal' in 1973.

While British engagement with the Commonwealth was hindered by successive UK governments' approach to white supremacist regimes in South Africa and Rhodesia, the release of Mandela combined to the end of the Cold War gave a boost to British politicians' agency. Linkages to the Commonwealth became key to recent British politicians' ontological security as figures such as Robin Cook and Tony Blair spoke of Britain's moral place in the international community and their dedication to healing 'the scar on the conscience of the world' with regard to Commonwealth Africa. Interestingly, however, Abrahamsen (2005) demonstrates how the Blair government's approach to Africa became increasingly securitised, in the sense of interventions being viewed through a security prism. In fact, Blair increasingly viewed development and poverty reduction efforts associated with the MDGs as a means of stabilising otherwise 'dangerous' societies, especially in African nations with high proportions of Muslim citizenries. This uneasy blend of security and humanitarian concerns could also be found in the approach of the Cameron government, the latter being of particular importance in his rebranding of the Conservative Party while in opposition in the 2000s too.

As the chapter has also illustrated, the political salience of the Commonwealth impacted upon the Brexit referendum. Brexiteer politicians such as James Cleverly and Daniel Hannan—and Nigel Farage—drew upon imperial romanticism and appeals to the African Commonwealth to inoculate the Brexit campaign from criticisms of xenophobia. These politicians' discursive appeals to Africa and to imperial nostalgia have subsequently impacted upon the Global Britain project and the importance of Africa to UK officials in the post-referendum period. Nevertheless, while British narratives of 'assisting' Commonwealth Africa remain key to UK politicians' ontological security, the next chapters' assessment of UK policies demonstrates that Global Britain exacerbates situations of neo-colonialism and global coloniality. Rather than being a solution to ill-being in African situations, the British state and its Global Britain project are an impediment to the continent's realisation of a more genuine and sustained form of 'development'. Britain amid the 'new scramble for Africa' denudes African countries' empirical sovereignty. This is despite Brexiteers narratives about the importance of the UK's own (regained) sovereignty for 'win–win' prosperity and independence within UK-Africa ties.

Bibliography

Abrahamsen, R. (2005). Blair's Africa: The Politics of Securitization and Fear. *Alternatives: Global, Local, Political, 30*(1), 55–80.

BBC News. (2018, August 27). Theresa May to Visit Africa for First Time as Prime Minister. *BBC News.* https://www.bbc.co.uk/news/uk-politics-45318022. Accessed 6 March 2023.

Bell, D., & Vucetic, S. (2019). Brexit, CANZUK, and the Legacy of Empire. *The British Journal of Politics and International Relations, 21*(2), 367–382.

Beswick, D. (2019). Rehabilitating the "Nasty Party"? The Conservative Party and Africa from Opposition to Government. In D. Beswick, J. Fisher, & S. Hurt (Eds.), *Britain and Africa in the Twenty-First Century: Between Ambition and Pragmatism* (pp. 121–138). Manchester University Press.

Bishara, M. (2022, October 17). Opinion - Josep Borrell as Europe's Racist "Gardener". *Al Jazeera.*

Brown, W. (2019). Labour, International Development and Africa: Policy Rethinking in Opposition. In D. Beswick, J. Fisher & S. Hurt (Eds.), *Britain and Africa in the Twenty-First Century: Between Ambition and Pragmatism.* Manchester University Press

Brysk, A., Parsons, C., & Sandholtz, W. (2002). After Empire: National Identity and Post-colonial Families of Nations. *European Journal of International Relations, 8*(2), 267–305.

Calhoun, C. (2017). Populism, Nationalism and Brexit. In W. Outhwaite (Ed.), *Brexit: Sociological Responses* (pp. 57–76). Anthem Press.

Catterall, P. (2018). The Plural Society: Labour and the Commonwealth Idea 1900–1964. *The Journal of Imperial and Commonwealth History, 46*(5), 821–844.

Conservative Home. (2013, July 29). Daniel Hannan MEP: How the EU Pays to Keep Africa in Poverty. *Conservative Home*. https://conservativehome.com/2013/07/29/watch-danhannanmep-how-the-eu-pays-to-keep-africa-in-poverty/. Accessed 6 March 2023.

Daddow, O. (2018). Brexit and Britain's Role in the World. In P. Diamond, P. Nedergaard, & B. Rosamond (Eds.), *The Routledge Handbook of the Politics of Brexit* (pp. 208–222). Routledge.

Dathan. (2016, June 8). More Black People Will Be Allowed into Britain If We Leave the EU and Immigration Will Become a "Non-Issue" Says Nigel Farage. *The Daily Mail*. https://www.dailymail.co.uk/news/article-3630847/More-black-people-allowed-Britain-leave-EU-immigration-non-issue-says-Nigel-Farage.html. Accessed 6 March 2023.

Gallagher, J. (2011). *Britain and Africa under Blair: In Pursuit of the Good State*. Manchester University Press.

Grosfoguel, R. (2002). Colonial Difference, Geopolitics of Knowledge, and Global Coloniality in the Modern/Colonial Capitalist World-System. *Review (fernand Braudel Center), 25*(3), 203–224.

Groves, J. (2013, January 1). Britain's Aid Millions Help the Most Corrupt Regimes in the World it is Revealed as Cameroon's Target is Finally Hit. *The Daily Mail*.

Gruhn, I. (1976). The Lomé Convention: Inching towards interdependence. *International Organization, 30*(2), 241–262.

Haastrup, T., Duggan, N., & Mah, L. (2021). Navigating Ontological (In)Security in EU–Africa Relations. *Global Affairs, 7*(4), 541–557.

Hannan, D. (2016, June 21). Free Britain to Trade with the World. *The Financial Times*. https://www.ft.com/content/6d4a444a-36f5-11e6-a780-b48ed7b6126f. Accessed 6 March 2023.

Holmes, J. (1962). The Impact on the Commonwealth of the Emergence of Africa. *International Organization, 16*(2), 291–302.

Hyam, R. (1998). The Parting of the Ways: Britain and South Africa's Departure from the Commonwealth, 1951–61. *The Journal of Imperial and Commonwealth History, 26*(2), 157–175.

The Independent. (2018, January 22). Margaret Thatcher Believed South Africa should be a "Whites-Only-State", says Former Chief Diplomat. *The Independent*.

Johnson, B. (2022, June 19). The Commonwealth Gives Britain a Boost. *The Telegraph*. https://www.telegraph.co.uk/news/2022/06/19/commonwealth-gives-britain-boost/. Accessed 6 March 2023.

Koegler, C., Kumar, P., & Tronicke, M. (2020). The Colonial Remains of Brexit: Empire Nostalgia and Narcissistic Nationalism. *Journal of Postcolonial Writing, 56*(5), 585–592.

Láng, I. (1979). The Conflict between American and British Commercial Policies Prior to World War II. *Acta Historica Academiae Scientiarum Hungaricae, 25*(3/4), 267–297.

Leroux, M. (2017, March 6). Ministers Aim to Build "Empire 2.0" with African Commonwealth. *The Times*.

McIntyre, D. (2000). Britain and the Creation of the Commonwealth Secretariat. *The Journal of Imperial and Commonwealth History, 28*(1), 135–158.

Mcintyre, W. D., Mole, S., Ashworth, L.M., Shaw, T. M., & May, A. (2007). Whose Commonwealth? Responses to Krishnan Srinivasan's The Rise, Decline and Future of the British Commonwealth. *The Round Table, 96*(388), 57–70.

McKinnon, D. (2004). After Abuja: Africa and the Commonwealth. *The Round Table, 93*(375), 403–409.

Murphy, P. (2011). Britain and the Commonwealth: Confronting the Past—Imagining the Future. *The Round Table, 100*(414), 267–283.

Murphy, P. (2018). *The Empire's New Clothes: The Myth of the Commonwealth*. Oxford University Press.

Murray-Evans, P. (2016). Myths of Commonwealth Betrayal: UK–Africa Trade Before and After Brexit. *The Round Table, 105*(5), 489–498.

Murray-Evans, P. (2018). Brexit and the Commonwealth: Fantasy Meets Reality. In P. Diamond, P. Nedergaard, & B. Rosamond (Eds.), *The Routledge Handbook of the Politics of Brexit* (pp. 197–207). Routledge.

Namusoke, E. (2016). A Divided Family: Race, the Commonwealth and Brexit. *The round Table, 105*(5), 463–476.

Ndlovu-Gatsheni, S. J. (2013). *Coloniality of Power in Post-Colonial Africa*. CODESRIA.

Ndlovu-Gatsheni, S. J. (2014). Global Coloniality and the Challenges of Creating African Futures. *Strategic Review for Southern Africa, 36*(2), 181–202.

Ndlovu-Gatsheni, S. J. (2015). *Empire, Global Coloniality and African Subjectivity*. Berghahn Books.

Nebehay, S. (2018, March 21). Executions, Torture, and Slave Markets Persist in Libya: UN. *Reuters*. https://www.reuters.com/article/us-libya-security-rights-idUSKBN1GX1JY. Accessed 6 March 2023.

Nelson, F. (2012, September 8). Justine Greening may be Tighter on International Aid. *The Spectator*. https://www.spectator.co.uk/article/justine-greening-may-be-tighter-on-international-aid/. Accessed 6 March 2023.

Nkrumah, K. (1965). *Neo-Colonialism: The Last Stage of Imperialism*. Panaf Press.

Nunn, A., & Price, S. (2004). Managing development: EU and African relations through the Evolution of the Lomé and Cotonou Agreements. *Historical Materialism, 12*(4), 203–230.

Obeng, S. (1979). *Selected Speeches of Kwame Nkrumah,* (Vol. 2). Afram Publishers.

Ølholm Eaton, M. (2020). We Are All Children of the Commonwealth': Political Myth, Metaphor and the Transnational Commonwealth "Family of Nations" in Brexit Discourse. *British Politics, 15,* 326–348.

Ølholm Eaton, M., & Smith, A. D. (2020). The Use of Historical Analogy in the 2017 Parliamentary Debates on the Future of Post-Brexit Commonwealth Trade. *Political Studies Review, 18*(4), 591–610.

Ovendale, R. (1995). MacMillan and the Wind of Change in Africa. *The Historical Journal, 38*(2), 455–477.

Połońska-Kimunguyi, E., & Kimunguyi, P. (2017). Gunboats of Soft Power": Boris on Africa and Post-Brexit "Global Britain." *Cambridge Review of International Affairs, 30*(4), 325–349.

Porteous, T. (2005). British Government Policy in Sub-Saharan Africa under New Labour. *International Affairs, 81*(2), 281–297.

Price, S., & Nunn, A. (2018). Managing Neo-Liberalisation through the Sustainable Development Agenda: The EU-ACP trade Relationship and World Market Expansion. In M. Langan & S. Price (Eds.), *Sustainable Development in Africa-EU relations* (pp. 24–39). Routledge.

Ramdani, N. (2019, April 11). Brexit Wasn't David Cameron's Worst Political Mistake—Bombing Libya Made the World A More Dangerous Place. *The Independent.* https://www.independent.co.uk/voices/libya-civil-war-david-cameron-gaddafi-bombing-brexit-a8863306.html. Accessed 6 March 2023.

Sakr, R. (2023). Regionalism as Development: The Lomé Conventions I and II (1975–1985). *Leiden Journal of International Law, 36*(1), 33–59.

Saunders, R. (2020). Brexit and Empire: "Global Britain" and the Myth of Imperial Nostalgia. *The Journal of Imperial and Commonwealth History, 48*(6), 1140–1174.

Siméon, O. (2019, May 9). British Protectionism Through the Ages: An Interview with David Todd. *Books & Ideas*. https://booksandideas.net/British-Protectionism-Through-the-Ages.html. Accessed 6 March 2023.

Taylor, I. (2000). Legitimisation and De-Legitimisation within a Multilateral Organisation: South Africa and the Commonwealth. *Politikon, 27*(1), 51–72.

Taylor, I. (2012). Spinderella on Safari: British Policies Toward Africa Under New Labour. *Global Governance, 18*(4), 449–460.
Thackeray, D., & Toye, R. (2019). Debating Empire 2.0. In S. Ward & A. Rasch (Eds.), *Embers of Empire in Brexit Britain* (pp. 15–24). Bloomsbury.
UK Government. (2016, September 29). 'Liam Fox's Free Trade Speech. *UK Government online.* https://www.gov.uk/government/speeches/liam-foxs-free-trade-speech. Accessed 6 March 2023.
UK Government. (2017, March 9). Commonwealth Trade Ministers Meeting: Towards a Free Trading Future. *UK Government online.* https://www.gov.uk/government/speeches/commonwealth-trade-ministers-meeting-towards-a-free-trading-future#:~:text=Liberation%20from%20poverty&text=I%20have%20long%20believed%20that,as%20a%20badge%20of%20honour. Accessed 6 March 2023.
UK Government. (2018, August 28). PM's Speech in Cape Town: 28 August 2018. *UK Government online.* https://www.gov.uk/government/speeches/pms-speech-in-cape-town-28-august-2018. Accessed 6 March 2023.
UK Government. (2020, January 17). Elizabeth Truss Champions "Lionesses of Africa". *UK Government online.* https://www.gov.uk/government/speeches/elizabeth-truss-champions-lionesses-of-africa. Accessed 6 March 2023.
UK Government. (2022a, June 23). PM Speech at the Commonwealth Business Forum. *UK Government online.* https://www.gov.uk/government/speeches/pm-speech-at-the-commonwealth-business-forum. Accessed 6 March 2023.
UK Government. (2022b, December 12). British Foreign Policy and Diplomacy: Foreign Secretary's Speech, 12 December 2022. *UK Government online.* https://www.gov.uk/government/speeches/foreign-secretarys-speech-12-december-2022. Accessed 6 April 2023.
UK Government. (2023a, March 9). UK to Host African Investment Summit in April 2024. *UK Government online.* https://www.gov.uk/government/news/uk-to-host-african-investment-summit-in-april-2024. Accessed 6 March 2023.
UK Government. (2023b). International Development in a Contested World: Ending Extreme Poverty and Tackling Climate Change. *UK Government.*
Vote Leave. (2016, April 27). Speech by James Cleverly MP: "How the EU's Common Agricultural Policy is Making Africans Poorer". *Vote Leave.* http://www.voteleavetakecontrol.org/speech_by_james_cleverly_mp.html. Accessed 6 March 2023.
Vickers, B. (2018). Implications of Brexit. In T. Shaw, L. Mahrenbach, R. Modi & Y. Xu (Eds.), *The Palgrave Handbook of Contemporary International Political Economy.* Palgrave.

Von Tunzelman. (2017, August 18). Who is to Blame for Partition? Above All, Imperial Britain. *New York Times*. https://www.nytimes.com/2017/08/18/opinion/india-pakistan-partition-imperial-britain.html. Accessed 6 March 2023.

Wellings, B. (2021). Brexit, Nationalism and Disintegration in the European Union and the United Kingdom. *Journal of Contemporary European Studies, 29*(3), 322–334.

Williams, P. (2005). Blair's Britain and the Commonwealth. *The round Table, 94*(380), 381–391.

Zarakol, A. (2010). Ontological (In)Security and State Denial of Historical crimes: Turkey and Japan. *International Relations, 24*(3), 3–23.

Zeffmann, H. (2022, July 28). Liz Truss Calls for More Commonwealth Trade. *The Times*. https://www.thetimes.co.uk/article/liz-truss-calls-for-more-commonwealth-trade-ms2chq9ld. Accessed 6 March 2023.

CHAPTER 3

Global Britain and Africa-UK Trade Relations

Introduction

The Brexit referendum was fought, in part, in relation to Leave narratives surrounding the need for a 'global' UK to offer African Commonwealth partners a fairer trading relationship. Figures such as Daniel Hannan (2016), Peter Lilley (2016) and Boris Johnson (2016) criticised the EU for its protectionist trade stance and argued that an independent UK trade policy would offer opportunities for 'development' in the Commonwealth. Moreover, since the Leave victory, UK prime ministers and cabinet ministers in their pursuit of the Global Britain project have re-emphasised this commitment. They have promised that the newly (re)formed UK Department for International Trade (DIT)—known as the Department for Business and Trade (DBT) since February 2023—will negotiate equitable trade agreements with African states that protect their level of access to British consumers and improve upon conditions vis-à-vis existing Africa-EU arrangements. Notably, Liam Fox promised that African countries would face no disadvantage upon the UK's legal withdrawal from the EU and would enjoy easy access to British markets under Brexit (UK Government, 2017a).

This chapter examines the trade relationship between the UK and African countries in the context of Brexit and the launch of Global Britain. It first provides historical background to the UK's recent negotiation of trade deals with African officialdom. Namely, it explores the significance of the EU's Economic Partnership Agreements (EPAs) in African, Caribbean and Pacific (ACP) countries in terms of the UK's withdrawal from pre-existing trade arrangements in relation to states such as Ghana. Moreover, it assesses the EU's own non-reciprocal trade schedules with African countries in relation to Everything But Arms (EBA) and the broader Generalised Scheme of Preferences (GSP). It underscores how diverging access to EBA between 'least developed countries' (LDCs) such as Uganda, and 'non-least developed countries' (non-LDCs) such as Kenya, has problematised integration efforts within African Regional Economic Communities (RECs). Importantly, it underscores the significant role played by Britain under New Labour in supporting the launch of EPA negotiations, with particular emphasis on then Directorate General (DG) Trade Commissioner, Peter Mandelson.

Following on from the historical contextualisation, the chapter then focuses upon UK politicians' promises in relation to trade policies enabled by the British withdrawal from the EU. It highlights pledges made by successive UK prime ministers and cabinet ministers about improving 'development' opportunities in the African continent via equitable trade arrangements. For instance, in terms of the UK government's (2021a) Integrated Review, *Global Britain in a Competitive Age*. In so doing, the chapter emphasises the UK's emphasis upon free market approaches to poverty reduction within a broader 'Post-Washington Consensus' (PWC) approach to international development (Fine, 2003; Öniş & Şenses, 2005). The chapter underscores that despite UK promises to improve upon EU trade policies towards Africa, that, nevertheless, the Global Britain project pursues the same problematic free trade agenda as the European Commission. Thereafter, the chapter explores the 'roll over' trade arrangements that the UK government has now established with African countries. This highlights especially the trade deal signed between British and Ghanaian officials amid accusations of British 'bullying' and bad faith (Burden, 2020; Merrick, 2020). It also assesses the 'development' merits of the UK's alternative to the EU GSP in terms of the newly launched UK Developing Countries Trading Scheme (DCTS). Finally, the chapter then considers the future trajectories of UK trade policy, particularly in relation to the African Continental Free Trade Area (AfCFTA) launched in 2019 by the African Union (AU). It considers British officials' desire to emulate EU plans for a Europe-Africa trade bloc—strategically 'piggybacking' on market opening between African countries themselves. In this context, the chapter emphasises the relevance of Nkrumah's (1965) critique of neo-colonialism—and the decolonial critique of global coloniality—for making sense of Global Britain's trade policies in Africa (Ndlovu-Gatsheni, 2015).

EU Free Trade Agendas in Africa: Assessing EPAs and EBA/GSP

The UK's withdrawal from the EU means that it is no longer party to a myriad of agreements and trade schemes between the EU and African states. During the lifetime of the Cotonou Agreement signed between EU officials and ACP countries in 2000, the European Commission vigorously pursued free trade deals with sub-regions of the ACP bloc. Namely in terms of Eastern Africa, Western Africa, Central Africa, Southern Africa, the Caribbean and the Pacific. Countries in North Africa such as Morocco and Tunisia have meanwhile been treated separately within EU trade policy agendas as non-ACP members. Several North African countries as part of Association agreements with the EU have committed themselves to signing free trade deals known as Deep and Comprehensive Free Trade Agreement (DCFTAs). This sits within the European Neighbourhood Policy (ENP) amid EU officials' ambitions for an eventual Euro-Mediterranean Free Trade Area (EMFTA) (Langan & Price, 2020).

In relation to African members of the ACP grouping south of the Sahara, the Cotonou Agreement mandated free trade deals known as EPAs. The European Commission argued that World Trade Organisation (WTO) rules meant that African countries would be required to acquiesce to trade liberalisation and tariff dismantling to maintain low tariff access to European consumers (Hurt, 2003; Nunn & Price, 2004). The previous granting of non-reciprocal trade preferences under the Lomé Conventions (1975–2000) signed between ACP countries and the then European Economic Community (EEC) was deemed to fall foul of WTO regulations since it constituted a form of discrimination against non-ACP developing countries (Grynberg, 1998; Hurt, 2003). In what Hurt (2003: 174) terms the EU's externalisation of responsibility for its own preferred policy direction towards free trade, EU officials thus blamed the WTO for the need for trade reciprocity in the timeframe of the Cotonou Agreement.

African negotiators for the eventual Cotonou Agreement were alarmed by this EU trade volte-face. Consequently, they issued the Libreville

Declaration in 1997 alongside other ACP ambassadors pointing to the economic damage and social relocation that would be visited upon their societies under free trade deals (Brown, 2000: 376). ACP officials argued that premature trade liberalisation under free trade agreements (FTAs)—or what became known as the EPAs—would have deleterious consequences for their manufacturers and agro-processors in terms of nascent industries. Producers in the Kenyan textiles industry, for example, would be unable to compete with imports originating from EU member states if protective tariffs were mandated for removal under an EPA (Traidcraft, 2005). ACP negotiators thus argued that EPAs would close down opportunities for economic diversification in former colonial contexts, instead perpetuating colonial patterns of trade in terms of dependence upon raw material and unprocessed agricultural exports to the European metropole (ibid.). Moreover, key figures such as President Abdoulaye Wade of Senegal pointed to the significance of import tariffs for government revenues and social expenditure within ACP countries. The dismantling of tariff schedules under EPAs would therefore not only pose a threat to jobs and livelihoods within vulnerable import-competing sectors but would have an immediate impact upon government spending in relation to public services such as health and education (Plank et al., 2021: 167). Meanwhile, President Muhummadu Buhari of Nigeria pointed to the likely decimation of dairy producers under the weight of subsidised imports from EU member states under EPAs (alluding to the EU Common Agricultural Policy) (Nigerian Tribune, 2022). ACP officials therefore queried how the EU could seek to impose premature free trade deals on former colonies under the wider framework of what became the Cotonou 'development' partnership. They sought to maintain non-reciprocal trade access to European consumers as had been enjoyed since the signing of the first Lomé Convention in 1975. Indeed, that Convention had been signed amid developing countries' calls for a more equitable trade environment as part of a New International Economic Order (NIEO) (Gruhn, 1976). The imposition of EPAs was therefore viewed by ACP officials and African civil society groups as a step back from earlier European commitments to level the playing field for former colonies in the aftermath of formal Empire (Chipaike & Knowledge, 2018; Trommer, 2011).

However, despite ACP officials' and civil society concerns—alongside doubts expressed by European parliamentarians and trade justice campaigners—the European Commission insisted that EPAs would be a requirement for ACP countries to maintain equivalent market access to Europe as had been enjoyed under the Lomé Conventions (see, for example, Greens-EFA, 2012). The EU therefore launched negotiations with sub-regions of the ACP bloc for the conclusion of EPAs. EU officials insisted, however, that the deals would be compatible with overarching 'development' norms outlined within the Cotonou Agreement. Specifically, the EPAs would include a 'sensitive goods basket' which would exempt sectors that were particularly vulnerable to European competition from liberalisation (up to 20% of commodity lines could be included) (Berends, 2016). Moreover, EU officials stated that phased liberalisation would provide ACP producers in import-competing sectors (in the 80% of goods subject to tariff dismantling) ample time to enhance their competitiveness, or else diversify into other productive activities (Koroma & Ford, 2006). In addition to this, they argued that EU provision of 'Aid for Trade' monies under the ACP-EU European Development Fund (EDF) would facilitate ACP countries' 'smooth and gradual' integration into global markets (Langan & Scott, 2011). As a result of such factors, the EPA deals were promoted as being commensurate with poverty reduction efforts. In fact, EU officials claimed that the competitiveness instilled by EPAs—combined to low tariff access to European consumers—would bring about job creation and social prosperity in Africa (GRAIN, 2017).

It should also be noted here that the EU under its Generalised Scheme of Preferences (GSP) for developing countries introduced an initiative in 2001 named Everything But Arms (EBA). The launch of EBA promised duty free and quota free (DFQF) access to European consumers for LDC countries irrespective of whether they committed to a free trade deal. EBA in this sense represented a non-reciprocal trade regime since the EU promised DFQF access to LDCs, such as Uganda, without mandating tariff reductions in return. Again, this was presented as evidence of the benevolence of EU trade policy in the context of wider normative 'pro-poor' commitments to the UN Millennium Development Goals (MDGs) in the timeframe of the Cotonou Agreement (European Commission, 2005a). The EU's wider GSP thus offered three tiers of access to developing countries: (i) the standard GSP for non-LDCs with tariff rates considerably higher in commodities such as cocoa paste and cocoa butter than ACP countries had enjoyed under Lomé; (ii) GSP 'Plus' with duty free access for non-LDCs that signed up to strict sustainable development and human rights commitments; and (iii) the EBA with DFQF access for LDCs (European Commission, 2023).

This complex picture of EU trade arrangements—the pursuit of EPAs—combined to the existence of the three tiers of GSP—forms the background upon which an independent UK trade policy now emerges. The UK as part of the EU had been a signatory to various EPAs with ACP countries including the fully fledged Caribbean Forum (CARIFORUM) EPA with Caribbean countries; an EPA with Southern African Customs Union (SACU) plus Mozambique; as well as so-called *interim* EPAs with African states including Ghana and Cote d'Ivoire. The UK's withdrawal from the EU removed it from such deals and meant that African countries would need to negotiate with British officials to maintain equivalent access to UK consumers. Brexit in this sense also complicated EU regional negotiations with African RECs such as the East African Community (EAC). EU talks with EAC officials for the conclusion of a full regional EPA had already been subject to disagreements emerging between the East African countries as to the advantages of a regional EPA (Mold, 2018). Countries such as Uganda and Tanzania that qualified as LDCs had little incentive to sign up to an EPA tariff liberalisation agenda, whereas non-LDCs such as Kenya desired an EPA to maintain low tariff access to European markets (ibid.). The withdrawal of the UK from the EU entrenched EAC divisions. Tanzania explicitly cited Brexit as yet more reason to refuse a regional free trade deal with the EU (Mbori & Gathii, 2020). Likewise, Nigeria within the Economic Community of West African States (ECOWAS) also found Brexit to be another barrier to the conclusion of a West African deal (Akinterinwa cited in The Sun Nigeria, 2016).

Before moving towards consideration of UK pledges to more equitable trade with African countries as part of the Global Britain project, it is important to note that the EU Trade Commissioner from 2004 to 2008 was UK New Labour architect, Peter Mandelson. Appointed by Prime Minister Blair as the UK's nominee for the European Commission, Mandelson was then directed to lead the Directorate General for Trade by President Jose Manuel Barroso (Cowell, 2004). Mandelson held responsibility therefore for the negotiation and conclusion of the EPAs by the original 31st December 2007 deadline. During his tenure, Commissioner Mandelson was one of the most enthusiastic and proactive proponents of the EPAs. At one summit, he was accused of shouting 'neo-colonial style' at a group of ACP ministers for their apparent reliance on foreign advisors (Monbiot, 2008). Mandelson repeatedly argued for the benefits of economic globalisation—understood as a synonym for trade liberalisation—for poverty reduction in the Global South. He explained that ACP economies would experience improved competitiveness upon opening their markets to the rigours of international trade. Moreover, he challenged civil society groups and other free trade sceptics in terms of their role in encouraging African leaderships to contest pro-poor trade deals with the EU. Speaking to the Civil Society Dialogue Group in Brussels in 2005, Mandelson argued that:

> EPAs are potentially a crucial, hugely positive contribution that Europe can and must make to trade and development. I am convinced of that. The purpose is the successful integration of the ACP economies in the global economy - and by that I mean putting the ACP on a ladder of prosperity that ends the grinding poverty which is the daily experience of so many ACP citizens. Until now, the EU-ACP relationship has simply not delivered on trade. It has adhered to the status quo and to a cycle of dependency. As result, these countries are not getting their fair share of the benefits of global economic integration. (cited in The Guardian, 2005)

Insisting that he welcomed the 'debate' offered by civil society activism on EPAs, nevertheless, he reportedly condemned the UK for being too heavily influenced by NGOs on trade policy matters (Sapp, 2005). Moreover, in alignment with Hurt's (2003) critique of the EU's 'externalisation of responsibility' for its own volte-face towards free trade deals, Mandelson denied that EU mercantilist instincts were at play. In a speech to the Trade Committee of the European Parliament, he directly cited WTO rules for being responsible for the demise of non-reciprocal trade under Lomé:

> Let me stress, up front, that our EPA agenda is emphatically not about opening markets to our own exports: it is about opening European, as well as crucial regional markets to developing countries and enabling them to take advantage of these opportunities. To comply with our WTO obligations there has to be an element of reciprocity in these agreements, but there will be no equality in these obligations. Our ACP partners will only be expected to open their markets progressively over a long period, and only as their capacity to trade allows. (European Commission, 2005b)

Mandelson clearly became frustrated by his failure to conclude EPAs will all of the negotiating sub-regions of the ACP bloc. Memorably, he deemed Nigeria to be an 'elephant sitting in the middle of the road' in terms of its refusal to acquiesce to tariff dismantling (Plank et al., 2021: 167). Nigerian officials and civil society continue to insist that an EPA would be incommensurate with the country's industrialisation strategy, which requires protective tariffs for emerging sectors unable to (yet) compete with more technologically advanced European rivals (Igechi, 2021).

Given Mandelson's prominent role in the 2000s, the argument deployed by Brexiteer campaigners that 'Europe' was responsible for unfair trade deals being imposed upon Commonwealth Africa—and that an independent UK trade policy would be able to rectify this—is amnesiatic (cf. Nicolaïdis, 2015). Their argument strategically 'forgets' the role of Britain in sponsoring EPAs across Africa. Moreover, it is odd that such critiques came from Conservative politicians whose party's own free market ethos was adopted by New Labour architects such as Mandelson in their 'Third Way' triangulation within UK and EU politics (Hale, 2011). In this context, the promises of Brexiteer politicians that UK withdrawal from the EU would open up opportunities for fairer trade with Africa were highly questionable from the outset. As the next section demonstrates, however, their promises since been reinforced by UK prime ministers and cabinet officials in their building of 'Global Britain', post-referendum.

GLOBAL BRITAIN AND PLEDGES TO PRO-POOR TRADE WITH AFRICAN COUNTRIES

Theresa May's official launching of a post-referendum Global Britain project came in her Lancaster House speech in January 2017. In this address, she emphasised her commitment to developing fruitful trade ties with Europe while also signalling the endeavour to build new linkages with 'old friends' and 'new allies':

> I want us to be a truly Global Britain – the best friend and neighbour to our European partners, but a country that reaches beyond the borders of Europe too. A country that gets out into the world to build relationships with old friends and new allies alike. I want Britain to be what we have the potential, talent and ambition to be. A great, global trading nation that is respected around the world and strong, confident and united at home. (May cited in UK Government, 2017b)

Since the launch of Global Britain, there has been pronounced discourse surrounding the importance of African countries for the UK's post-Brexit prosperity (as Chapter 2 noted in terms of UK elites' own ontological security). Moreover, there has been a normative focus on the ability of the UK to deliver pro-poor trade deals via the 'sovereign' exercise of an independent trade policy. In this vein, the (re)creation of the UK Department for International Trade (DIT) was hailed as an opportunity to support poverty reduction in emerging economies, not least in Commonwealth Africa. Rehearsing the logic of 'comparative advantages' inherent to a free trade ethos, DIT's (2017: 8) white paper *Preparing For Our Future UK Trade Policy* published in October 2017 argued that:

> The UK government has a long-standing commitment to support developing countries to reduce poverty through trade…This will help them to continue to benefit from trade by growing their economies, increasing incomes and reducing poverty. Helping to build developing countries' prosperity creates the conditions that allow commerce to flourish and in doing so, opens up opportunities for UK business in future markets.

Furthermore, the DIT white paper pledged that developing countries would not lose out from any transitional turbulence vis-à-vis the UK's withdrawal from EU trade deals. In addition to this promise, the white paper emphasised that 'free trade does not mean trade without rules' (DIT, 2017: 8). It insisted that developing countries would be allowed the policy space to impose safeguard measures where imports threatened sensitive industries. In another apparent sign of a willingness to take a nuanced approach to the benefits of free trade, the then Trade Minister, Liam Fox, in the foreword of the white paper commented upon the need for a fairer share of trade gains within the UK itself:

> We must recognise that whilst globalisation has spread prosperity and lifted millions out of poverty, some have felt left behind. Aligning our domestic Industrial Strategy and our trade ambitions will be key to delivering the innovative, competitive and growing economy that benefits individuals and communities, and will ensure the value of trade is shared more widely. (cited in DIT, 2017: 4)

Fox alluded here to arguments that the Brexit referendum had swung to a Leave victory on the back of voter discontent within post-industrial towns and cities within England. Namely, that the 'losers' of free trade—or of what some commentators dub the 'China effect'—had expressed their political discontent by voting against 'establishment' and/or 'centrist' politicians such as David Cameron or Hillary Clinton within the 'Global North' (Rama, 2003: 9; Rosenberg & Boyle, 2019). Such arguments were prominent at the time of the white paper's publication owing to the 2016 presidential election victory of Donald Trump in the USA. This was a US election in which Trump had blamed the Clintons for the North Atlantic Free Trade Agreement (NAFTA) and had promised to clamp down on 'unfair' trade from China (Edwards, 2018).

Nevertheless, despite evidence of a potentially nuanced approach to the benefits of free trade regimes within the DIT white paper, UK ministers and prime ministers have been less nuanced in their pronouncements on the need for African partners to sign free trade deals. One example was the speech delivered by then Minister for Africa, Andrew Stephenson, at a United Nations Global Compact (UNGC) event in January 2020. Stephenson spoke effusively of the benefits of win-win free trade for the UK and African economies. In particular, he referenced Africa's demographic trends and the need to integrate African youth into global markets for job creation and poverty reduction:

> By 2050, over 2 billion people will live in Africa and 1 in 4 global consumers will be African. Currently, African countries receive less than 4% of foreign direct investment and around 20 million jobs a year must be created to keep pace with that population growth. That is why I want to create mutually beneficial partnerships and help Africa move beyond aid, to trade. (Stephenson cited in UK Government, 2020)

This pro-poor rhetoric of win-win trade opportunities is further illustrated by Penny Mordaunt's language during her time as Minister of State for Trade Policy. Her written response to the House of Commons International Trade Committee's (ITC) enquiry on the impact of UK trade policy for developing countries pledged that:

> we can support countries to become more self-sufficient through trade, creating stronger trade and investment partners for the future. We will also deliver on our commitment… of enabling developing countries' integration into the global economy and achieving the Sustainable Development Goals. Furthermore, through our trade and economic partnerships the UK can

help to foster a global Network of Liberty that advances our values, such as free enterprise, openness, democracy and poverty reduction. (DIT, 2022)

Mordaunt articulated a liberal vision of free trade not only solidifying economic prosperity, but also providing a basis for co-operation among democratic nations. In this sense, her rhetoric alluded to a 'Kantian triangle of peace' in which free trade, democracy and cosmopolitan values would provide ingredients for a stable international order (Owen, 2004).

Conservative ministers, like their New Labour counterparts, have thus routinely argued for free trade to stimulate developing countries' economies and to integrate them into the global marketplace. Moreover, they insist that free trade policies will ensure that Britain is prosperous in the post-Brexit phase by enabling UK entrepreneurs to gain access to emerging markets (see, for instance, Trevelyan cited in UK Government, 2022). This rhetoric is not isolated to the UK. It reflects a broader Post-Washington Consensus (PWC) narrative about making 'globalisation works for the poor' (Stiglitz, 2007). At times, this PWC discourse notes challenges about the need for greater technical assistance to help developing countries to deal with hygiene standards and other non-tariff barriers, or the need for Aid for Trade to enhance trade infrastructure (such as ports and roads). Nevertheless, there is strong PWC emphasis on the benefits of comparative advantages for ensuring that countries in the 'Global South' concentrate capital on efficient industries (Stiglitz, 2005: 30). This reflects the PWC approach to poverty reduction that, in keeping with many of the tenets of neoliberalism, emphasises the pre-eminence of the private sector and a free market within poverty reduction (Sheppard & Leitner, 2010: 188). The compatibility of such PWC thinking with the ideologies of the Conservative Party and New Labour reflects a free market consensus on the need for private sector development (PSD) within open markets.

One potential exception, however, is recent UK politicians' focus upon the DCTS as a post-Brexit replacement of the EU's EBA initiative. The logic of the DCTS as a non-reciprocal trade scheme implies that there is some danger in premature market opening for the most vulnerable economies. Namely, the logic of the DCTS and EBA is that LDCs in Africa and beyond may require policy space to build up their nascent industries before engaging in tariff cutting (Gil-Pareja et al., 2019). Moreover, there were hopes within UK civil society and academia that the DIT would use the opportunity of Brexit for a reformulation of UK trade policy to better recognise the legitimate place of tariffs within a developmentalist approach in the 'Global South'. There have been calls not only to introduce a similar system to the EU EBA regime—now found within the DCTS—but to expand access to such a non-reciprocal system for 'non-LDCs' (Grady, 2017: 80; Hurt, 2022: 8; Ikpe, 2017: 43–44; Luke et al., 2022; Razzaque, 2017: 60). Hurt (2022: 8) argued that the UK could do this within WTO regulations by adopting more inclusive definitions of what constitutes a 'vulnerable' developing economy. Some also pointed here to the existence of the US African Growth and Opportunity Act (AGOA) as a non-reciprocal scheme that did include a wider array of African states than allowed under EBA (Razzaque, 2017: 60). As the next section demonstrates, however, there has been widespread dismay from UK civil society groups—and African commentators—that the UK government has not offered more generous definitions in its approach to the DCTS.

Global Britain and Trade Deals in Africa After EU Withdrawal

A number of academic and policy commentators predicted that the UK would place a relatively low priority on post-Brexit trade deals with African countries (see, for example, Razzaque, 2017: 59). Many commentators cited figures indicating the modest percentages that African trade constituted vis-à-vis the UK's total global trade. The UK Treasury in 2019 indicated that UK exports to Africa totalled £18.5 billion, which was equivalent to 2.7% of total UK exports. UK imports from Africa meanwhile totalled £16.7 billion, accounting for 2.3% of total UK imports (Taylor, 2021). Despite these modest trade figures, the DIT did actively pursue trade agreements with African counterparts. Even if in material terms, trade flows between the UK and Africa are smaller compared to, for example, China-UK equivalents, trade deals with African Commonwealth countries held genuine significance for UK officials. This owed in part to the symbolic resonance of establishing post-Brexit arrangements with 'old friends'. It also owed to UK officialdoms' ontological security, as discussed in Chapter 2. Moreover, DIT's approach reflected the immediacy of certain African countries' trade dependency. For instance, Kenya actively sought out a UK agreement to protect access to British supermarkets for its lucrative cut flower industry (Suess, 2019:

3). Ghana meanwhile sought access for its own producers, notably in terms of cocoa and tuna exports (UK Government, 2021b).

By 2021, the UK DIT had secured nine trade agreements in Africa (UK Government, 2022). This included seven country-to-country agreements with Ghana, Kenya, Cote d'Ivoire, Cameroon, Egypt, Morocco and Kenya. It also included two regional agreements. First, with the Eastern and Southern Africa (ESA) bloc now covering three fully ratifying states—Mauritius, Seychelles and Zimbabwe. Second, with the Southern African Customs Union plus Mozambique (SACUM) now covering Botswana, Eswatini, Lesotho, Mozambique, Namibia and South Africa (UK Government, 2023a). These agreements were signed during the premiership of Boris Johnson—with Liz Truss as then Trade Minister—and have been hailed as evidence of the UK's continuing partnership with emerging economies (ibid.). Additionally, the deals were hailed as important for securing jobs in developing countries. Liz Truss' successor as Trade Minister, Anne-Marie Trevelyan, delivered a speech in July 2022 in which she lauded the deals as evidence of a strong UK-Africa partnership:

> the UK is responding to the Continent's growth story. This partnership is about truly understanding Africa's needs and exploring how our businesses can support them through projects that create jobs, support inclusion and sustainability and bring lasting value. In turn this will build the Continent's economic strength… Equally, our partnership is about opening up new opportunities for UK businesses… There can be no doubt that Africa is the future. (UK Government, 2022)

These deals played an important part within the UK government's media messaging about Global Britain's apparent successes. For instance, Liz Truss hailed the agreements on her social media. Right-leaning newspapers such as *The Daily Express* also praised these deals 'in the bag' (Falvey, 2021). This pro-Brexit narrative was sustained in relation to the announcement of the UK's intention to provide DFQF access to non-LDCs. This soon evolved into the DCTS and was hailed as evidence of the UK's normative role within Africa (UK Government, 2022).

Nevertheless, despite these apparent 'success stories', there has been much criticism of the 'development' implications of the DIT's approach. There has been particular concern about the consequences of the 'roll over' EPAs with countries such as Ghana, Kenya and South Africa. The UK's failure to address concerns surrounding EPAs in its own bespoke deals has been seen as a missed opportunity (Trade Justice Movement, 2022). As noted earlier, the EU's EPAs are highly controversial and were contested by African officials. As a result, only the SACUM and ESA regional agreements in Africa are in partial effect with the EU. As noted, this has led to the signing of unilateral EPAs with countries such as Ghana and Kenya, leading to regional fragmentation within their RECs. The UK's decision to replicate 'cut and paste' EPAs is thus highly questionable particularly in the context of Brexiteer promises and ministers' pro-poor rhetoric.

Moreover, in the situation of Ghana, there were criticisms that the UK government had 'bullied' the country into a free trade deal (Merrick, 2020). The DIT's aggressive approach led to tensions with the UK Foreign, Commonwealth and Development Office (FCDO) which sought to avoid a diplomatic fallout (ibid.). Despite these inter-ministry tensions, the UK ceased trading with Ghana under the DFQF terms of the EU interim EPA and instead applied UK standard GSP rates in January 2021 (Reuters, 2020). The UK government at one stage apparently threatened to place Ghana on 'WTO terms' which would have meant even more punitive tariffs under the UK Global Tariff (UKGT) (Lanktree, 2020). The default to the standard GSP meant that the Ghanaian government faced intense pressure to acquiesce to a 'rushed' UK EPA (War on Want, 2021). Industries in Ghana such as the banana and tuna sectors found that their access to British consumers had overnight become much more expensive (ibid.). The House of Lords International Agreements Committee (IAC, 2021) explained the impact of this upon Ghanaian banana producers:

> The UK is a substantial export market for Ghana's banana producers, accounting for approximately 25% of the country's total banana exports by value. For two months bananas from Ghana were subject to a substantial tariff import duty of £95 per tonne, with some Ghanaian companies reporting, as a consequence, over £20,000 of additional weekly costs.

Under pressure to assist their exporters, the Ghanaian government by March 2021 had acquiesced to the text of a UK EPA—given a rebranding as the interim Trade Partnership Agreement (TPA) (High Commission of Ghana, 2021). This was despite Ghanaian officials' earlier reservations and calls from civil society campaigners to allow Ghanaian exporters access under the equivalent of EBA or GSP+ in which DFQF rules would apply as part of non-reciprocal trade arrangements (IRDC, 2021: 95). Campaigners argued that countries such as Ghana could classify as vulnerable economies and be exempted from liberalisation commitments under WTO rules if the UK government had the political will to make the case. And this opportunity was facilitated by the fact that the UK had regained an independent seat at the WTO (ibid.).

The failure of UK DIT to reconsider EPAs is especially problematic in the light of growing empirical evidence as to their impact upon nascent manufacturing and agro-processing (Stender et al., 2021). In the case of South Africa and its SACUM neighbours, the poultry sector has been a *cause célèbre* of the difficulties associated with premature market opening. Southern African countries have experienced declining poultry farms due to cheap frozen chicken entering their markets from European origins (Nkukwana, 2018). Cheap wings and thighs, which are often cheaper to dump upon African markets than to sustainably dispose of within Europe itself, are responsible for decimating local poultry businesses. Southern African states responded to the threat posed to livelihoods by applying higher tariffs under the so-called safeguard clause included within the text of the EU EPA (SACU, 2022). This same clause is included within the UK deal. However, the EU lodged a legal challenge to the implementation of the safeguard clause. An arbitration panel then found in favour of the EU (European Commission, 2022). This one example is compounded by a recent evaluation of EU EPAs in Africa by Stender et al. (2021: 1511–1512), which concludes that:

> the disruptive effects on domestic markets and industrialization prospects that our findings imply, especially in the agricultural sector in Africa, [are] doubled by concerns that the losses of customs revenues in ACP countries due to agreed tariff reductions… are simultaneously reducing the financial leeway of governments. Positive developmental impacts of the EPAs are thus unlikely to come with unleashing market forces.

Additionally, the UK government has been regularly warned about the likely implications of replicated EPA deals. For example, Hurt (2022) in written evidence to the ITC explicitly warned about the incompatibilities of EPAs with African states' aspirations to diversify their economic base. Hurt pointed to the AU's approach to economic growth and the requirements for its external trade partners to respect African policy space:

> [The AU's] 'Agenda 2063' plan has at its core the aim of 'transforming Africa's economies through beneficiation from Africa's natural resources, manufacturing, industrialization…' This vision will only be realised if the external environment is conducive to such an approach. It is therefore important that the UK… allows the 'policy space' for domestic and regional development strategies that are not focused on external trade liberalization. (Hurt, 2022: 5)

Such warnings have now turned to disappointment, as voiced by the Trade Justice Movement (2022):

> It was a great shame that the UK did not seize the opportunity provided by its newly independent trade policy… A number of these [EPA] agreements were already contentious. There was concern about their likely impacts on Least Developed Countries (LDCs) and regional integration, but the government chose to side-line these concerns and press ahead with replicating flawed agreements.

In a similar vein, the House of Lords' International Relations and Defence Committee (IRDC, 2021: 6) advised the UK government that:

> We also identify leaving the EU as an opportunity for the UK to re-cast its trade relationships in the region, and remedy some of the defects in the EU's Economic Partnership Agreements. We were surprised to hear that no detailed work has yet been done to consider how to offer better access to African exporters.

Despite these appeals, the UK government continues to pursue EPAs. For instance, the text of the Kenya EPA allows for members of the EAC to accede to the agreement within five years (Mutambo & Kitimo, 2020). Moreover, the UK trade envoy to Nigeria lauded the UK's strong desire to initiate a free trade deal (Kedem, 2021). While that deal has not yet come to fruition, there is little indication that the UK government is prepared to rethink trade liberalisation.

Furthermore, the terms of the UK's DCTS Comprehensive System for LDCs such as Uganda have also come under criticism for 'double standards' in comparison with terms offered to developed country partners such as Australia and New Zealand (ITC, 2022). Namely, the DCTS includes strict protocols regarding respect for labour standards and human rights. It offers the UK the ability therein to suspend LDC states accused of breaching these norms from DFQF access to British consumers. By contrast, agreements with 'developed' nations, while noting international norms on labour standards, do not contain a mechanism by which either party can be suspended. The ITC in the House of Commons wrote to Trade Minister, Kemi Badenoch, in November 2022 outlining their concerns regarding such apparent double standards. They called for a more consistent approach. They also sought reassures about the monitoring processes surrounding evaluations of developing countries' compliance with such social clauses (ibid.).

Moreover, officials from the 'Global South' have articulated concerns with the inclusion of such conditionalities within trade deals, fearing that they provide countries in the 'Global North' with opportunities for veiled protectionism (Hafner-Burton et al., 2019: 1275; IRDC, 2021: 96). These concerns surrounding the makeup of the DCTS are compounded by the scheme's failure to adopt a more inclusive definition of vulnerable economies, meaning that countries such as Ghana cannot benefit from full DFQF access under the DCTS Comprehensive Scheme (equivalent to EU EBA). Instead, they must sign an EPA or default to less preferential access under the standard GSP, known now as UK DCTS Standard Preferences (UK Government, 2023b). This accounted for the situation of Ghanaian banana producers who suffered a tariff hike from January 2021 until the signing of the Ghana-UK EPA (TPA) in March 2021. The UK government has since refused to refund Ghanaian producers for the tariffs they incurred during this transitional period, despite earlier assurances from ministers about protecting developing countries from Brexit turbulence (Banana Link, 2021).

Meanwhile, the one apparent UK concession to 'development' in relation to DCTS Comprehensive Preferences—more lenient rules of origin and cumulation for LDC members compared to the EU's GSP—is arguably a device by which UK negotiators hope to incentivise EPAs for non-LDCs. Relaxed rules of origin allow for DCTS LDC members to more readily create regional value chains with non-LDC EPA signatories without incurring penalties when later accessing UK markets (UK Government, 2022). While potentially beneficial for LDCs, this has the impact of incentivising non-LDCs to sign EPAs so that they can then more easily build value chains in their region with their LDC counterparts, and access UK markets on low tariff rates. Such incentives for 'bad' trade deals like EPAs are a questionable development gain. Whetherit is possible to successfully build regional value chains in value-added sectors such as textiles under conditions of EPA import flooding is also highly questionable. As the next section explains, the early direction of UK trade policy bodes ill for Global Britain's claim to assist 'old friends' in Africa.

Neo-colonial Trajectories for Global Britain's Trade with Africa?

The indications arising from Global Britain's signing of nine free trade deals with eighteen African countries—combined to its refusal to open up its definition of LDCs under the DCTS Comprehensive Preferences—bode ill for the trajectory of UK trade with African states. Despite Brexiteer discourse that Brexit would allow an independent UK trade policy to redress the difficulties associated with EU trade agendas, UK elites have opted instead to replicate the EU's PWC approach to 'development' embodied in EPAs. In this process, they have replicated legitimising narratives surrounding the supposed benefits of free trade for job creation, private sector growth, and social prosperity resulting from trickle-down. In this context, they have highlighted the benefits arising from comparative advantages in the global economy and have sought to ensure African economies 'smooth' transition to free trade in a post-Brexit period. In this process, they have placed pressure upon countries such as Ghana to sign an unilateral interim EPA with the UK, despite that country's reservations about the consequences of trade opening for integration with other ECOWAS members (Merrick, 2020).

Worryingly, the UK continues to push for yet more EPAs. It continues to negotiate with Nigeria—the country that Peter Mandelson named the 'elephant sitting on the road'—for the conclusion of a full regional EPA in West Africa (Plank et al., 2021: 167). The wording of the text of the unilateral Ghanaian EPA (TPA) is such as to allow for the easy transformation of that deal into a regional agreement (UK Government, 2021). This is also the case in East Africa with regard to Kenya's standalone EPA—signed by Kenya's government to safeguard their flower exports to British supermarkets. As noted, that agreement allows a five-year period for members of the East African Community (EAC) to join the deal. This is despite the fact that LDCs such as Uganda and Tanzania—afforded DCTS Comprehensive Preferences—have little incentive to sign up to strict liberalisation timetables as would be mandated under a region-wide EPA. The UK thus continues to stoke tensions within the EAC and ECOWAS with its differential treatment of LDCs and non-LDCs.

And while the granting of non-reciprocal DFQF access to countries such as Uganda may appear a benevolent concession on the part of Global Britain, such arrangements are not a sound basis for long-term planning since they are given at the sole discretion of the UK (Tanaka, 2020: 6). DFQF access may be quickly revoked if a LDC contravenes conditionalities in terms of respect for human rights and/or labour standards (ibid.).

As noted, countries in the 'Global South' have also protested that conditionalities as found within the UK DCTS are unjust. They fear that suspension may be cynically invoked by for protectionist purposes. This lay behind the decision of the WTO Singapore Ministerial Conference in 1996 to reject the inclusion of 'social clauses' within trade deals (Wilkinson & Hughes, 2000: 262). Developing country governments additionally point to double standards (ibid.). For example, the UK and EU have given copious aid and DFQF trade access to President Yoweri Museveni in Uganda despite his regime's alleged kidnapping and torture of opponents (Titeca, 2022: 2). Conversely, the UK and the EU punished the regime of President Robert Mugabe of Zimbabwe for similar alleged abuses (Vines, 2012). This differential treatment—combined to UK/EU failure to sanction violent regimes in countries such as Saudi Arabia and Israel—raises doubts as to UK/EU elites' ability to fairly enforce conditionalities (Amnesty International, 2015, 2023). Critics also indicate that the provision of DFQF access for LDCs focused upon the export of colonial era commodities may entrench their dependency on low value trade (Gamberoni, 2007: 16). Schemes such as the UK DCTS Comprehensive Preferences are therefore potentially more about maintaining UK/EU supplies of cheap raw materials than about 'development'. European corporations' haphazard attempts to eliminate child labour within supply chains originating in LDCs (for instance, cocoa production) underscore that the impetus for granting DFQF status by European governments is not necessarily borne out of a desire to facilitate achievement of the UN SDGs (Deam, 2020).

Adding to these concerns is the recent decision of the UK government to de facto disband the House of Commons' ITC. This multi-party committee has consistently called for greater parliamentary scrutiny of Brexit trade agreements. However, given the merging of the department for trade with the department for business under Prime Minister Sunak, the government has decided to merge the two distinct committees that shadow these departments' activities (Trade Justice Movement,

2023). Ostensibly, this is a rational reconfiguration of committee structures. However, the government's approach has been to disband the ITC and to grant the existing business committee competencies to evaluate trade policy. The expertise developed within the ITC over the last seven years since the Brexit referendum is being lost (ibid.). Meanwhile, a singular committee already tasked with oversight of UK business policies will now have to simultaneously evaluate UK trade deals. British civil society groups have condemned this move and have accused the government of seeking to minimise proper parliamentary scrutiny (see, for example, WWF, 2022). Indeed, trade deals are signed and ratified without a guaranteed parliamentary vote. Combined to this fact, the government does not meaningfully engage UK civil society during negotiation processes (ibid.). Closing the ITC and minimising opportunities for civil society engagement bodes ill for a UK trade policy that prioritises poverty reduction in Africa.

One further element of concern is that the UK government is now mirroring the language of the European Commission about the future benefits of the African Continental Free Trade Area (AfCFTA) for trade deals in Africa (UK Government, 2022). EU and UK officials view the AU's intra-African liberalisation agenda as an opportunity to obtain a free trade deal with the continent. British officials have therefore articulated support for the AfCFTA, viewing it as a future platform for uniting regional EPAs into one UK-Africa free trade deal. As Hurt (2022) indicates, however, the logic of the AU initiative would be undermined by premature trade liberalisation vis-à-vis external players. The logic of the AfCFTA is to build new industries within African regional value chains. This is only possible if fledgling industries are first protected behind robust tariff walls. If premature free trade deals are signed and tariffs dismantled, then such new industries will likely collapse under the weight of foreign imports emanating from the UK and/or EU member states. The UK's cynicism here—in discursively and materially supporting AU's integration efforts—with a view to future 'piggybacking' onto the agreement bodes ill for poverty reduction objectives.

In this context, the warnings of Kwame Nkrumah (1965; cited in Obeng, 1979) appear wholly relevant for assessing Global Britain's post-Brexit trade agenda. As Nkrumah predicted, the UK is pursuing trade policies that prematurely lock in African economies into free trade patterns that do not allow them the policy space to protect emerging industries. African producers are compelled under EPA import flooding to rely upon exports of primary exports that do not compete with UK/EU agribusiness or manufacturing interests—such as cocoa and cut flowers. And where UK/EU agribusiness interests do compete with African primary production—as in the case of the poultry industry in Western and Southern Africa—European governments resist any efforts to raise tariffs as per ostensible safeguard clauses. Added to this, the UK and the EU have both engaged in 'bullying' tactics using the threat of tariff escalations to compel African governments to comply with free trade demands. Recently, this was seen in the case of Ghana which defaulted to the standard UK GSP in January 2021—meaning that producers in sectors such as fair-trade bananas found much higher taxes imposed upon their cargo when entering Britain (Banana Link, 2021). This threatened to make them uncompetitive given the already low margins received in British supermarkets for their fruit exports. The Ghanaian government, under pressure from its primary producers—and dependent on colonial style exports to the former coloniser—had little choice but to accede to an EPA (TPA) with the UK (Merrick, 2020). As Nkrumah predicted, UK aid monies have also been combined with the pressure of trade negotiations and threats regarding defaults to the standard GSP. As the next chapter explores, such utilisations of aid monies to incentivise African governments' acquiescence to trade deals, that leave them with less government revenues in the long run, does not bode well for the UK's commitment to the UN SDGs. Nor is it conducive to African countries' exercise of empirical sovereignty.

Moreover, the decolonial critique provided by Ndlovu-Gatsheni (2015) provides further insight. Not only is the coloniality of power cultivated by UK officials in the sense of threats concerning GSP default combined to aid leverage. But the coloniality of knowledge is also cultivated in the sense that UK officialdom actively disseminates 'common sense' understandings of free trade deals as being compatible with poverty reduction. Rhetoric from trade ministers such as Liam Fox and Penny Mordaunt emphasises that African economies can hope to benefit from trade liberalisation since comparative advantages nominally take effect. This PWC discourse of 'win-win' free trade is not confined to UK officials. The EU has routinely deployed similar rhetoric, especially during Peter Mandelson's tenure as Commissioner for Trade. As per Ndlovu-Gatsheni's (2015) warnings, Euro-American elites promote Western knowledge constructs and seek to impose them onto their African counterparts. In this case, the rhetoric of pro-poor free trade encourages African governments to accede to trade deals.

With credit to AU officials, there is a developmentalist logic within the AfCFTA in the sense that free trade applies only between the AU member states themselves. There is thus the hope that a common African customs union will impose protectionist tariffs upon external parties whose exports might otherwise undermine industrialisation within Africa (Hurt, 2022; Ndlovu-Gatsheni, 2014). Nevertheless, if not carefully monitored, the AfCFTA could move towards a position that merely facilitates free trade with more industrialised external entities. This is what the UK and EU hope in terms of the conclusion of a future bicontinental free trade zone. This would wholly negate any developmentalist rationale within the AfCFTA project. African officials in this context could act upon Ndlovu-Gatsheni's warnings about Western impositions of 'common sense' agendas onto African projects. As Ndlovu-Gatsheni (2014: 190) notes, previous pan-African initiatives often failed by mimicking or acquiescing to Western norms. Note, for example, the New Partnership for African Development (NEPAD) in the 2000s that assumed that the private sector would provide trickle-down growth in free market conditions. Concerned African officials and civil society groups could proactively guard the AfCFTA from the predations of the UK or EU in terms of these external actors' aspirations to 'piggyback' onto intra-African liberalisation.

Conclusion

Brexiteer politicians in part fought the referendum on promises that a sovereign UK trade policy would yield dividends for Commonwealth Africa. In contrast to the apparently protectionist and exploitative EU approach, the UK in a post-Brexit context would be positioned to offer more equitable trade conditions to 'old friends' in the 'Global South'. In the years following the referendum, UK prime ministers and their cabinet colleagues have regularly re-emphasised such discourse. The UK has pledged itself to working in a win-win fashion with African partners to deliver a fairer international trade environment conducive to job creation, investment and social prosperity. In particular, the UK's launch of DCTS Comprehensive Preferences for LDCs was hailed as a contribution to poverty reduction. Moreover, the signing of nine trade deals with eighteen African countries (to date) has been presented by UK ministers as material evidence of the UK's prioritisation of emerging markets.

However, there are serious grounds upon which to contest Global Britain's discourse. The UK decision to replicate EPAs has meant that countries such as Ghana have been pressurised to commit to strict tariff liberalisation schedules. This is despite African officials' concerns about the implications of UK EPAs for regional integration. It is also despite growing evidence surrounding the impact of reciprocal free trade deals for nascent industries (Stender et al., 2021). Moreover, it goes against ample evidence surrounding the importance of tariff revenues for government spending across social sectors. Furthermore, the UK's downgrading of Ghana to GSP standard status evidenced a 'bullying' approach. The UK government's refusal to reimburse Ghana's fair-trade banana producers for the higher tariffs they faced is further evidence of a disjuncture between UK elites' 'development' rhetoric and the material consequences of UK trade policies. Additionally, the UK government's failure to provide more generous definitions of vulnerable developing countries has ensured that countries such as Ghana do not have the option of utilising the DCTS Comprehensive Preferences schedule. Instead, the UK is only willing to provide such status to the very poorest—and least diversified—economies such as Uganda. For LDCs, non-reciprocal regimes may even act as a disincentive to diversification. And even if LDC producers began to challenge UK commercial interests through acquiring competitiveness in a sensitive sector, the British government within the DCTS reserves the right to 'graduate' such a product into a higher tariff band (UK Government, 2022). Again therefore, the UK's development pledges in terms of its post-Brexit trade policy appear highly questionable.

In this context, the warnings of Nkrumah (1965; cited in Obeng, 1979) prove highly relevant. The UK is utilising EPAs to prise open emerging economies irrespective of the damage free trade deals cause in terms of closing-down policy space for developmentalism and industrialisation. Moreover, the UK—following the example of the European Commission—seeks to unite disparate EPAs into a singular free trade deal with AU members. Such 'piggybacking' onto the AfCFTA would fatally undermine the AU's attempts to build economies of scale behind protective tariff walls. It would wholly undermine diversification and instead—through import flooding—ensure that African countries remain reliant upon exports of primary commodities and low value-added goods. In this process, the UK has cultivated the coloniality of knowledge by disseminating hegemonic discourses surrounding the compatibility of free trade agendas and poverty reduction in a PWC setting. African officials are in many cases forced to adopt such knowledge frameworks, or else face discipline in terms of the UK's exercise of the coloniality of power vis-à-vis higher tariff schedules and/or aid withdrawal. This latter question of the combination of UK aid monies to trade deals is the subject of the next chapter. It underscores the ongoing relevance of the concept of neo-colonialism and the decolonial critique for making sense of UK interventions in Africa.

Bibliography

Amnesty International. (2015, December 16). *European Parliament Prize Exposes EU Inaction on Saudi Arabia's Human Rights Abuses*. Amnesty International website. https://www.amnesty.eu/news/european-parliament-prize-exposes-eu-inaction-on-saudi-arabia-s-human-rights-abuses-0952/. Accessed 14 April 2023.

Amnesty International. (2023, March 20). *EU Needs to Acknowledge the Reality of Israeli Apartheid*. Amnesty International Website. https://www.amnesty.org/en/latest/news/2023/03/eu-needs-to-acknowledge-the-reality-of-isr aeli-apartheid/. Accessed 14 April 2023.

Banana Link. (2021, February 9). *Ghana Signs Post-Brexit Trade Deal With UK, But No Agreement on Tariff Refund*. Banana Link Website. https://www.bananalink.org.uk/news/ghana-signs-post-brexit-trade-deal-with-uk-but-no-agreement-on-tariff-refunds/. Accessed 14 April 2023.

Berends, G. (2016). What Does the EU-SADC EPA Really Say? An Analysis of the Economic Partnership Agreement Between the European Union and Southern Africa. *South African Journal of International Affairs, 23*(4), 457–474.

Brown, W. (2000). Restructuring North-South Relations: ACP-EU Development Co-operation in a Liberal International Order. *Review of African Political Economy, 27*(85), 367–383.

Burden, L. (2020, November 15). Ghana Loses Faith on UK Trade Deal. *The Telegraph*. https://www.telegraph.co.uk/business/2020/11/15/ghana-loses-faith-uk-trade-deal/. Accessed 14 April 2020.

Chipaike, R., & Knowledge, M. (2018). The Question of African Agency in International Relations. *Cogent Social Sciences, 4*(1), 1–16.

Cowell, A. (2004, July 24). Blair Appoints Close Advisor to Represent Britain in Europe. *New York Times*. https://www.nytimes.com/2004/07/24/world/blair-appoints-close-adviser-to-represent-britain-in-europe.html. Accessed 6 April 2023.

Deam, A. (2020). Children, Chocolate, and Profits: A Policy-Oriented Analysis of Child Labor and the Chocolate Industry Giants. *Intercultural Human Rights Law Review, 15*, 257–281.

Department for International Trade. (2017). *Preparing for Our Future UK Trade Policy*. HM Stationery Office.

Department for International Trade. (2022, February 28). *Written Evidence to the International Trade Committee from the Right Honourable Penny Mordaunt*. Department for International Trade.

Edwards, J. (2018). Make America Great Again: Donald Trump and Redefining the U.S. Role in the World. *Communication Quarterly, 66*(2), 176–195.

EPA Monitoring. (2018, March 12). *The Complications of "Rolling Over" Current EPAs into "Cut and Paste" Bilateral "UK Only" Trade Deals*. EPA Monitoring Website. https://epamonitoring.net/the-complications-of-rolling-over-current-epas-into-cut-and-paste-bilateral-uk-only-trade-deals/. Accessed 14 April 2023.

European Commission. (2005a). *EU Report on Millennium Development Goals 2000–2004: EU Contribution to the Review of the MDGs at the UN 2005 High Level Event*. European Commission.

European Commission. (2005b, May 23). *Peter Mandelson EU Trade Commissioner Remarks to the Trade Committee of the European Parliament, Brussels*. European Commission.

European Commission. (2022, August 3). Panel Rules in Favour of EU on Southern African Customs Union's Safeguard on EU Poultry Cuts. *News Article*. https://policy.trade.ec.europa.eu/news/panel-rules-favour-eu-southern-african-customs-unions-safeguard-eu-poultry-cuts-2022-08-03_en. Accessed 14 April 2023.

European Commission. (2023). *Generalised Scheme of Preferences*. European Commission.

Falvey, D. (2021, February 5). Another Brexit Deal in the Bag! Britain Signs Lucrative £1.2 Bn Trade Agreement with Ghana. *Daily Express*. https://www.express.co.uk/news/politics/1393808/brexit-news-brexit-trade-deal-ghana-liz-truss-eu-trade. Accessed 14 April 2023.

Fine, B. (2003). Neither the Washington Nor the Post-Washington Consensus: An Introduction. In B. Fine, C. Lapavitsas, & J. Pinkus (Eds.), *Development Policy in the Twenty-first Century* (pp. 17–43). Routledge.

Gamberoni, E. (2007). *Do Unilateral Trade Preferences Help Export Diversification?* (HEI Working Paper, No. 17/2007, pp. 1–27). Graduate Institute of International Studies.

Gil-Pareja, S., Llorca-Vivero, R., & Martínez-Serrano, J. (2019). Reciprocal vs Nonreciprocal Trade Agreements: Which Have Been Best to Promote Exports? *PLoS ONE, 14*(2), 1–15.

GRAIN. (2017, August 21). *Colonialism's New Clothes: The Economic Partnership Agreements with Africa*. GRAIN. https://grain.org/en/article/5777-colonialism-s-new-clothes-the-eu-s-economic-partnership-agreements-with-africa. Accessed 6 April 2023.

Grady, M. (2017). Supporting African Development Agendas in Our Future Trading Relationships. In Royal African Society (Ed.), *The Future of Africa-UK Trade and Development Cooperation Relations in the Transitional and Post Brexit Period: A Report of the All-Party Parliamentary Africa Group* (pp. 78–81). Royal African Society.

Greens/EFA. (2012, December 6). Free Trade Agreements and Human Rights: The EU's Double Standards. *Greens/EFA in the European Parliament*. https://www.greens-efa.eu/en/article/news/free-trade-agreements-and-human-rights. Accessed 6 April 2023.

Gruhn, I. (1976). The Lomé Convention: Inching Towards Interdependence. *International Organization, 30*(2), 241–262.

Grynberg, R. (1998). The WTO Incompatibility of the Lome Convention Trade Provisions. *Asia Pacific School of Economics and Management Working Paper Series, 98*(3), 1–29.

The Guardian. (2005, January 20). Full Text: Peter Mandelson's Speech. *The Guardian*. https://www.theguardian.com/politics/2005/jan/20/development.internationalaidanddevelopment. Accessed 6 April 2023.

Hafner-Burton, E., Mosley, L., & Galantucci, R. (2019). Protecting Workers Abroad and Industries at Home: Rights-Based Conditionality in Trade Preference Programs. *Journal of Conflict Resolution, 63*(5), 1253–1282.

Hale, S. (2011). Discourse, Policy… and Ideas: An Obituary of the Third Way in Britain. *European Political Science, 10*, 488–500.

Hannan, D. (2016, June 21). Free Britain to Trade with the World. *The Financial Times*. https://www.ft.com/content/6d4a444a-36f5-11e6-a780-b48ed7b6126f. Accessed 6 March 2023.

High Commission of Ghana. (2021, March 2). *Ghana Signs Trade Partnership Agreement with the United Kingdom*. High Commission of Ghana Website. https://ghanahighcommissionuk.com/GHANA-SIGNS-TRADE-PARTNERSHIP-AGREEMENT-WITH-THE-UNITED-KINGDOM. Accessed 14 April 2023.

Hurt, S. (2003). Co-Operation and Coercion? The Cotonou Agreement Between the European Union and ACP States and the End of the Lomé Convention. *Third World Quarterly, 24*(1), 161–176.

Hurt, S. (2022). Written Evidence from Dr Stephen Hurt (Oxford Brookes University). In International Trade Committee (ITC) *Written Evidence: UK Trade Approach Towards Developing Countries*. UK Parliament. https://committees.parliament.uk/work/1700/uk-trade-approach-towards-developing-countries/publications/written-evidence/. Accessed 14 April 2023.

Igechi, G. (2021). Should Nigeria Join the European Union's Economic Partnership Agreement with the Other ECOWAS States? *Review of African Political Economy, 48*(169), 462–472.
Ikpe, E. (2017). The Development Objectives of EPAs and Emerging Lessons for UK-Africa Trade and Development Relations. In Royal African Society (Ed.), *The Future of Africa-UK Trade and Development Cooperation Relations in the Transitional and Post Brexit Period: A Report of the All-Party Parliamentary Africa Group* (pp. 42–46). Royal African Society.
International Agreements Committee of the House of Lords. (2021). *Scrutiny of International Agreements: Interim Partnership Agreements with Ghana and Cameroon*. HM Stationary Office.
International Relations and Defence Committee of the House of Lords. (2021). *The UK and Sub-Saharan Africa: Prosperity, Peace and Development Co-operation*. HM Stationery Office.
International Trade Committee of the House of Commons. (2022, November 7). *MPs Warn of Double Standard in Trade Approach to Developing Countries*. UK Parliament Website. https://committees.parliament.uk/committee/367/international-trade-committee/news/174192/mps-warn-of-double-standard-in-trade-approach-to-developing-countries/. Accessed 14 April 2023.
Johnson, B. (2016, May 9). *The Liberal Cosmopolitan Case to Vote Leave*. Vote Leave. http://www.voteleavetakecontrol.org/boris_johnson_the_liberal_cosmopolitan_case_to_vote_leave.html. Accessed 6th March 2023.
Kedem, S. (2021, May 17). Mixed Reactions to "Absolutely Huge" UK-Nigeria Trade Deal. *African Business*. https://african.business/2021/05/trade-investment/mixed-reactions-to-absolutely-huge-uk-nigeria-trade-deal. Accessed 14 April 2023.
Koroma, S., & Ford, J. (2006). *The Agricultural Dimension of the ACP-EU Economic Partnership Agreements* (FAO Commodities and Trade Technical Paper No. 8, pp. 1–116). FAO.
Langan, M., & Price, S. (2020). Imperialisms Past and Present in EU Economic Relations with North Africa. *Interventions, 22*(6), 703–721.
Langan, M., & Scott, J. (2011). *The False Promise of Aid for Trade* (Brooks World Poverty Institute Working Paper, No. 160). University of Manchester.
Lanktree, G. (2020, October 21). Ghana Won't Sign New Trade Deal in 2020. *Politico*.
Lilley, P. (2016, May 26). The Truth About Britain's Trade Outside the European Union. *The Telegraph*. https://www.telegraph.co.uk/politics/2016/05/26/the-truth-about-britains-trade-outside-the-european-union/. Accessed 6 March 2023.
Luke, D., Bashi, J., & MacLeod, J. (2022). *Submission by the African Trade Policy Programme, Firoz Lalji Institute for Africa, London School*

of Economics. Written Evidence: UK Trade Approach Towards Developing Countries. UK Parliament. https://committees.parliament.uk/writtenevidence/106536/pdf/. Accessed 14 April 2023.

Mbori, H., & Gathii, J. (2020, February 26). Analysis of the Kenya-UK Economic Partnership Agreement. *AfroEconomics Law*. https://www.afronomicslaw.org/category/analysis/bilateralizing-eu-eac-epa-introductory-legal-analysis-kenya-uk-economic. Accessed 6 April 2023.

Merrick, R. (2020, December 20). Brexit: Final Bid to Prevent Huge Tariffs Ruining African Farmers Amid Allegations of UK "Bullying". *The Independent*. https://www.independent.co.uk/news/uk/politics/brexit-tariffs-africa-ghana-farmers-b1766278.html. Accessed 6 March 2023.

Mold, A. (2018). The Consequences of Brexit for Africa: The Case of the East African Community. *Journal of African Trade, 5*(1–2), 1–17.

Monbiot, G. (2008, September 8). Protect and Survive. *The Guardian*. https://www.monbiot.com/2008/09/09/protect-and-survive/. Accessed 6 April 2023.

Mutambo, A., & Kitimo, A. (2020, November 10). EAC Partner States Get Five Years to Join Kenya-UK Trade Deal. *The East African*. https://www.theeastafrican.co.ke/tea/business/eac-partner-states-get-five-years-to-join-kenya-uk-trade-deal-3017058. Accessed 14 April 2023.

Ndlovu-Gatsheni, S. J. (2013). *Coloniality of Power in Post-colonial Africa*. CODESRIA.

Ndlovu-Gatsheni, S. J. (2014). Global Coloniality and the Challenges of Creating African Futures. *Strategic Review for Southern Africa, 36*(2), 181–202.

Ndlovu-Gatsheni, S. J. (2015). *Empire, Global Coloniality and African Subjectivity*. Berghahn Books.

Nicolaïdis, K. (2015). Southern Barbarians? A Post-Colonial Critique of EUniversalism. In K. Nicolaïdis, B. Sébe & G. Maas (Eds.), *Echoes of Empire: Memory, Identity and Colonial Legacies*. IB Tauris.

Nigerian Tribune. (2022, February 17). Africa EU Relationship Not Encouraging Job Creation—Buhari. *Nigerian Tribune*. https://tribuneonlineng.com/africa-eu-relationship-not-encouraging-job-creation-%E2%80%95-buhari/. Accessed 6 April 2023.

Nkrumah, K. (1965). *Neo-colonialism: The Last Stage of Imperialism*. Panaf Press.

Nkukwana, T. T. (2018). Global Poultry Production: Current Impact and Future Outlook on the South African Poultry Industry. *South African Journal of Animal Science, 48*(5), 869–884.

Nunn, A., & Price, S. (2004). Managing Development: EU and African Relations Through the Evolution of the Lomé and Cotonou Agreements. *Historical Materialism, 12*(4), 203–230.

Obeng, S. (1979). *Selected Speeches of Kwame Nkrumah* (Vol. 1). Afram Publishers.

Öniş, Z., & Şenses, F. (2005). Rethinking the Emerging Post-Washington Consensus. *Development and Change, 36*, 263–290.

Owen, J. (2004). Democratic Peace Research: Whence and Whither? *International Politics, 41*, 605–617.

Plank, F., Keijzer, N., & Niemann, A. (2021). Outside-in Politicization of EU–Western Africa Relations: What Role for Civil Society Organizations? *JCMS: Journal of Common Market Studies, 59*, 161–179.

Rama, M. (2003). *Globalization and Workers in Developing Countries* (World Bank Policy Research Working Paper, No. 2958). World Bank.

Razzaque, M. (2017). Post-Brexit UK-Africa Trading Relationship: Can It Be More Development-Friendly Than EPAs. In Royal African Society (Ed.), *The Future of Africa-UK Trade and Development Cooperation Relations in the Transitional and Post Brexit Period: A Report of the All-Party Parliamentary Africa Group* (pp. 58–61). Royal African Society.

Reuters. (2020, December 31). *UK and Ghana to Miss Brexit Trade Deadline, But Deal Close.* Reuters. https://www.reuters.com/article/britain-eu-ghana-idUSL8N2JB1SY. Accessed 10 June 2023.

Rosenberg, J., & Boyle, C. (2019). Understanding 2016: China, Brexit and Trump in the History of Uneven and Combined Development. *Journal of Historical Sociology, 32*, 32–58.

Saap, M. (2005, May 19). *Mandelson Takes Tough Line on Poor Countries.* EUObserver. https://euobserver.com/news/19101. Accessed 14 April 2023.

SACU. (2022). Southern African Customs Union—Safeguard Measure Imposed on Frozen Bone-In *Chicken Cuts from The European Union: First Written Submission of the Southern African Customs Union.* SACU. https://www.sacu.int/docs/publications/2022/First_Written_Submission_of_the_SACU_non-confidential.pdf. Accessed 14 April 2023.

Sheppard, E., & Leitner, H. (2010). Quo Vadis Neoliberalism? The Remaking of Global Capitalist Governance After the Washington Consensus. *Geoforum, 41*(2), 185–194.

Stender, F., Berger, A., Brandi, C., & Schwab, J. (2021). The Trade Effects of the Economic Partnership Agreements between the European Union and the African, Caribbean and Pacific Group of States: Early Empirical Insights from Panel Data. *JCMS: Journal of Common Market Studies, 59*, 1495–1515.

Stiglitz, J. (2005). More Instruments and Broader Goals: Moving Toward the Post-Washington Consensus. In UNU-Wider (Ed.), *Wider Perspectives on Global Development* (pp. 16–48). Palgrave.

Stiglitz, J. (2007). Rich Countries, Poor People? *New Perspectives Quarterly, 24*(1), 7–9.

Suess, J. (2019, May). The UK's Policy Towards Africa Post-Brexit. *Policy Centre for the New South Policy Brief* PB-19/17. Policy Centre for the New South.

The Sun Nigeria. (2016, June 26). Brexit Aftermath: How It Affects Nigeria. *The Sun Nigeria.*

Tanaka, K. (2020). The EU's EBA Scheme and the Future of Cambodia's Garment Industry. *Perspective*, No. 14. ISEAS-Yusof Ishak Institute.

Taylor, R. (2021, October 25). *Promoting Trade and Business Opportunities with Africa.* House of Lords Library Website. https://lordslibrary.parliament.uk/promoting-trade-and-business-opportunities-with-africa/. Accessed 14 April 2023.

Titeca, K. (2022). *EU Uganda Relations: Friction, Change or Business as Usual?* (Egmont Policy Brief No. 296). Royal Institute for International Relations. https://repository.uantwerpen.be/docman/irua/c3263a/191963.pdf. Accessed 14 April 2023.

Trade Justice Movement. (2022). Written Evidence from the Trade Justice Movement. In International Trade Committee (ITC) *Written Evidence: UK Trade Approach Towards Developing Countries.* UK Parliament. https://committees.parliament.uk/work/1700/uk-trade-approach-towards-developing-countries/publications/written-evidence/. Accessed 14 April 2023.

Trade Justice Movement. (2023, March 23). *Stifled in the Cradle: Commons Treaty Scrutiny Delivered a New Blow.* Trade Justice Movement Website. https://www.tjm.org.uk/blog/2023/stifled-in-the-cradle-commons-treaty-scrutiny-delivered-a-new-blow. Accessed 14 April 2023.

Traidcraft. (2005). *EPAs Through the Lens of Kenya.* Traidcraft.

Trommer, S. (2011). Activists Beyond Brussels: Transnational NGO Strategies on EU–West African Trade Negotiations. *Globalizations, 8*(1), 113–126.

UK Government. (2017a, June 24). *Government Pledges to Help Improve Access to UK Markets for World's Poorest Countries Post-Brexit.* UK Government Online. https://www.gov.uk/government/news/government-pledges-to-help-improve-access-to-uk-markets-for-worlds-poorest-countries-post-brexit. Accessed 14 April 2023.

UK Government. (2017b, January 17). *The Government's Negotiating Objectives for Exiting the EU: PM Speech.* UK Government Online. https://www.gov.uk/government/speeches/the-governments-negotiating-objectives-for-exiting-the-eu-pm-speech. Accessed 14 April 2023.

UK Government. (2020, January 22). *Minister for Africa's Speech at the UN Global Compact.* UK Government Online. https://www.gov.uk/government/speeches/minister-of-state-speech-at-un-global-compact-event. Accessed 14 April 2023.

UK Government. (2021a). *Global Britain in a Competitive Age: The Integrated Review of Security, Defence, Development and Foreign Policy.* HM Stationery Office.

UK Government. (2021b, April 20). *Continuing the UK's Trade Relationship with Ghana*. UK Government Online. https://www.gov.uk/government/publications/continuing-the-uks-trade-relationship-with-ghana-parliamentary-report/continuing-the-uks-trade-relationship-with-ghana-web-version. Accessed 14 April 2023.

UK Government. (2022, July 6). *A UK-Africa Trading Partnership for the 21st Century*. https://www.gov.uk/government/speeches/a-uk-africa-trading-partnership-for-the-21st-century. Accessed 14 April 2023.

UK Government. (2023a, February 3). *'UK Trade Agreements in Effect' 'A UK-Africa Trading Partnership for the 21st Century*. UK Government Online. https://www.gov.uk/guidance/uk-trade-agreements-in-effect. Accessed 14 April 2023.

UK Government. (2023b). *Preference Tiers under the Developing Countries Trading Scheme (DCTA)*. UK Government.

Vines, A. (2012). The Effectiveness of UN and EU Sanctions: Lessons for the Twenty-First Century. *International Affairs, 88*(4), 867–877.

War on Want. (2021, February 4). *Empire 2.0: UK Trade Deals Squeeze Wealth from the Global South*. War on Want Website. https://waronwant.org/news-analysis/empire-20-uk-trade-deals-squeeze-wealth-global-south. Accessed 14 April 2023.

Wilkinson, R., & Hughes, S. (2000). Labor Standards and Global Governance: Examining the Dimensions of Institutional Engagement. *Global Governance, 6*, 259–277.

WWF. (2022, January). *WWF Briefing—Public and Parliamentary Scrutiny of Free Trade Agreements*. WWF. https://www.wwf.org.uk/sites/default/files/2022-09/Scrutiny-of-Trade-Agreements-July-22.pdf. Accessed 14 April 2023.

CHAPTER 4

Global Britain and UK Aid Policy Towards Africa

INTRODUCTION

UK elites have articulated moral 'development' narratives that aim to bolster Global Britain's soft power in the post-Brexit period. These narratives have emphasised a British exceptionalism in terms of the UK's apparent outstanding commitment to free trade, democracy and the rule of law (Petrikova & Lazell, 2019; Połońska-Kimunguyi & Kimunguyi, 2017; Price, 2018). Global Britain is construed as a normative actor whose engagement with other states is conducive to a more stable and prosperous international realm. Additionally, British exceptionalism has been combined to UK elites' focus upon African countries in terms of their ontological security and 'mission civilisatrice' (cf. Połońska-Kimunguyi & Kimunguyi, 2017). In this context, Britain is construed as an 'old friend' of African states that is willing to assist them on the road to economic and social prosperity (UK Government, 2017a). The UK also is presented as a more trustworthy partner for African officials than certain other 'emerging powers', notably China. Moreover, Theresa May as Prime Minister committed the UK to fulfil its existing pledges in terms of EU financial commitments to Africa. Notably, in terms of honouring UK contributions to the European Development Fund (EDF) as it was winded down as per the ending of the Cotonou Agreement between the EU and African, Caribbean and Pacific (ACP) countries (Price, 2018).

This chapter thus assesses UK elites' narratives on African 'development' in relation to aid delivery. It examines how UK contributions to Aid for Trade and investment are construed by UK elites as contributions to poverty reduction within a just form of Africa-UK relations. In this discussion, the chapter highlights the role of the now defunct Department for International Development (DfID), as well as the newly enlarged Foreign Commonwealth *and Development* Office (FCDO, previously FCO). Furthermore, it problematises UK elites' discourse in the context of an apparent 'realist' or 'nationalist' shift amid the tying of aid to UK geopolitical interests (Olivie & Perez, 2017). Brexiteer politicians' aid fatigue and their emphasis on the need for aid monies to 'win' Brexit trade deals are contrasted with an ethical self-portrayal within UK government documents. This includes the UK Government's (2022) *Strategy for International Development*. Moreover, when usages of UK aid are examined in countries such as Ethiopia and Rwanda, the 'pro-poor' rhetoric of British elites comes further into question. In keeping with the warnings of Ndlovu-Gatsheni (2013, 2014, 2015) and Nkrumah (1965) on global coloniality and neo-colonialism, British aid can be seen to serve UK interests in a fashion that regularly has negative consequences for African citizenries. Aid acts as a 'revolving credit' which returns to Global Britain in the form of increased profits amid a 'new scramble for Africa' (Carmody, 2016; Nkrumah, 1965: xv).

The discussion is structured as follows. The first section provides historical context by assessing UK aid and 'development' contributions to Africa in the 2000s under New Labour, followed by Conservative Prime Minister David Cameron (2010–2016). This underscores the humanitarian rhetoric deployed by both New Labour and Conservative politicians in their depiction of Britain as a moral actor committed to justice and poverty reduction vis-à-vis Africa, the 'scar on the conscience of the world' (Blair cited in Porteous, 2005: 289). It highlights the policy focus of DfID under New Labour and its emphasis upon Aid for Trade. This is understood in terms of New Labour's 'Third Way' orientation, blending a commitment to free markets with ostensible social justice objectives (ibid.: 296). DfID's commitment to Aid for Trade is also seen as in keeping with the UK government's then emphasis upon aid delivery via multilateral institutions at a global governance level. In the context of Aid for Trade, this illustrated DfID's and UK officials' willingness to work with the World Trade Organisation (WTO) to make aid work for 'pro-poor' trade deals vis-à-vis the Doha Development Round (DDA). David Cameron's later commitment to the maintenance of DfID—and his pledge to meet the United Nations (UN) aid target of 0.7% of Gross National Income (GNI)—is understood in terms of the Conservative Party's electoral need to distance itself from the 'nasty party' image that had demarcated it from New Labour in the 2000s (Beswick, 2019).

The second section of the chapter assesses the impact of the Brexit vote amid a xenophobic English nationalism (Calhoun, 2017). It emphasises that hostility towards 'illegal migrants' found parallel in terms of Brexiteer politicians' ambivalence (if not outright hostility) towards aid for poorer citizenries in the 'Global South'. In keeping with Boris Johnson's condemnation of aid as a 'giant cashpoint in the sky', Brexiteer politicians' electoral success is built in part upon populist appeals to—and the media cultivation of—aid fatigue among sections of the British electorate (Savage, 2022). The section proceeds to consider early predictions about Brexit marking a 'critical juncture' for UK aid and development policy (Nwankwo, 2018). It underscores debates that the UK might move from a 'cosmopolitan' to a more 'realist' or even 'nationalist' approach to aid-giving in the post-Brexit era (Olivie & Perez, 2017). It also highlights early pledges from the Theresa May government that Global Britain—while pursuing British interests in the 'Global South'—would fulfil its obligations to EU development spending (with resonance for the final years of the ACP-EU EDF).

The third section examines the direction of UK aid policy after the Brexit result. It highlights the closure of DfID amid a merger with the renamed FCDO. It argues that aid policy has moved towards what might be described as a more openly 'realist' or 'nationalist' phase amid UK cuts to Official Development Assistance (ODA)—and increased emphasis on bilateral rather than multilateral spending. Nevertheless, parallels with pre-Brexit aid policy must be acknowledged in terms of the consistency of a securitisation agenda even during the self-styled 'cosmopolitan' phase under New Labour. In this discussion, it highlights the tying of UK aid delivery to post-Brexit trade deals, commercial opportunities and wider UK geopolitical interests. Finally, the fourth section of the chapter concludes by examining the implications of Global Britain's neo-colonial agenda. It underscores that Ndlovu-Gatsheni's (2015) and Nkrumah's (1965) conceptual focus on the coloniality of power and neo-colonialism remains central to the critique of British aid. It also emphasises how Global Britain's use of aid monies may undermine poverty reduction, human rights and sovereignty in African countries—not least in terms of the pursuit of Brexit Economic Partnership Agreement (EPA) trade deals and the signing of migration compacts. The final section also highlights the utility of the concepts of the coloniality of knowledge and the coloniality of being for assessing UK elites' treatment of racialised 'others' in the African continent.

From Blair to Brexit: A 'Humanitarian' Phase in UK Aid Policy?

Following the Brexit referendum, there have been debates as to whether the UK has now lost its 'superpower' status in terms of a supposedly positive reputation in international development circles (Wickstead, 2019). Moreover, that the UK is now possibly witnessing a turn to a more realist or nationalist phase of aid delivery compared to a more humanitarian or cosmopolitan phase during the administrations of Tony Blair, Gordon Brown and perhaps even David Cameron (cf. Olivie & Perez, 2017). This relates to the fact that New Labour drew heavily upon a 'global cosmopolitan' discourse of aid largesse to bolster their electoral advantage and to cultivate the UK's external image as a caring 'Cool Britannia' (Pugh et al., 2013: 195). New Labour came to power upon a promise to move away from the cynical utilisations of aid under the governments of Major and Thatcher. Scandals involving the combination of UK aid to arm sales in relation to the UK's funding of the Pergau Dam in Malaysia had tarnished the reputation of Britain in the 1990s (Ambreena, 2019). The Blair government as part of an 'ethical foreign policy' promised to reorientate UK aid towards humanitarianism. This discourse was soon linked to what became the UN Millennium Development Goals (MDGs) in the 2000s (Połońska-Kimunguyi & Kimunguyi, 2017).

One major contribution of the incoming Blair government to this ostensible ethical shift was the establishment of DfID. Much of the criticisms of the preceding government's approach emanated from concerns that the Foreign and Commonwealth Office (FCO) too eagerly tied aid to British economic and security interests. The creation of a separate department devoted to poverty reduction and humanitarian relief was seen by the Blair government as a means of establishing a new institution, along with a new working culture, that would facilitate a more ethical approach (cf. Hall, 2012). As opposed to the 'male, pale and stale' paternalistic culture of the FCO, the newly established DfID was headed by a prominent New Labour woman, Clare Short, and encouraged diversity in recruitment (FCO, 2019: 10). The new department was represented within Blair's cabinet despite the earlier appeals of the FCO that this division of labour would cause it problems in terms of its core diplomatic functions. The FCO during the Blair era found the poverty reduction focus of DfID problematic in terms of its own 'human rights' approach to engagements in Africa (Porteous, 2005: 285; 286).

Adding to this apparently progressive volte-face was Tony Blair's own early interest in poverty reduction in Africa. Blair famously referred to the African continent as a 'scar on the conscience of the world' and alongside Gordon Brown, the then Chancellor of the Exchequer, cultivated a 'pro-poor' New Labour discourse and self-image (Porteous, 2005; Pugh et al., 2013). One illustration of Blair and Brown's joint interest in Africa's development came with the G8 Gleneagles Summit of 2005 in which donors committed to debt relief pledges, amid later criticisms that these commitments had not been fulfilled (Lazell, 2023: 12; Taylor, 2012: 457). This coincided with UK civil society activism for debt relief as part of a popular *Make Poverty History* movement which appeared to verify the electoral advantages of New Labour's humanitarian language (Rugendyke, 2007). Blair's meetings with celebrity campaigners such as Bono and Bob Geldof solidified an egalitarian New Labour image of ending poverty in African countries (*The Irish Times*, 2003). Moreover, from the WTO Hong Kong Summit in 2005 onwards, the UK became a firm advocate of Aid for Trade—a modality in which aid would be used for improving economic competitiveness and job creation (Langan & Scott, 2014). This amplified a New Labour 'Third Way' politics in which free markets could supposedly be made to work for 'the poor', whether in African countries or domestically within the UK (Porteous, 2005: 296).

Moreover, the apparent successes of Blair and Brown on 'development' issues influenced then Leader of the Opposition, David Cameron, to voice his own commitment to poverty reduction in Africa (Beswick, 2019). Upon becoming the Conservative Party leader, Cameron sought to de-toxify the party's brand by pledging support to progressive causes, including the UN MDGs. Later upon becoming Prime Minister in 2010, he followed through with a commitment to raise UK aid spending to meet the UN target of 0.7% GNI (ibid.). He also maintained DfID as an independent government department, despite sentiments within the FCO, and his own party, that aid spending should be returned to the latter organisation. As discussed in Chapter 2, Cameron—alongside Blair and Brown—voiced a strong commitment to the development of the

Commonwealth, with high-profile visits to African countries. As such, this era—from Blair to the end of the Cameron government—has been described as a period in which the UK acted as a 'superpower' in the development field amid the successful cultivation of DfID's reputation internationally (Wickstead, 2019).

Nevertheless, this positive depiction of UK aid and development policies from Blair to Cameron is highly problematic in the context of how UK—and wider EU—aid policy became securitised in the aftermath of 9/11 (Abrahamsen, 2005; Olivie & Perez, 2020). As Abrahamsen (2005) makes clear, the Blair government increasingly invoked a security discourse in its presentation of UK aid spending after 9/11. Blair's experience of the UK's interventions in Kosovo and Sierra Leone, combined to the launch of Western nations' 'anti-terror' campaign, led Blair to espouse aid spending as part of efforts to create 'stability' in countries that might otherwise be susceptible to radicalisation (cf. PorteoColoniality of Power in Post-Colonialus, 2005: 288). UK aid expenditure became increasingly driven not by poverty reduction, but by UK security motivations deriving from the perceived risk' posed by African countries, and African migrants, within a globalised 'war on terror' (Abrahamsen, 2005; Bello, 2022). Poverty reduction became increasingly seen as a 'means' and not an ultimate 'ends' of UK aid interventions as a security imperative came to the fore (discussed more in Chapter 7). British elites' securitised aid discourse became woven throughout the speeches not only of Blair himself but of his successors in Downing Street. Indeed, security agendas pervaded DfID's own approach to poverty reduction efforts (Bello, 2022; Petrikova & Lazell, 2022).

A securitised emphasis on aid spending coincided with the UK's increasingly assertive use of aid in relation to its perceived economic imperatives in Africa—notably as part of the EU's drive for free trade deals in the 2000s (the Economic Partnership Agreements, EPAs). As the second largest contributor to the EU's European Development Fund (EDF), UK aid became entwined with EU budget support and Aid for Trade that were used to leverage African officials' acquiescence to free trade deals (Langan, 2011; Langan & Scott, 2014). For example, in West Africa, the creation of the EPA Development Programme (EPADP) in West Africa sought to facilitate trade agreements in the interests of European commerce (Langan, 2023; Langan & Price, 2015). Moreover, aid suspension in the 2000s became used to 'punish' regimes deemed to be non-compliant with European geopolitical interests such as Zimbabwe, while friendlier regimes with similarly problematic human rights records (such as Uganda) received large amounts of aid (Porteous, 2005: 295; Crawford & Kacarska, 2019). Under the Cameron government, meanwhile, aid increasingly was oriented towards support for the private sector and for the mitigation of migration. This has been viewed as a shift to a more interests-based approach to aid expenditure in the 2010s (Lazell, 2023).

Recent debates about whether the UK since Brexit has shifted to a more 'realist' or 'nationalist' phase in its approach to aid thus require historical context. Britain's so-called superpower status during the 2000s and early 2010s needs to be problematised (Wickstead, 2019). While there was discursive focus on poverty reduction, nevertheless, UK policy agendas from Blair to Brexit did reflect British economic and geopolitical interests (Gallagher, 2011: 87; Porteous, 2005: 289). DfID's focus on Aid for Trade as a legitimating route towards WTO and EPA free trade deals—as part of a wider Post-Washington Consensus (PWC)—is but one example of how New Labour used aid as leverage for economic advantages. The next section, however, underscores how Brexiteer discourse and populist sentiment drew upon—and cultivated—aid fatigue. A xenophobic English nationalism found expression against migrants coming to the UK, which found further expression in terms of scepticism towards humanitarian spending in the 'Global South'. This has had consequences in terms of post-Brexit governments' approach to aid-giving in Africa.

Brexiteer Populism and Aid Fatigue in the UK Context

By the time of the Brexit referendum, British politicians on the populist right such as Nigel Farage and Boris Johnson had long cited their concerns with British aid policy. During the early years of the Blair government, Johnson—while on a trip to Uganda—posited one early example of right-wing populist aid scepticism (Połońska-Kimunguyi & Kimunguyi, 2017). He expressed that the 'mess' in Africa was because British officials were no longer running their former colonies. He stated that development dilemmas would be resolved through a 'return' of British elites (Johnson, 2002). This return could be secured, Johnson wrote, through British investment—on the understanding that Britons would not be made to feel any 'guilt' (ibid.). The United Kingdom Independence Party (UKIP) under Farage and other leaders also cited their concerns with aid expenditure (Watts, 2014). These populist sentiments were combined to heavy media coverage of perceived misuse of aid in Africa and India. One tabloid newspaper campaign lambasted DfID's funding of what it described as the 'Ethiopian Spice Girls' as part of a gender empowerment campaign (Brown, 2013; Groves, 2015). The same newspaper campaigned against UK aid to India on the basis that the country's government had launched a space programme (Chamberlain, 2015; Reid, 2011).

The Leave campaign's focus on migration during the referendum was thus matched by Brexiteer elites' scepticism regarding aid expenditures. A xenophobic form of English nationalism informed hostility both towards migrants in the UK and the use of British taxpayers' monies for 'development' (Wellings, 2019). This populist sentiment soon found traction within elements of the British electorate. This was in large part owing to a domestic austerity politics enacted by the Cameron government, in which his Chancellor, George Osborne, cut expenditure on social services and welfare provision. A politics of resentment gained momentum in which the alleged loss of British jobs to migrants—and the supposed misuse of taxpayers' monies in the 'Global South'—worked to encourage support for populist politicians of the right, as well as for the Leave campaign (Rhodes & Hall, 2019; Virdee & McGeever, 2018). While the Brexit referendum did not forcefully highlight EU aid expenditures as a liability for the UK taxpayer, nevertheless a generally xenophobic mood contributed to the Leave majority within England and Wales. As Chapter 7 details, anxieties about migration dating back to Blair's securitised discourse on 'fragile states' in the 'Global South' played a key role in facilitating the Leave vote (cf. Bello, 2022).

In this context, early commentary on the implications of Brexit focused not only upon the technical element of UK withdrawal from EU development architectures—notably the EDF facility for ACP countries—but queried what direction would now be taken by UK aid policy. Olivie and Perez (2017, 2020) highlighted three possible scenarios described in turn as (i) cosmopolitan, (ii) realist and (iii) nationalist options. The cosmopolitan option would see the UK maintain its commitment to poverty reduction associated with the United Nations' (UN) Sustainable Development Goals (SDGs) and to the maintenance of 0.7% GDI spending. It would involve the UK's fulsome engagement with multilateral agencies devoted to 'development' (ibid.). The realist option, meanwhile, was seen as one in which the UK would maintain aid expenditure levels but increasingly shift to bilateral aid models. British aid would also be increasingly geared towards UK economic and foreign policy priorities. The nationalist scenario, meanwhile, was one in which aid fatigue would see a depletion of UK aid expenditure and a falling back in terms of previous British commitments to the UN target of 0.7% GNI. It would also see a retrenchment of UK elites' commitment to poverty reduction in the 'Global South' as part of an insular and inward post-Brexit trajectory (ibid.).

Accordingly, the question of UK withdrawal from the EU became enmeshed in a wider debate surrounding the political scenarios that would motivate British aid policy in the post-Brexit era. Continued UK engagement with the EU for joint aid delivery was seen to sit neatly with the cosmopolitan option where Global Britain would continue to play a 'leadership' role in terms of international development. Theresa May's Lancaster House speech and its promise that the UK would continue to positively engage the EU appeared to signal that this cosmopolitan option might be viable (Olivie & Perez, 2020: 205). Moreover, in her Florence speech, May sought to dispel EU member state fears that the UK would now renege on its promised contributions to projects under the current EU budget:

> I am conscious that our departure causes… uncertainty for the remaining member states… I do not want our partners to fear that they will need to pay more or receive less… The UK will honour commitments we have made during the period of our membership… we will also want to continue working together in ways that promote the long-term economic development of our continent. This includes continuing to take part in those specific policies and programmes which are greatly to the UK and the EU's joint advantage. (UK Government, 2017a)

May's promise appeared to leave open the possibility of the UK's ongoing involvement with the EDF, not only in terms of honouring existing commitments under the 11th iteration, but potentially in terms of future EDFs too.

Nevertheless, the possibility of an ongoing UK/EU joint effort on 'development' did not come to fruition. First, the EU's decision to 'budgetise' development spending towards the ACP bloc closed-down future UK involvement (Price, 2019). The EDF historically had been a member state-funded device outside of the formal EU budget. However, this had led to complaints from the European Parliament that its parliamentarians did not have sufficient oversight of EDF spending priorities. Moreover, the European Commission's decision to, in effect, close down the EDF as an only-ACP mechanism for aid disbursement and to create a global aid fund (with regional envelopes)—the Neighbourhood Development and International Cooperation (NDICI) instrument—within the formal EU budget ended the possibility of the UK's post-Brexit involvement in ACP-EU aid disbursement (ibid.: 8).

Furthermore, domestic pressures ensured that May would take a path closer to the 'realist' or 'nationalist' options. Given that May had campaigned for Remain, the Prime Minister appointed leading Brexiteer politicians to key positions (Mold, 2018). In terms of DfID, May appointed an aid sceptic—Priti Patel—to the development post. Patel made clear her views that UK aid disbursal via multilateral programmes ought to be reduced unless institutions such as the World Bank could evidence better value for money (Quinn, 2016). Additionally, she made plain that, in the post-Brexit era, aid monies ought to align more to the pursuit of UK interests, explicitly in terms of trade deals. Speaking in Kenya during her first visit to Africa as development secretary, Patel explained that:

> The government's approach is focused on ensuring that we drive taxpayer value - so when it comes to multilateral organisations… if they are not performing then obviously we'll look at the contributions that we give to them… soft power is exactly where DfID… and our aid…come together to deliver in our national interest and deliver for Britain when it comes to free trade agreements but also life post-Brexit. (cited in BBC News, 2016)

Patel's appointment was joined to that of Boris Johnson as Foreign Secretary, Liam Fox as Trade Minister and David Davis as Brexit secretary. All three of these fellow Brexiteers had voiced aid sceptic views, echoing a wider discourse within the Conservative right. A 'realist' outlook was soon reflected by May herself at the Hamburg Summit in 2017 in which she pledged that Aid for Trade would take pre-eminence within DfID's future approach (Kohnert, 2018: 122). Patel meanwhile suggested the merging of DfID with the Trade Ministry for the pursuit of trade deals (Price, 2018: 424). The likelihood of May pursuing a 'cosmopolitan' approach to aid was also dimmed by her own political posturing. As Prime Minister she embraced the populist language of her Brexiteer colleagues—appealing to a xenophobic English nationalism that condemned 'citizens of nowhere' (The Spectator, 2016). This cemented her earlier populist appeals during her tenure in the Home Office under David Cameron, in which she had authorised 'Go Home Vans' to target neighbourhoods where perceived 'illegal migrants' were present (Taylor, 2022). This notorious campaign constituted part of her 'hostile environment' that especially targeted British citizens of Caribbean descent, as part of what is now termed the Windrush Scandal (ibid.).

The potential of a 'cosmopolitan' aid scenario was further eroded with the appointment of Boris Johnson as Prime Minister in 2019. Johnson had expressed aid sceptic views in the 2000s. He had also articulated an imperial romanticism mixed with racialised remarks about black Commonwealth citizens (Igbini et al., 2020: 8). As Prime Minister, he condemned aid as a giant 'cashpoint in the sky' and made a symbolic and material move towards a more 'realist' agenda by merging DfID and the FCO into the FCDO (Savage, 2022). This did away with the New Labour ministry that had nominally been founded as a shift away from the blending of aid and interests that underpinned multiple scandals in the 1990s. The closure of DfID was marked by wide dismay among civil society. In June 2020 when the merger took place, the chief executive of Oxfam (2020) queried how this aligned to an open 'Global Britain':

> It is scarcely believable that... the Prime Minister has decided to scrap DfID. This decision puts politics above the needs of the poorest people and will mean more people around the world will die unnecessarily from hunger and disease. The Foreign Office may be excellent at diplomacy, but it has a patchy record of aid delivery and is not as transparent as DfID. To be a truly 'Global Britain' we need to do more to live up to our values, not turn our backs on them.

As the next section explains in relation to aid cuts, the tying of aid to trade agreements, the renewed focus on bilateral instruments, especially the BII, and the pursuit of UK commercial interests via aid in countries such as Ethiopia, the UK pursues an increasingly 'realist' or indeed 'nationalist' agenda in the post-Brexit era.

A 'Realist' or 'Nationalist' Turn in UK Aid After Brexit?

UK aid and development policies since the Brexit referendum do appear to have taken an increasingly 'realist' or even 'nationalist' stance. It is important to note, however, that this does not imply that UK aid policy has ever truly been 'cosmopolitan'. Even the Blair government cannot be deemed to have met the criteria of a genuinely 'cosmopolitan' aid agenda. The securitised discourse combined with the Aid for Trade agenda embedded in UK aid disbursal in the 2000s is good illustration of how UK development policies have always had a 'realist' tone (Abrahamsen, 2005). Or what can be more accurately be described as a neo-colonial character, with aid focused upon swaying officials in 'developing countries'—either in terms of complying with British security agendas, or with UK economic objectives such as EU EPA trade deals (Langan, 2019). Brexit therefore marks less a 'critical juncture' for a policy volte-face than an event that has intensified existing trends (cf. Nwankwo, 2018).

Specifically, UK aid policy after Brexit appears to be even more 'realist' in outlook. The closure of DfID has been combined to a move away from aid delivery within multilateral forums towards bilateral delivery via UK ministries and institutions. This is clearly outlined in the UK Government's (2022) *Strategy for International Development* which states that a hallmark of Global Britain's policy is to do 'proportionately more through country and bilateral programmes, being a more responsive development partner to countries' needs and more consciously geopolitical in approach'. Indeed, the UK government aims that 75% of all UK aid will now be delivered on a bilateral basis (Bond, 2020). This emphasis on a 'geopolitical' approach interestingly mirrors the language of the European Commission which has promised that the EU too will take a more 'geopolitical' stance—as part of a 'new scramble' for African resources (Carmody, 2016; EEAS, 2016). The UK's 2022 document goes on to insist that:

> We want to have more and closer bilateral partnerships that support countries to succeed as open, free nations. To underpin this, FCDO will substantially rebalance its ODA investments from multilateral towards bilateral channels. By 2025 FCDO intends to spend around three-quarters of its funding allocated at the 2021 Spending Review through country

programmes. This will allow FCDO to focus funding on UK priorities and control exactly how taxpayers' money is used to support these. (UK Government, 2022)

Peck (2023: 163) rightly notes here that the UK strategy reflects the logic of the Brexit referendum, especially regarding 'sovereign' policy choices:

> The [international development] strategy is infused with echoes of the discursive logics of Brexit... This time it is not only the UK taking back control; through its development interventions it is facilitating other countries to do so... This shift towards bilateral partnerships presents a more individualistic, sovereign (and perhaps nationalistic) approach to development, a move away from global bodies to strategic partnerships with countries of the UK's choosing.

Populist language about regaining sovereign futures and 'taking back control' have seeped into aid policy discourse, as articulated by the UK government under Boris Johnson.

Moreover, the Johnson government's decision to cut ODA spending—with the approval of the then Chancellor of the Exchequer, Rishi Sunak—has contributed towards a 'nationalist' element. Despite legislation introduced by the Cameron government which aimed to enshrine the 0.7% target, the Johnson government cited circumstances after the pandemic to facilitate an aid cut to 0.5% GNI (Lulat, 2022: 13). The rapid reduction has meant that UK embassies have had to take decisions to suspend—or to prematurely end—various humanitarian projects. Worley (2022) explains the impact in Rwanda:

> Former Foreign Secretary Dominic Raab cut the aid budget for Rwanda from £62 million in 2019 to less than £30 million in 2021... resulting in a £4.6 billion shortfall in the budget. The aid cuts disproportionately affected bilateral programs and countries in the African continent, according to official statistics.

The aid cut—combined to the closure of DfID—has been interpreted as a symbolic blow to the 'superpower' status of Global Britain as a development protagonist (cf. Wickstead, 2019). It has also meant reduced UK commitment to UN programmes. The bilateral aid target has been condemned by UK civil society groups including Bond International

(2020) who state that 'multilateral funding offers a proven and effective way to pool resources and act collectively to alleviate poverty at scale, while bilateral spending can increase country ownership... Placing arbitrary limits on either could ultimately be counter-productive'.

UK aid funding has further come under scrutiny in relation to trade deals and 'Aid for Trade' schemes since Brexit. The Independent Commission for Aid Impact (2022) estimates that the British government spent £9 billion on Aid for Trade between 2015 and 2020. By contrast in 2011, DfID's total Aid for Trade spending amounted to £1 billion per annum (Rauf, 2011). This ramping up of Aid for Trade was first signposted by Priti Patel as development minister and has come to be reflected in official government policy. UK aid is openly being used as leverage for the signing of post-Brexit trade arrangements despite legislation that states that the primary focus of aid must be poverty reduction (Ambreena, 2019: 41; 44). Aid for Trade nominally involves aid expenditure on improving competitiveness among business communities in the 'Global South'. It was a mechanism devised during the WTO Doha Round to 'level the playing field' and ensure that trade liberalisation would work for developing economies. This is despite mounting evidence about the negative impact of premature free trade deals in terms tariff dismantling and import flooding in Africa and beyond (see, for instance, Stender et al., 2021 on EU EPAs). Nevertheless, in 2020, the UK's ambassador to the WTO and United Nations (UN) in Geneva expressed the government's strong support for this aid modality in strictly 'pro-poor' terms:

> The United Kingdom strongly believes that aid for trade is vital to the future of the global trading system. While the past half-century has changed the WTO, our commitment to development within it has not. The United Kingdom believes that targeted technical assistance, linked to stable and predictable rules, allow cross-border trade to transform economies, unlock growth, and reduce poverty. (UK Government, 2020)

Such rhetoric mirrors the pro-poor discourse of the Blair government, which as noted was a keen sponsor of Aid for Trade alongside DfID. In the post-Brexit context, this aid modality has found renewed support among Brexiteer politicians who believe that such aid can (i) lubricate the signing of trade deals and (ii) legitimise such deals as being about 'poverty reduction'.

Despite the enthusiasm of UK governments, however, there are concerns with the strategic usages of Aid for Trade by Global Britain and more widely in terms of usages by the international donor community. Namely, there is concern that Aid for Trade can amount to 'boomerang aid' in the sense that monies are spent upon business sectors in which the donor country is heavily involved. For example, EU Aid for Trade expenditure on the cut flower industry in East Africa during the Cotonou Agreement has been seen to assist Dutch commercial interests, given the role of flower auctions in the Netherlands (Langan, 2011). Similarly, donor expenditure on infrastructure and trade facilitation (including support to trade negotiations) can be seen to serve donors' interests. Better roads, ports and electricity supplies allow foreign investors to more easily operate within the recipient country, as well as to export valuable goods (for instance, critical raw materials) back to the donor country (Langan & Scott, 2014). Facilitation of trade deals also can work in the interests of foreign donors, as can the conditioning of Aid for Trade upon recipient acquiescence to controversial policy adoption, for example privatisation agendas in Ethiopia (discussed in more detail below).

In this context, the UK government's (2022) announcement within its *Strategy for International Development* that it will increasingly focus on Aid for Trade—as well as foreign direct investment (FDI)—has led to alarm among anti-poverty campaigners. The chair of the House of Commons' International Development Committee (IDC), Sarah Champion, outlined the dangers of this modality for African countries:

> We all want our exporters to do well and to create jobs in the UK. But aid for trade is dangerous. It can distort the core, legally stipulated purpose of our assistance—which is to support the poorest and most vulnerable whether in the countries of sub-Saharan Africa or in Ukraine. Supporting the poorest in the world should not be conditional on a trade deal or agreeing to investment partnerships. (cited in Taylor, 2022)

This concern has been echoed by UK civil society organisations, including Bond (2020), an NGO network, whose chairperson stated that 'the strategy's shortcomings signal the UK's loss of leadership in global development'. This echoed Bond's earlier criticism of Priti Patel when she expressed her desire that aid would be tied to Brexit trade deals:

> All Bond members… would argue strongly that there is significant research and experience to suggest that when aid is used as a bargaining tool for securing trade and contracts, and works primarily in the interests of the donor, it results in profoundly detrimental experiences for those living in poverty. (Harris, 2016)

Scepticism thus exists within British civil society as to whether Global Britain's international development approach remains compliant with 2002 legislation that enshrines poverty reduction as the core goal of aid spending. Ambreena (2019) concludes that a tightening of legal barriers to improper usages of aid may be necessary in the UK parliamentary context:

> Is the legal framework for aid sufficiently robust to protect public money at a time when it might constitute a slush fund for making friends and influencing new partners? It remains an open question what this country's international role, standing and intentions will be after Brexit. But there can be little doubt that its aid policies will be affected. And in my view, there is reason to doubt whether the current legal framework can withstand the challenges that lie ahead.

Moreover, fears about the potential for UK governments to misuse aid monies are borne out in the post-Brexit period. Perhaps most notably, the UK government continued to provide aid to the regime of Prime Minister Abiy Ahmed in Ethiopia despite allegations of gross human rights abuses in the Tigray War. The Abiy administration has embarked upon a free market strategy that conforms with donors' prescriptions and shies away from the developmentalist approach of his predecessors, including former Prime Minister Meles Zenawi of the Tigray People's Liberation Front (TPLF) (Fourie, 2015; Rynn, 2023: 15). The UK government supported Abiy's Prosperity Party (PP) during the Tigray War and enabled him to embark on a wide-ranging privatisation agenda, including the Ethiopian telecoms industry. This has paved the way for the UK firm, Vodafone, to win a lucrative contract as part of an international consortium for telecoms provision within the Ethiopian market (Rynn, 2023: 16). The British embassy heralded this corporate win as being in part due to their Aid for Trade support to industrial parks within the country (ibid.). This winning consortium is also being supported by British International Investment (BII) (formerly the Commonwealth Development Corporation [CDC] group, which is discussed in more detail in the next chapter). CDC/

BII is wholly owned by the FCDO. This involvement led to a group of concerned Tigrayan academics writing to the British government to express their concerns that CDC/BII monies might be misused by the Ethiopian regime for furthering its human rights abuses (Leigh Day, 2021).

The tandem of UK government and corporate involvement in Ethiopia, however, is despite other donors—including the European Commission—suspending aid to the regime as a result of its abuses, including widespread rape and abuse of women and girls (Amnesty International, 2021). There are also concerns that the rapid liberalisation and privatisation agenda may further stoke societal and political tensions given their controversial nature:

> Critics... have noted the lack of a societal consensus on the PP's rapid privatisation and liberalisation agenda, and expressed doubts about the intentions of a government which has no shame in using policy agendas to isolate opponents. For supporters of the... government's economic model, there is also suspicion that introducing foreign competition will lead to expatriation of profits. (Rynn, 2023: 17)

The strategic use of UK aid in Ethiopia by Global Britain appears to contravene human rights and to add fuel to internal conflict despite the rhetoric of UK documents such as *Global Britain in a Competitive Age* (2021) and the *Strategy for International Development* (2022). The former document's promise that the UK will sit at the heart of a network of like-minded countries and flexible groupings, committed to protecting human rights and upholding global norms, appears hollow in the Ethiopian situation.

Again though, this is not to say that aid usage in the pre-Brexit period was wholly 'humanitarian'. In 2014, an Ethiopian citizen sued the UK government for facilitating human rights abuses via aid towards a forced villagisation process:

> In this 2014 case, an Ethiopian national known only as Mr O had claimed that funding provided by DfID for a Protection of Basic Services (PBS) Programme coordinated by the World Bank had contributed to human rights abuses by the Ethiopian government through a forced villagisation programme that led to evictions, forced removals, and the alienation of the land of farmers. (Ambreena, 2019: 49)

In that case, DfID latterly suspended its support to the World Bank initiative. There appears no current sign, however, that the FCDO will withdraw support from the Abiy regime.

Furthermore, the *entrenchment* of a 'realist' or 'nationalist' approach to aid in the post-Brexit era has been illustrated by the UK government's decision to categorise domestic spending on accommodation and the broader maintenance of migrants within the UK as constituting Official Development Assistance (ODA). While this is technically not an infringement of the Organisation for Economic Co-operation and Development's (OECD) Development Assistance Committee (DAC) rules, nevertheless, the UK's approach has been viewed as a violation of the spirit of ODA— and as a means of reducing aid expenditure on humanitarian programmes in the 'Global South' (Bond, 2020). Additionally, its approach is seen to send a dangerous signal to other OECD governments that might now choose to categorise domestic support for migrants in this way, to lower aid commitments elsewhere (Amnesty International, 2022a: 5). UK civil society groups have condemned the UK government's cynical actions (ibid.).

Combined to this, the UK government has been heavily criticised for its controversial migration 'externalisation' agreement with Rwanda (Worley, 2022). Namely, the UK government seeks to send male migrants to Rwanda for processing and accommodation as part of a populist appeal by the Sunak government to 'stop small boats' (IRC, 2023). The £120 million agreement, seeking to discourage attempts by migrants from Calais to UK shores, involves an opaque 'Memorandum of Understanding' with the Rwandan government and apparently is not being counted in terms of ODA (Goddard, 2023; Gower et al., 2022: 22–23). The deal is seen to fall foul of human rights imperatives, not least due to the forcible removal of migrants to a country with a recent history of genocide and attacks on LGBT+ communities (Amnesty International, 2022b). The £120 million being given for economic development objectives in Rwanda must also be contextualised in terms of the UK's official ODA cutbacks, which included the curtailing of humanitarian projects for women and girls (Worley, 2022). Any 'new' monies under the migration compact are partly mitigated by lost ODA funding as a result of the UK government's decision to renege on its earlier promises to meet the UN 0.7% GNI target for delivering the UN SDGs. The Rwandan government's acquiescence to this internationally notorious deal may itself be partly motivated by a desire to financially counteract the prior aid cut.

The entrenchment of a 'realist' or 'nationalist' approach is also seen in terms of the UK government's post-Brexit emphasis upon the Commonwealth Development Corporation (CDC)—now renamed British International Investment (BII) (Lulat, 2022: 14). This British development finance institution (DFI) is owned by the FCDO and seeks to 'de-risk' investments in Africa by providing loans and guarantees for UK firms wishing to invest. In this capacity, BII seeks to achieve a multiplier effect, with its role being to reassure British capital that investments in African contexts will be secure and recoverable (Kohnert, 2018; Price, 2018). The enhanced role of BII within the post-Brexit vision of international development is also mirrored in a European context where the European Commission has increasingly emphasised the need for 'aid blending'—namely the use of ODA monies to support European DFIs including the European Investment Bank (EIB) (Bougrea et al., 2022). The EU's Global Gateway initiative operates via aid blending, hoping to leverage in investments in lucrative infrastructure and business projects in Africa as a challenge to China's own Belt and Road initiative (ibid.). The UK's BII is thus a competitor not only to European DFIs, but also to Chinese investors within the 'new scramble' for African resources (cf Carmody, 2016). As the next chapter illustrates, CDC/BII investments—and their counting as a form of ODA/aid spending—promote UK commercial interests with little regard for genuine poverty reduction. Often investments run contrary to the 'development' needs of recipient countries, especially in relation to the mining sector where poor labour and environmental standards jeopardise the well-being of workers and local communities (Simpere, 2010). As the next section discusses, the overall picture of UK aid policy in the post-Brexit era conforms to Nkrumah's (1965) and Ndlovu-Gatsheni's (2015) warnings regarding neo-colonialism and global coloniality.

Global Britain, Aid and Global Coloniality

The direction of UK aid and development policy in the post-Brexit era fuses together elements of the 'realist' and 'nationalist' scenarios laid out by Olivie and Perez (2017). There is the usage of aid monies to achieve 'realist' geopolitical and economic goals for Global Britain in its engagement with African countries. For example, the use of monies to incentivise Brexit trade deals as outlined by Priti Patel and the use of aid to secure a migration compact with Rwanda underscore that 'realist' motivations are at the heart of Global Britain's aid expenditure. Moreover, as the case of Ethiopia exemplifies, the use of UK aid monies to secure benefits for UK firms occurs even in situations of civil war and alleged human rights violations (amid circumstances where other Western donors suspend aid). There is thus clearly a 'realist' element to Global Britain's aid in the sense that hard interests trump normative concerns when UK policy-makers approach conflict situations such as in Ethiopia.

Nevertheless, there is also a 'nationalist' element in the sense of mounting aid fatigue among UK elites—note Brexiteer politicians such as Johnson—as well as among segments of the UK electorate influenced by media campaigns against alleged wastage. This 'nationalist' component to aid is also seen in terms of the UK's ODA cutbacks despite previous legislation that had sought to enshrine the UN's 0.7% GNI target. It is further witnessed in terms of the domestic utilisation of 'ODA' to support accommodation and expenses for migrants within the UK's own borders, at the expense of overseas humanitarian initiatives that have been scaled back— for instance, gender equality programmes in Rwanda (Worley, 2022). Additionally, the UK Government's (2022) declared intention to spend more monies via bilateral channels as opposed to multilateral agencies (such as UN bodies) signals both a 'realist' and a 'nationalist' tendency in the sense of opening up more opportunities for aid conditionality, as well as demonstrating an insular attitude to global governance institutions.

However, any assessment of the 'realist' and 'nationalist' elements within Global Britain's approach to aid must be historically contextualised and combined to a decolonial critique of neo-colonialism and global coloniality. As the chapter has discussed, the era of Britain's supposed 'superpower' status in development under Blair, Brown and Cameron did not conform to 'cosmopolitan' credentials in terms of usages of aid monies (Wickstead, 2019). While New Labour discursively endorsed a pro-poor approach, nevertheless, usages of aid monies conformed to UK economic and (perceived) security interests. After 2005, the Blair government and DfID became firm supporters of Aid for Trade strategies—namely aid aligned to the pursuit of free trade agreements at both the multilateral level of the WTO and EU EPAs in Africa (Rauf, 2011). Moreover, in the post-9/11 context, UK aid discourse emphasised the need to stabilise so-called fragile states in Africa and to limit conflict-driven migration (Abrahamsen, 2005; Bello, 2022). Today's securitised rhetoric surrounding migration was preceded by New Labour's emphasis on the development-security linkage in their approach to the 'war on terror'.

In relation to Nkrumah's (1965) and Ndlovu-Gatsheni's (2015) warnings regarding neo-colonialism and global coloniality, the post-Brexit direction of UK aid delivery confirms their fears as to Euro-American elites' recourse to aid as leverage. As Nkrumah (1965: xv) predicted in the 1960s, UK elites are utilising aid as a form of 'revolving credit' in which short-term aid expenditure aims to secure longer-term profits in the shape of inequitable trade deals such as Brexit EPAs. Moreover, aid denudes recipient sovereignty and stokes internal domestic tensions, as with UK aid to an Ethiopian regime that was conducting privatisation agendas while waging war on Tigray. Global Britain's decision to continue aid to the Ethiopian regime has won dividends for UK firm Vodafone while bringing into question the UK's own professed reputation for its commitment to human rights (Rynn, 2023). This reputational damage to the UK was solidified by the decision of other Western donors—such as the European Commission—to suspend aid to Ethiopia given mounting human rights allegations—including systematic rape (Amnesty International, 2021). The UK's use of aid here can therefore—in Ndlovu-Gatsheni's (2015) terms—be seen as evidence of the coloniality of power in which British elites exert financial and political pressure on African countries to acquiesce to their geopolitical and geoeconomic interests.

The concepts of the coloniality of knowledge and the coloniality of being also help us to understand UK elites' approach to aid in the post-Brexit era. In terms of the coloniality of knowledge, the Global Britain project has emphasised the centrality of free trade and economic liberalisation to African countries' prosperity. In keeping with a donor Post-Washington Consensus (PWC), UK elites emphasise the compatibility of Brexit EPA free trade deals to poverty reduction (Öniş & Şenses, 2005; UK Government, 2017b). They emphasise that UK aid to the private sector in African states—via infrastructural improvements and support for trade policy formation—will create livelihoods conducive to social prosperity (UK Government, 2020). Aid for Trade initiatives here become central to the UN SDGs as per Brexiteer—and earlier, New Labour—discourse in a PWC setting. This constitutes the coloniality of knowledge in the sense of the cultivation of a 'common sense' free market approach to development that is latterly combined to aid conditionalities. Officials in Ethiopia, for instance, pursue highly controversial privatisation strategies in the face of domestic opposition as they align to Western donors' free market preferences. In return, they receive aid and investment from the UK irrespective of alleged gross human rights violations. Indeed, Tigrayan academics feared that British investment would facilitate more regime crimes in the conflict zone (Leigh Day, 2021). Ethiopian officials' adoption of Western style policy agendas also assists them to lever in foreign direct investment from Western companies such as Vodafone. Ethiopian officials' move away from the successful developmental state strategies of earlier administrations, such as that of Meles Zewawi, is thereby underpinned by Western aid and FDI. The UK similarly overlooks human rights abuses in countries such as Uganda which also adhered to laissez-faire free market strategies conducive to UK corporate engagement. For example, British firm Tullow Oil, which is involved in Uganda's lucrative energy sector, is discussed more in Chapter 6 (The Independent, 2020).

The concept of the coloniality of being also finds resonance in terms of UK elites' 'mission civilisatrice' in Africa (cf. Połońska-Kimunguyi & Kimunguyi, 2017). As exemplified by Blair's declaration that Africa constituted a 'stain on the conscience of the world' and by Johnson's numerous racialised remarks, UK elites continue to view the African continent as being in need of British salvation. Whether in terms of the 'old racism' that fixates on alleged biological differences, or the 'new racism' that fixates on alleged cultural differences, the Global Britain project is permeated by racialised imaginaries drawn from Empire (Grosfoguel, 2002). Furthermore, UK elites' securitised rhetoric regularly demeans African persons as 'illegal' migrants (McConnon, 2022). Global Britain's notorious Rwanda deportation policy in this sense aligns to a broader European antipathy towards racialised migrants, as reflect within remarks Josep Borrell's much condemned 'garden' and 'jungle' speech (Bishara, 2022). In this context, debates surrounding the 'realist' and 'nationalist' elements within Global Britain's aid approach need to acknowledge UK elites' racialised mission civilisatrice as a driving factor for Global Britain's neo-colonial interventions in Africa. The associated concepts of the coloniality of power, knowledge and being can help to interrogate the reasons for the UK's ongoing neo-colonial approach to the continent, even with the rise of insular sentiment within the UK electorate itself.

Conclusion

This chapter has examined aid and development policy in the context of UK elites' launch of the Global Britain project. It has engaged debates that the UK has since lost its 'superpower' status in international donor circles by abandoning a cosmopolitan concern for multilateral aid spending and humanitarian projects. In particular, the closure of DfID amid ODA cutbacks appears to signal that Global Britain is turning towards 'realist' or even 'nationalist' policy options in terms of promoting UK economic and security interests—while appealing to populist pressures to scale back aid spending on 'corrupt' recipients. Moreover, the UK's securitised approach to migration—combined to externalisation strategies embodied in the UK-Rwanda migration compact—underpins an argument that Global Britain has moved away from a humanitarian ethos associated with the *Make Poverty History* campaign in the 2000s under New Labour and now takes a more 'assertive' approach to international development. This argument is also bolstered by recent policy documents released by the Johnson and Sunak governments, notably the UK Government's (2021, 2022) *Global Britain in a Competitive Age* and the *Strategy for International Development*.

However, it is important to contextualise this apparent shift to 'realist' or 'nationalist' policy positions in terms of historical trajectories. UK aid policy under Blair—and as pursued by DfID—did align to securitisation agendas in the wake of 9/11. Blair's pursuit of free trade deals combined to Aid for Trade marked a 'realist' focus upon UK economic interests—for example in relation to EU EPAs negotiated by New Labour's own Peter Mandelson. It would be wrong therefore to assume that the UK previously abided by a cosmopolitan aid agenda and that Brexit has augured in a radically different approach to 'development' in Africa. What instead has occurred is an entrenchment of neo-colonial usage of UK aid monies in which the coloniality of power, knowledge and being combines to perpetuate existing power asymmetries. The use of British aid monies in Ethiopia, despite the war in Tigray, is perhaps the clearest example. In this case, UK aid largesse was used to support the Ethiopian government in its pursuit of privatisation agendas to the benefit of a British company, despite mounting allegations of human rights abuses in the civil war. Brexiteer politicians' emphasis upon Aid for Trade aligned to free trade deals also illustrates the neo-colonial character of Global Britain's approach. Aid for Trade—given its New Labour lineage—also exemplifies some of the consistencies—as opposed to divergences—in the UK's approach since the Brexit referendum. The next chapter continues this interrogation of UK aid policy in the sense of development finance and the UK's DFI (the CDC group, renamed BII). It illustrates that British commercial appetites underpin the BII's role irrespective of supposed poverty reduction goals articulated as part of the Global Britain project.

Bibliography

Abrahamsen, R. (2005). Blair's Africa: The Politics of Securitization and Fear. *Alternatives: Global, Local, Political, 30*(1), 55–80.

Ambreena, M. (2019). The Legal Framework for UK Aid After Brexit. *Current Legal Problems, 72*(1), 37–57.

Amnesty International. (2021). *"I Don't Even Know If They Realised I Was a Person": Rape and Sexual Violence in the Conflict in Tigray, Ethiopia*. Amnesty International.

Amnesty International. (2022a). *Submission to International Development Committee Aid Spending in the UK, November 2022*. Amnesty International.

Amnesty International. (2022b, June 17). Rwanda: Commonwealth Leaders Must Oppose UK's Racist Asylum Seeker Deal. *Amnesty International News*. https://www.amnesty.org/en/latest/news/2022/06/rwanda-commonwealth-leaders-must-oppose-uks-racist-asylum-seeker-deal/. Accessed 29 May 2023.

BBC News. (2016, October 25). Aid to be Cut Unless It Is Value for Money, Says Patel. *BBC News*. https://www.bbc.co.uk/news/uk-politics-37758164. Accessed 29 April 2023.

Bello, V. (2022). The Spiralling of the Securitisation of Migration in the EU: From the Management of a 'Crisis' to a Governance of Human Mobility? *Journal of Ethnic and Migration Studies, 48*(6), 1327–1344.

Beswick, D. (2019). Rehabilitating the "Nasty Party"? The Conservative Party and Africa from Opposition to Government. In D. Beswick, J. Fisher, & S. Hurt (Eds.), *Britain and Africa in the Twenty-First Century: Between Ambition and Pragmatism* (pp. 121–138). Manchester University Press.

Bishara, M. (2022, October 17). Opinion—Josep Borrell as Europe's Racist "Gardener"'. *Al Jazeera*.

Bond. (2020). *The UK Government's Strategy for International Development: Bond's Analysis of What It Says and What Needs to Happen Next*. Bond.

Bougrea, A., Orbie, J., & Vermeiren, M. (2022). The New European Financial Architecture for Development: Change or Continuity? *European Foreign Affairs Review, 27*(3), 337–360.

Brown, L. (2013, November 15). How You Pay £4M to Fund the Ethiopian Spice Girls: New Aid Storm Over Project That's Even Ridiculed in African Country. *The Daily Mail.* https://www.dailymail.co.uk/news/article-2508063/UK-pay-4m-fund-Ethiopian-Spice-Girls-New-aid-project-Yegna-ridiculed.html. Accessed 29 April 2023.

Calhoun, C. (2017). Populism, Nationalism and Brexit. In W. Outhwaite (Ed.), *Brexit: Sociological Responses* (pp. 57–76). Anthem Press.

Carmody, P. (2016). *The New Scramble for Africa.* Polity Press.

Chamberlain, G. (2015, February 11). Lunar-cy! India Gets Enough Cash in British Aid to Allow it to Send a £250 Million Rocket to the Moon… Even Though Government Promised to Stop It. *The Daily Mail.* https://www.dailymail.co.uk/news/article-2947400/Lunar-cy-India-gets-cash-British-aid-send-250million-rocket-moon.html. Accessed 29 April 2023.

Crawford, G., & Kacarska, S. (2019). Aid Sanctions and Political Conditionality: Continuity and Change. *Journal of International Relations and Development*, 22, 184–214.

EEAS. (2016, November 30). Africa and the EU. *EEAS Strategic Communications* 30 November 2022. https://www.eeas.europa.eu/eeas/africa-and-eu_en. Accessed 29 April 2023.

FCO. (2019). *Foreign and Commonwealth Office (FCO) Diversity and Equality Report 2018–19*. FCO.

Fourie, E. (2015). China's Example for Meles' Ethiopia: When Development 'Models' Land'. *The Journal of Modern African Studies, 53*(3), 289–316.

Gallagher, J. (2011). *Britain and Africa Under Blair: In Pursuit of the Good State.* Manchester University Press.

Goddard, J. (2023, January 26). UK-Rwanda Asylum Agreement: Why Is It a Memorandum of Understanding and Not a Treaty? House of Lords Library. In *Focus.* https://lordslibrary.parliament.uk/uk-rwanda-asylum-agreement-why-is-it-a-memorandum-of-understanding-and-not-a-treaty. Accessed 29 May 2023.

Gower, M., Butchard, P., & McKinney, C. J. (2022, December 22). The UK-Rwanda Migration and Economic Development Partnership. *House of Commons Library Research Briefing.* https://commonslibrary.parliament.uk/research-briefings/cbp-9568/. Accessed 29 May 2023.

Grosfoguel, R. (2002). Colonial Difference, Geopolitics of Knowledge, and Global Coloniality in the Modern/Colonial Capitalist World-System. *Review (Fernand Braudel Center), 25*(3), 203–224.

Groves, J. (2015, June 19). Ethiopian Spice Girls Project in Line for £16M More of Our Foreign Aid Despite Warning That It May be a Waste of Money. *The Daily Mail*. https://www.dailymail.co.uk/news/article-3130623/Ethiopian-Spice-Girls-project-line-16m-foreign-aid-despite-warning-waste-money.html. Accessed 29 April 2023.

Hall, I. (2012). Building the Global Network? The Reform of the Foreign and Commonwealth Office under New Labour. *The British Journal of Politics and International Relations, 15*(2), 228–245.

Harris, A. (2016). *Post-Brexit Aid Policy: What Is Aid for Trade? And What Is It Not?* Bond.

Igbini, M., Oluka, N., & Oharisi, A. (2020). Nigeria and the United Kingdom Diplomatic Relations: The Emerging Issues in the Post-Brexit Era. *International Journal of Research and Scientific Innovation, 7*(7), 1–8.

Independent Commission for Aid Impact. (2022). *Approach Paper: UK Aid for Trade*. ICAI.

International Rescue Committee. (2023). *Why Rishi Sunak's "Stop the Boats" Bill Won't Work*. https://www.rescue.org/uk/article/why-rishi-sunaks-stop-boats-bill-wont-work Accessed 15 November 2023.

Irish Times. (2003, May 22). Geldof and Bono to Discuss Africa with Blair. *Irish Times*. https://www.irishtimes.com/news/geldof-and-bono-to-discuss-africa-with-blair-1.478500. Accessed 23 April 2023.

Johnson, B. (2002, February 2). Africa Is in a Mess, But We Can't Blame Colonialism. *The Spectator*. https://www.spectator.co.uk/article/the-boris-archive-africa-is-a-mess-but-we-can-t-blame-colonialism/. Accessed 23 April 2023.

Kohnert, D. (2018). More Equitable Britain-Africa Relations Post-Brexit: Doomed to Fail? *Africa Spectrum, 53*(2), 119–130.

Langan, M. (2011). Uganda's Flower Farms and Private Sector Development. *Development and Change, 42*(5), 1207–1240.

Langan, M. (2019). Africa's Trade with Brexit Britain: Neo-colonialism Encounters Regionalism? In D. Beswick, J. Fisher, & S. Hurt (Eds.), *Britain and Africa in the 21st Century: Between Ambition and Pragmatism* (pp. 35–53). Manchester University Press.

Langan, M. (2023). The Double Movement in Africa: A Nkrumah-Polanyi Analysis of free Market Fatigue in Ghana's Private Sector. *Review of International Political Economy, 30*(2), 463–486.

Langan, M., & Price, S. (2015). Extraversion and the West African EPA Development Programme: Realising the Development Dimension of ACP–EU trade? *The Journal of Modern African Studies, 53*(3), 263–287.

Langan, M., & Scott, J. (2014). The Aid for Trade Charad. *Cooperation and Conflict, 49*(2), 143–161.

Lazell, M. (2023). UK Aid to Africa: "Nationalisation" and Neoliberalism. *Canadian Journal of Development Studies* (Early view ed., pp. 1–20).
Leigh Day. (2021). *Tigrayan Group in the UK Raises Serious Concerns About CDC Investments in Ethiopia Telecoms*. Leigh Day. https://www.leighday.co.uk/news/news/2021-news/tigrayan-group-in-uk-raises-serious-concerns-about-cdc-investment-in-ethiopia-telecoms/. Accessed 4 September 2023.
Lulat, Y. G-M. (2022, November 20). *The View from Africa of Britain, Populism, and Brexit: A Blessing in Disguise?* https://ssrn.com/abstract=4282367. Accessed 29 April 2023.
McConnon, E. (2022). People as Security Risks: The Framing of Migration in the UK Security-Development Nexus. *Journal of Ethnic and Migration Studies, 48*(6), 1381–1397.
Mold, A. (2018). The Consequences of Brexit for Africa: The Case of the East African Community. *Journal of African Trade, 5*(2–1), 1–17.
Olivie, I., & Perez, A. (2017). *Possible Impacts of Brexit on EU Aid and Humanitarian Policies*. European Commission.
Olivie, I., & Perez, A. (2020). The Impact of Brexit on Aid: EU and Global Development Assistance Under a Realist UK Scenario. *Journal of Contemporary European Studies, 16*(2), 200–217.
Ndlovu-Gatsheni, S. J. (2013). *Coloniality of Power in Post-Colonial Africa*. CODESRIA.
Ndlovu-Gatsheni, S. J. (2014). Global Coloniality and the Challenges of Creating African Futures. *Strategic Review for Southern Africa, 36*(2), 181–202.
Ndlovu-Gatsheni, S. J. (2015). *Empire, Global Coloniality and African Subjectivity*. Berghahn Books.
Nkrumah, K. (1965). *Neo-colonialism: The Last Stage of Imperialism*. Panaf Press.
Nwankwo, C. F. (2018). Brexit: Critical Juncture in the UK's International Development Agenda? *Open Political Science, 1*(1), 16–19.
Öniş, Z., & Şenses, F. (2005). Rethinking the Emerging Post-Washington Consensus. *Development and Change, 36*(2), 263–290.
Oxfam. (2020, June 16). *Reaction to Merger of Department for International Development with Foreign Office*. Oxfam GB Media Centre. https://www.oxfam.org.uk/media/press-releases/reaction-to-merger-of-department-for-international-development-with-the-foreign-office/. Accessed 29 May 2023.
Peck, S. (2023). A "Distinct UK Offer": The Geographies of the FCDO's International Development Strategy 2022. *The Geographical Journal, 189*, 161–167.
Petrikova, I., & Lazell, M. (2019). The Securitisation of UK and DfID Programmes in Africa: A Comparative Case Study of Cameroon, Central African Republic, Ethiopia, Kenya and Uganda. In D. Beswick, J. Fisher, & S. Hurt (Eds.), *Britain and Africa in the Twenty-First Century: Between Ambition and Pragmatism* (pp. 73–98). Manchester University Press.

Petrikova, I., & Lazell, M. (2022). "Securitized" UK aid Projects in Africa: Evidence from Kenya, Nigeria and South Sudan. *Development Policy Review*, *40*(1), 1–42.

Połońska-Kimunguyi, E., & Kimunguyi, P. (2017). "Gunboats of Soft Power": Boris on Africa and Post-Brexit "Global Britain." *Cambridge Review of International Affairs*, *30*(4), 325–349.

Porteous, T. (2005). British Government Policy in Sub-Saharan Africa under New Labour. *International Affairs*, *81*(2), 281–297.

Price, S. (2018). Brexit and the UK-Africa Caribbean and Pacific Aid Relationship. *Global Policy*, *9*, 420–428.

Price, S. (2019). The Impact of Brexit on EU Development Policy. *Politics and Governance*, *7*(3), 72–82.

Pugh, J., Gabay, C., & Williams, A. (2013). Beyond the Securitisation of Development: The Limits of Intervention, Developmentisation of Security and Repositioning of Purpose in the UK Coalition Government's Policy Agenda. *Geoforum*, *44*, 193–201.

Quinn, B. (2016, 25 October). Priti Patel Warns Aid Organisations Must Provide Value for Money or Face Cuts. *The Guardian*. https://www.theguardian.com/global-development/2016/oct/25/priti-patel-warns-aid-organisations-must-provide-value-for-money-or-face-cuts-development-secretary-post-brexit. Accessed 15 April 2023.

Rauf, A. (2011). *United Kingdom's Support for Trade Facilitation*. DfID.

Reid, S. (2011, December 2). How India Squanders British Aid: We Give £1.4 Bn to a Country That Has Its Own Space Programme. *Daily Mail*. https://www.dailymail.co.uk/news/article-2068930/How-India-squanders-British-aid--1-4bn-country-space-programme.html. Accessed 29 April 2023.

Rhodes, B., & Hall, N. (2019). Racism, Nationalism and the Politics of Resentment in Contemporary England. In J. Solomos (Ed.), *Routledge International Handbook of Contemporary Racisms* (pp. 284–299). Routledge.

Rugendyke, B. (2007). Making Poverty History? In B. Rugendyke (Ed.), *NGOs as Advocates for Development in a Globalising World*. Routledge.

Rynn, S. (2023, February). *On Shifting Ground: An Appraisal of UK Engagement in Ethiopia* (RUSI Occasional Paper). RUSI.

Savage, M. (2022, November 6). Boris Johnson's Attacks Behind Fall in Support for Foreign Aid, Says Minister. *The Guardian*. https://www.theguardian.com/politics/2022/nov/06/boris-johnsons-attacks-behind-fall-in-support-for-overseas-aid-says-minister. Accessed 29 April 2023.

Simpere, A. (2010). *The Mopani Copper Mine Zambia*. Counter Balance.

Stender, F., Berger, A., Brandi, C., & Schwab, J. (2021). The Trade Effects of the Economic Partnership Agreements Between the European Union and the African, Caribbean and Pacific Group of States: Early Empirical Insights from Panel Data. *Journal of Common Market Studies*, *59*, 1495–1515.

Taylor, D. (2022, May 25). From "Go Home" Vans to Windrush Scandal: A Timeline of UK's Hostile Environment. *The Guardian*. https://www.theguardian.com/uk-news/2022/may/25/from-go-home-vans-to-windrush-scandal-a-timeline-of-uks-hostile-environment. Accessed 29 May 2023.

Taylor, I. (2012). Spinderella on Safari: British Policies Toward Africa Under New Labour. *Global Governance, 18*(4), 449–460.

The Independent. (2020, October 23). How Uganda Lost Out in Lucrative Tullow Oil Deal. *The Independent*. https://www.independent.co.ug/end-of-an-era-how-uganda-lost-out-in-lucrative-tullow-oil-deal/. Accessed 29 May 2023.

The Spectator. (2016, October). Full Text: Theresa May's Conference Speech. *The Spectator*. https://www.spectator.co.uk/article/full-text-theresa-may-s-conference-speech/. Accessed 29 April 2023.

UK Government. (2017a). *PM's Florence Speech: A New Era of Cooperation and Partnership Between the EU and UK*. UK Government Online. https://www.gov.uk/government/speeches/pms-florence-speech-a-new-era-of-cooperation-and-partnership-between-the-uk-and-the-eu. Accessed 29 April 2023.

UK Government. (2017b). *Trade White Paper: Our Future UK Trade Policy*. HM Stationery Office.

UK Government. (2020). *UK Statement to the WTO Committee on Trade and Development—48th Session on Aid for Trade*. UK Government Online. https://www.gov.uk/government/speeches/uk-statement-to-the-wto-committee-on-trade-and-development-48th-session-on-aid-for-trade. Accessed 31 May 2023.

UK Government. (2021). *Global Britain in a Competitive Age: The Integrated Review of Security, Defence, Development and Foreign Policy*. HM Stationery Office.

UK Government. (2022). *Strategy for International Development*. HM Stationery Office.

Virdee, S., & McGeever, B. (2018). Racism, Crisis, Brexit. *Ethnic and Racial Studies, 41*(10), 1802–1819.

Watts, J. (2014, December 5). Nigel Farage: Slash 80% of Foreign Aid to Pay UK's Deficit Bill. *The Evening Standard*. https://www.standard.co.uk/news/politics/farage-slash-80-per-cent-of-foreign-aid-to-pay-uk-s-deficit-bill-9905529.html. Accessed 29 April 2023.

Wellings, B. (2019). *English Nationalism, Brexit and the Anglosphere: Wider Still and Wider*. Manchester University Press.

Wickstead, M. (2019). The UK: An Aid Superpower at a Crossroads. In I. Olivie & A. Perez (Eds.), *Aid Power and Politics* (pp. 73–88). Routledge.

Worley, W. (2022, April 26). *UK-Rwanda Project Called "Uglier Version of Development Diplomacy"*. Devex. https://www.devex.com/news/uk-rwanda-project-called-uglier-vision-of-development-diplomacy-103083. Accessed 30 June 2023.

CHAPTER 5

Global Britain and Development Finance in Africa

Introduction

Since the launch of the Global Britain project in the wake of the 2016 referendum, UK elites have promised that 'development' assistance will be delivered to African partners in the form of enhanced finance for job creation and infrastructure. With the launch of 'UK-African Investment Summits' (UK-AIS) in the UK from 2020 onwards, the Global Britain project is presented as one that leverages the financial capabilities of the British state for poverty reduction and economic growth within African countries (Eaton, 2020). The UK is therefore presented as a benevolent force, helping 'old friends' to achieve their potential within globalised markets and to meet the demands of demographic change in terms of provision of employment for youth (Daddow, 2018). Moreover, the UK is presented as an influential global actor that competes with other 'great powers' for access to markets and resources within Africa. Through the provision of development finance at concessional rates, Global Britain aims to become a partner of choice for its African partners such as Ethiopia and Nigeria—as outlined in the Foreign, Commonwealth and Development Office (FCDO)'s recent published *Integrated Review* (UK Government, 2021). In this scenario, the UK's nationally owned development finance institution—British International Investment

© The Author(s), under exclusive license to Springer Nature Switzerland AG 2023
M. Langan, *Global Britain and Neo-colonialism in Africa*,
https://doi.org/10.1007/978-3-031-42482-3_5

(BII)—originally known as the Colonial—then Commonwealth Development Corporation (CDC)—is envisaged as a key institution for delivering the UN Sustainable Development Goals (SDGs) in Africa (BII, 2023a).

However, this normative image of Global Britain—via the CDC/BII—acting as an enlightened development actor in the African continent is highly problematic. There is much concern that UK investments do not prioritise poverty reduction as a primary objective for the provision of finance (Bracking, 2009; Gilbert, 2022; Global Justice Now, 2020; Hildyard & Oloko, 2015). Rather that UK elites utilise CDC/BIII to assist economic production in areas that benefit UK citizens—for example, in terms of the stable supply of foodstuffs and raw commodities from Africa (Gilbert, 2022: 307). Moreover, that the CDC/BII's commitment to profit in terms of 'bankable' projects—combined to lucrative salaries for their staff—means that the social impact agenda of the UN SDGs is not the chief motivating factor in their decision-making (Bracking, 2009: 77; Global Justice Now, 2020: 17). There are also concerns about the CDC/BII's exit strategies (or lack therefore) in which the wellbeing of workers within previously invested companies are not taken into sufficient account when divestments occur (Global Justice Now, 2020: 25).

Furthermore, there is a deep concern about the implications of the 'financialisation of development' for African countries' policy space to pursue developmental state models amid a 'new scramble' for the continent's resources (Carmody, 2016; Trelstad, 2016: 357, 434). Namely, that British development finance (amid other sources) may go towards sectors and industries that do not align to—or else conflict with—the long-term economic strategies of the host country. By utilising land, resources, and workers within UK-financed endeavours without sufficient co-ordination with central government authorities in the country in question, UK elites may be undermining developmental state models. Indeed, developmental state strategies would necessitate government prioritisation of industries deemed to have a potential comparative advantage vis-à-vis industrialisation and diversification away from colonial patterns of production and exchange (Edigheji, 2005; Mkandawire, 2001). UK finance may be 'locking in' African countries into dependence upon traditional export models while closing-down options for developmentalism. There are also concerns that while development finance from Global Britain may be given at concessional rates, that nevertheless, such forms of 'aid' may be conditioned upon political influence in particular African states (cf. Hildyard & Oloko, 2015). And perhaps more worryingly that the counting of this form of 'development' provision as Official Development Assistance (ODA) means that donors can reduce humanitarian aid while protecting their soft power image as benevolent actors in Africa (Attridge & Engen, 2019: 12). This allows Western donors within the Organisation for Economic Co-operation and Development (OECD) (which sets the rules for ODA criteria) to satiate growing aid fatigue within their domestic electorates by pivoting to development finance and emphasising 'win–win' profitability for their own businesses.

In this context, the chapter examines the efficacy of UK finance for 'development' goals. It first assesses recent debates concerning the 'financialisation of development'. It considers whether this type of 'aid' is compatible with poverty reduction. The second section assesses the role of UK development finance in historical context, from the creation of the Colonial Development Corporation (CDC) in 1948 to the operation of the Commonwealth Development Corporation (also CDC). This focuses upon the growing emphasis on UK development finance and private sector development (PSD) as part of the Department for International Development's (DfID) poverty reduction goals during the New Labour and David Cameron government eras (Mawdsley, 2015). The third section then examines UK development finance in terms of the launch of the Global Britain project. It underscores how BII has become central to UK public diplomacy narratives. The final section then considers the meaning of this form of UK intervention in Africa in terms of the warnings of Nkrumah (1965) and Ndlovu-Gatsheni (2015) in relation to neo-colonialism and global coloniality.

THE FINANCIALISATION OF DEVELOPMENT AND THE WALL STREET CONSENSUS

External financing for private sector initiatives—such as agribusiness plantations and large infrastructure projects—has long been central to debates about economic growth and 'development' in Africa. From African states' attainment of juridical independence in the early Cold War, liberation leaders such as Nkrumah concerned themselves with the question of how to attract capital for major projects such as the Volta Dam in Ghana (Noer, 1984). Such projects, it was hoped, would meet citizens' desire for better living conditions and the creation of jobs, while avoiding scenarios in which foreign donors dominated the economy—and hence the polity—of the African country in question. In this context, Nkrumah argued that certain forms of controlled foreign finance could be a benefit for economic diversification and industrialisation. This could happen so long as foreign investors understood that their capital would be subordinated to national plans devised by African central governments. And that the profitability of such projects would likewise be suitably taxed by the government (Nkrumah, 1963: 170, 1965: 9; Obeng, 1979a: 90, 99, 1979b: 354–355).

In the early period of juridical 'decolonisation', many African states such as Nigeria and Kenya created their own nationally owned development banks (Goga et al., 2019: 4; Lazarinni, 2015: 237). These were given a mandate to provide government finance to projects deemed central to national development. This was seen in other regions, perhaps most famously in East Asia, where national development banks played a key role as part of developmental state strategies (Alem et al., 2017). Indeed, nationally owned development banks were pivotal to developmental state strategies in the Cold War period as several countries utilised targeted finance to industry as a means of spurring forward economic development. With the onset of the debt crisis and the Washington Consensus in the 1980s, however, many indebted states found that they no longer had the capital to invest within nationally owned banks (Thorne & Du Toit, 2009: 680). Structural adjustment programmes (SAPs) supported by the World Bank and International Monetary Fund (IMF) were implemented in many indebted African nations, emphasising a 'small state' laissez-faire approach to development (Mailafia, 1997). Allegedly bloated governments were instructed to impose austerity measures vis-à-vis social spending and restrain themselves from further 'interference' with the development of the economy (ibid).

However, despite the World Bank's and IMF's emphasis upon the need for domestic fiscal restraint in African states, Western donors continued to operate their own externally oriented DFIs with a view to providing finance and investment within African economies. Organisations such as the UK's Commonwealth Development Corporation (CDC)—owned by the British state—continued their self-appointed 'mission civilisatrice' to invest capital within profitable enterprises and infrastructural projects (cf. Połońska-Kimunguyi & Kimunguyi, 2017: 327, 343; Bracking, 2009). Meanwhile, SAP reforms and the creation of a private sector 'enabling environment' were deemed central to African countries' ability to attract foreign private capital deemed necessary for scaling up viable industries. While domestic planning and local government investment were viewed as being contrary to market logic and austerity, nevertheless, Western DFIs continued to make highly profitable investments. This was particularly the case with industries associated with colonial plantation economies and infrastructure projects conducive to the extraction of raw materials and minerals from indebted African countries (ibid). In the 1990s, Western governments emphasised that such development interventions would continue to assist the emergence of viable private sector enterprises in Africa, with organisations such as the CDC group deemed central to this task.

Interestingly, however, the donor community's private sector focus soon became merged with an increasingly 'pro-poor' and humanitarian discourse in the aftermath of the East Asian Financial Crisis. Joseph Stiglitz's formulation of a so-called Post-Washington Consensus (PWC) that acknowledged the need for (limited) state intervention to redress barriers to growth (including to improve education and health vis-à-vis labour productivity) gained intellectual traction (Mawdsley, 2015; Onis & Senses, 2005). The role of Western DFIs in Africa continued but was accompanied by increased focus upon budget support and other forms of government-to-government (G2G) assistance such as debt forgiveness under the World Bank's Highly Indebted Poor Countries Initiative (HIPC) (Cassimon & Van Campenhout, 2007). As part of this PWC, donors emphasised the need for African aid recipients to adhere to 'good governance' criteria involving both financial rectitude and respect for human rights. DFIs such as the World Bank (2009) and its International Finance Corporation (IFC), meanwhile, emphasised that their provision of capital to social infrastructure projects including clean water initiatives were compatible with the United Nations (UN) Millennium Development Goals (MDGs). DFIs presented their work as compatible with poverty reduction within a PWC vision of free market enterprise cojoined to (limited) state intervention to redress market inefficiencies and failures.

However, since the Global Financial Crisis (GFC)—as well as the growing influence of China in the African continent via its Belt and Road Initiative (BRI)—scholars such as Gabor (2021) and Alami et al. (2021) have argued that we are entering a new donor 'development' paradigm built upon the financialisation of development. Namely that since the 'credit crunch' and the crisis faced by many large Western commercial banks, there has been an increased acceptance of the legitimate position of the state in the provision of countercyclical finance to the private sector and for 'de-risking' private investments via guarantees and loans (Trelstad, 2016: 431–432). The growing acceptance of the role of the state in buttressing private sector investments has been witnessed both in terms of Western donors' own economic recovery from crisis—for instance, note the role of the European Central Bank (ECB) in stabilising private sector recoveries within the dominant EU member states' socio-economic sectors—and in terms of donors' approach to the 'Global South' (Talani, 2017a; Talani, 2017b). As part of what Gabor (2021) terms the Wall Street Consensus, Western governments are increasingly seeking to de-risk private sector investments into 'fragile states' by providing loans and guarantees that attract investors into sectors otherwise deemed too high risk.

In the context of the African continent, therefore, Western donors' DFIs increasingly emphasise that their provision of capital is being used to lever in additional investments from private commerce (Giordano & Ruiters, 2016: 568). The provision of finance from a DFI to a business or infrastructure project is seen to provide other investors with confidence that their investments will be 'bankable'. Western DFIs in this capacity increasingly now 'blend' public aid monies from their host nation(s) with private finance in the delivery of capital to, for instance, energy projects within the African continent (Mawdsley, 2015: 340). Often this is achieved via the use of private equity funds located in secrecy jurisdictions, where third-party fund managers deploy the finance derived from the DFI—alongside that of commercial investors—into an African initiative (Bracking, 2012: 287). Investors then acquire equity and derivatives associated with that African enterprise or infrastructural project. In time they also hope to gain in terms of the profitable onward sale of a going business concern to another company, or bloc of investors (ibid).

The use of private equity funds by DFIs is controversial since host communities surrounding the investments—as well as workers—often find it difficult to seek redress for any labour rights violations or environmental abuses that may occur (Bracking, 2012: 275). The opaque nature of private equity funds—combined to the transient nature of the investments—mean that workers and communities cannot easily hold investors accountable—since the companies often founded with private equity investments inevitably involve multiple stakeholders (Kelk & Copestake, 2022: 2). As noted in the previous chapter, there is also concern that donors' counting of DFI finance as ODA means that there will be less monies available for humanitarian projects, for instance, those funded via donor ODA contributions to UN programmes (Mawdsley, 2015: 356). In an era of right-wing populism and aid scepticism, the use of Western aid monies for DFI expenditure as part of 'win–win' profitability for Western investors—and ostensible jobs for African beneficiaries—is seen as a threat to more 'traditional' forms of aid.

Furthermore, there is debate as to whether the financialisation of development responds to the priorities of African governments themselves. The OECD DAC committee argues that the provision of finance responds to African officials' demands for easier access to credit and for investment into infrastructure and productive economic sectors (cf. Mawdsley, 2015: 344). Critical scholars, however, query whether high concentrations of foreign capital in extractive industries and infrastructure is compatible with state-led developmental models that led to poverty reduction in countries such as South Korea during the Cold War (Alami et al., 2021: 1295). Foreign investment into colonial patterns of production—and into infrastructure conducive to extraction—appears to sit uneasily with the policy space for progressive African governments to pursue diversification strategies (RIAO-RDC et al., 2021: 4). Whether DFIs from the West can contribute to the realisation of developmental states in Africa is further doubted by these critical voices given the types of investments already witnessed prior to the onset of the Wall Street Consensus (Gilbert, 2022: 312). The history of Western DFI investments into agribusiness, low-waged manufacturing and extractive industries bodes ill for any progressive collaboration between Western capital and African governments committed to economic diversification under democratic developmental state models.

Moreover, it is in the context of the Wall Street Consensus and the financialisation of development that the UK government has emphasised its desire for Global Britain to leverage additional capital into African economies (UK Government, 2018a). Aligning with the emerging donor consensus, the UK government (2018b) insists that its financing of African economic growth via the BII (formerly CDC) will lead to job creation, falling migration rates and higher economic output. Perhaps paradoxically in the context of Brexit, this Western donor consensus involves the EU itself. The EU Commission similarly emphasises the centrality of organisations such as the European Investment Bank (EIB) and member state DFIs for African development in conjunction with its new 'Global Gateway' fund (Bougrea et al., 2022). This sits as the EU's rival instrument to China's Belt and Road Initiative (BRI). The next section turns to the history of the CDC as Britain's central DFI in relation to Africa and developing regions.

UK Development Finance and CDC Prior to the 2016 Referendum

The UK's external development finance arm began as the Colonial Development Corporation (CDC) in 1948 and tasked itself with improving agricultural, industrial and infrastructure assets within British colonies in the aftermath of World War Two (WW2). In 1963, the group was rebranded as the Commonwealth Development Corporation (CDC) given the wave of juridical 'decolonisation' that had taken place in Africa and Asia (Gilbert, 2022: 306). While Western European states benefitted from injections of finance under the US Marshall Plan, their colonies had not benefitted from such US largesse (Bracking, 2009: 66–68). Under pressure from liberation movements, the UK government decided to establish a financial arm to invest in colonial projects with the aim of stabilising food supplies to the metropole and (ostensibly) of ameliorating the worst conditions of poverty in the colonies (ibid: 68).

It was hoped that the CDC's efforts would satiate anti-British sentiment and enable colonised territories to remain within the imperial 'family'. Whereas India had won its independence in 1947, the British government believed that African territories would remain part of the UK's imperial arrangements for decades to come. In this sense, CDC was established to respond to—and to deal with—a 'legitimacy crisis' in the colonies (ibid: 67). As Bracking (2009: 67) explains, the idea behind CDC had been voiced as early as 1943 amid the pressures of war. Its creation also coincided with the launch of 'international development' as a Western project in the 'Third World' under the Truman inaugural address in 1949 (ibid: 67). In accordance with Truman's mission to end 'underdevelopment' and to 'modernise' societies in the 'Global South', the UK government adopted development rhetoric about the need to improve conditions within its colonies through job creation and economic growth.

As Gilbert (2022: 300) notes, however, the reality of CDC interventions in the immediate post-war period often did more to impoverish local populations—while subsidising the nascent British welfare state through extracted profits. As per Nkrumah's (1965: xv) warnings, Gilbert (2022: 300) notes that 'aid' in the case of CDC became a type of revolving credit returning increased profits back to British coffers. He notes that it continues to operate in this fashion too:

> the UK is… repurposing quasi-governmental organisations which evolved as organs of colonial administration, at times complicit in the undermining of colonies' tax bases and welfare regimes for the benefit of Britain's nascent welfare state in the post-war period, and continuing to provide opportunities for aid money to recirculate among elites in the Global North. (ibid)

Financing of commercial projects and infrastructure in Africa by CDC did not necessarily translate into 'improved conditions' for local citizenries in the Cold War period.

In this 'development' guise, the CDC as part of a British post-war mission civilisatrice embarked on financing commercial ventures in African colonies. As BII (2023) explains, its first investment was to establish colonial Zambia's first cement works in 1949. By 1952, it had established a cattle ranch venture in Botswana. In Kenya, it invested in the Kenya Tea Development Authority in 1962. In this process, it helped to pioneer the concept of satellite contract farming (Bracking, 2009: 69). By the 1970s, it had expanded beyond investing in the British Commonwealth, providing loans to an Indonesian airline in 1971–72 (BII 2023a). By the late 1980s, it had made its first investments in India and Pakistan (ibid). In Ghana, meanwhile, it undertook its first initiative to attract third-party private capital by establishing Ghana Venture Capital in 1992 (ibid). This marked the beginning of the CDC's attempts to 'leverage' third-party investments by 'de-risking'. In the late 1990s, the CDC group invested in Celtel, which emerged as a lucrative provider of mobile-phone services (ibid). By 2004, under instructions from DfID, the group ceased to offer direct loans and direct equity (ICAI, 2019). Instead, it operated solely through intermediary private equity funds. By the end of 2007, it was working with 42 independent fund managers across 100 separate funds (Bracking, 2009: 79). It also embarked upon a failed privatisation initiative whereby a private arm—'ACTIS'—comprised of former CDC staff—sought to operate independently from DfID (ibid: 76). This privatisation was reversed after the electoral demise of New Labour.

However, while DfID cultivated a positive reputation for its apparent humanitarian stance, the CDC group, attracted much negative attention. UK NGOs such as War on Want (2006) began to bring public attention to the hitherto little-known entity and its use of taxpayers' monies in its pursuit of 'bankable' operations in Africa. In particular, the CDC group's 2013 investment of US $34.14 million into Feronia Inc.—a Canadian company operating palm oil plantations via a subsidiary firm (named PHC) in the Democratic Republic of Congo (DRC)—earned it much opprobrium (Global Justice Now, 2020; Human Rights Watch, 2019). In 2016, CDC defended this investment in a written submission to the House of Common's International Development Committee (2016):

> Our investment supports the on-going rehabilitation of an existing 102-year-old plantation business which, prior to the acquisition by Feronia in 2009, had suffered over a decade of under-investment due to the civil conflict in the DRC. Feronia contributes to the DRC's reduction of imports of staple goods and to local food security by increasing the availability of edible oil and crop products in the country. All of the palm oil, rice and arable crops produced by Feronia are consumed solely within the domestic market.

This pro-poor rationale of 'developing' the DRC and providing jobs for its citizens was invoked to defend the CDC's decision-making process.

However, the negative publicity this investment attracted was due to the appalling conditions apparently faced by its poorly paid 10,000 workers, some of whom alleged that they were unable to afford three meals a day for their families (Human Rights Watch, 2019: 7; FMO, 2023). Poor conditions also included run down housing that was reported to have led to the death of an eleven-year-old child (RIAO-RDC, 2021:10). Most egregiously, the plantations operated on contested lands which were acquired from the colonial Belgian authorities by Lord Leverhulme in April 1911—one of the founders of the modern-day Unilever company (ibid: 18). Feronia Inc. had bought the operation in 2009 from Unilever (ibid: 3). The involvement of CDC group—and then subsequently other European DFIs—complicated the claims of Congolese campaigners seeking the return of their lost lands since the expiring concessions were 'fragmented… into multiple titles to serve as security for their loans, without the knowledge of local communities and in violation of DRC law' (World Rainforest Alliance, 2022). Moreover, the CDC group later withdrew—to much criticism of its apparent lack of an exit strategy in terms of ensuring the wellbeing of the workers that had toiled during their investment in the plantations (discussed in more detail in the next section) (ibid).

The CDC group's apparent lack of appropriate care and attention to workers is compounded by its actions in the case of its investments into a Zambian agribusiness operation involving production of food crops on plantations. The invested company, MDC, was founded as a venture between CDC and the Zambian government in the 1980s (Public Bill Committee, 2016). It remained active in the New Labour era but was liquidated in 2006 'because it could not meet the higher targets of return demanded by its investments demanded by its owners, CDC' (Mujenja & Wonani, 2012: 26). As a result, its plantations came under the ownership of a different company named ETC Bio Energy, and later, were sold to Zambeef (ibid). Worker testimonies allege that wages fell in the transfer from CDC to ETC, and that social provisions such as company funds towards school fees were withdrawn. One worker lamented that:

> My second born is in secondary school but the fees are really taxing for us. In those days MDC used to contribute to school fees, around K150,000 ($30) for secondary pupils depending on one's job grade. But this is all gone now. In MDC people used to be paid overtime but now this does not happen. Many people receive K500,000 ($100). If one is paid K700,000 ($140), he or she must be a supervisor riding a motorbike. No one here gets more than K1,000,000 ($200) a month except those bosses that drive vehicles. (ibid: 38)

Another expressed that the lack of staged wage payments and the withdrawal of a clinic had negatively impacted upon their family (ibid: 38).

Perhaps even more worryingly, there are allegations that during its operation, the CDC-invested MNC not only caused environmental damage through heavy use of chemicals pesticides but also damaged the health of local communities through inadequate disposal methods:

> MDC relies heavily on chemical weed killers. These chemicals are applied through aerial means. This method of application creates the possibility for the chemicals to be blown far beyond the farm with consequent damage to the atmosphere. A related problem is the safe disposal of used containers for pesticides and other toxic substances. Poorly disposed used containers are a real danger to the surrounding communities who pick up these containers and start reusing them for such things as water and food storage.

The villagers are often not aware of the dangers inherent in the use of such containers. (ibid 50)

Such claims are mirrored in the case of Feronia Inc. and its subsidiary in the DRC, where CDC-invested palm oil operations involved heavy use of pesticides which allegedly resulted in serious health effects for workers and local communities in terms of alleged contamination of drinking water (Human Rights Watch, 2019: 2). CDC/BII's claims to create decent jobs thus must be accompanied by a caveat regarding the durability of the supposed benefits given the transient nature of its investments, the health impact of business operations and the lack of appropriate exit strategies. The ability of communities negatively affected by historical CDC investments to seek redress from this British 'development' arm is doubtful.

Furthermore, the CDC group attracted much criticism in the 2000s for its decision in 2004 to channel finance via private equity funds based in secrecy jurisdictions. The move away from direct loans and equity meant that there was a lack of transparency about the types of investments that were being made with use of British taxpayers' monies (Global Justice Now, 2020: 4). The use of tax havens, meanwhile, meant that the initiatives funded by the CDC-backed private equity funds often paid little revenue to the governments in the countries in which they conducted their activities. The UK Parliament's International Development Committee noted that 80% of CDC investments were made via tax havens in 2010 (Gilbert, 2022: 309). The 'development' gains of private sector activity were thus undermined by lack of appropriate taxation revenues for government welfare services. By contrast, the National Audit Office (NAO) in 2008 'raised concerns about CDC sitting on £1.4 billion in cash, held in the UK Debt Management Office exceeding its total overseas investments' (ibid: 307). The NAO queried why these funds had not been provisionally allocated towards 'development' projects in partner countries as per the CDC's remit. Following on from this, the UK Parliament's Public Accounts Committee queried why the Chief Executive of an organisation commitment to job creation and poverty reduction in the 'Global South' was accruing a salary of £970,000 in 2007 (ibid: 307).

The complicity of the CDC group in convoluted private equity funds—controlled by third-party managers—and the group's own high rates of remuneration provoked a public backlash. As a result, a series of 2011 reforms under the then Development Secretary, Andrew Mitchell, took place. As a report issued by Global Justice Now (2020: 4) explains:

> In 2011, then secretary of state for international development Andrew Mitchell set out a new vision for CDC. His reforms were supposed to make CDC more "socially and environmentally responsible", with fewer investments in "harmful tax regimes" and greater transparency. CDC would ditch its old model, cutting out the 'middlemen' in the private equity funds that seemed to be behind so much of the controversy, and instead invest directly in private sector projects in developing countries, buying shares in companies and giving loans and guarantees.

These reforms brought back the CDC group's earlier model of direct investments—albeit not banning the use of private equity funds. Instead, what occurred was a rebalancing of the scale of investments between direct and indirect funding models. As the case of the CDC group's investments in Feronia Inc. demonstrates, however, direct investments do not necessarily correlate with 'development' objectives either.

Despite dubious gains for workers and local communities, by March 2013 the then Development Secretary, Justine Greening, indicated that DfID's strategy for African countries would focus even more on private sector development (PSD) (Mawdsley, 2015: 340). She 'promised an agenda for change using the language of investment, market making and the necessity of a structural rebalancing from the public to the private sector' (ibid: 349). Soon the aid budget adjusted to reflect this PSD prioritisation. Spending on 'economic development' rose to £1.8 billion by 2015/16 and was almost double what had been spent in this area in 2012/13. Spending on economic development thus reached approximately one-fifth of the total aid budget (ibid: 349). This coincided with the broader turn within the donor community to financialised aid in the aftermath of the global financial crisis. It also followed on from the 2011 OECD Busan meeting which declared a need to amplify funding for the UN SDGs 'from billions to trillions' (ibid: 342). DFIs such as Britain's CDC group were hailed as vital vehicles for delivering the infrastructural development and private sector growth necessary for attaining the goals. This trend was consolidated by China's launch of the BRI in 2013 which indicated to OECD donors that they would have to provide large sums of finance to compete with Chinese 'debt diplomacy' amid a new scramble for African resources (Loft, 2022: 15; Carmody, 2016). The financialisation of aid, however, has intensified in the wake of the 2016 referendum as the next section discusses in relation to UK elites' pursuit of 'Global Britain'.

GLOBAL BRITAIN AND BRITISH INTERNATIONAL INVESTMENT (BII)

The launch of the Global Britain project has entailed UK elites' seeking to demonstrate the relevance of the British state on the international stage. Prime Minister Theresa May promised in 2018 that the UK would utilise its financial expertise and links with the City of London to become the chief investor in the African continent within the G7 by 2022 (UK Government, 2018b). This followed on from the UK's 2017 announcement of an injection of £3.5 billion into the CDC group under May and her DfID Secretary Priti Patel. This action sought to evidence the UK government's support towards the tangible delivery of enhanced investments in Africa (Attridge, 2019: iii). Notably here, the 'portfolio of the CDC Group… increased from US$ 4.7 billion to US$ 7.1 billion in the five years between 2016 and 2020' (CDC cited in Kelk & Copestake, 2022: 1). The Independent Commission for Aid Impact (ICAI) also highlighted the increasing significance of the CDC/BII group in terms of overall UK aid delivery. A ICAI (2019) report makes clear that:

> CDC has become an increasingly important channel for UK aid. Between 2015 and 2018, CDC received investments of new capital from DfID totalling £1.8 billion, and further capital injections of up to £703 million per annum are planned until 2021. CDC's net assets are projected to increase from £2.8 billion in 2012 to above £8 billion by 2021 as a result of these capital injections and earnings.

In keeping with the ICAI discussion of CDC/BII net assets, the development minister, Andrew Mitchell, confirmed in June 2023 that the group had in recent years received injections totalling £6 billion (International Development Committee, 2023).

Amid the pursuit of the Global Britain project, meanwhile, the CDC group was rebranded as British International Investment (BII) in 2022 to align more closely to the projection of UK public diplomacy within recipient countries. This coincided with the renaming of the FCO as the FCDO as DfID was folded into the larger ministry under the premiership of Boris Johnson. Despite Johnson's downgrading of May's ambition to become the largest G7 investor in the African continent to instead become the 'partner of choice', his government launched a UK African Investment Summit in 2020 (UK Government, 2020). A second summit is due to be held in April 2024 (UK Government, 2023). The first summit brought together UK and African dignitaries with business leaders to discuss areas of commercial co-operation and to leverage new investments. Such events are framed by UK officials as evidence of Global Britain's commitment to poverty reduction through stimulation of private sector-led economic development (ibid). UK discourse has, meanwhile, emphasised the 'win–win' benefits of such arrangements for British taxpayers and businesses in the form of profitable investments (ibid).

CDC/BII, meanwhile, has echoed this 'pro-poor' narrative. Its *Investing to Transform Lives: Strategic Framework 2017–2021* justified its mission in Africa in terms of attracting private investors and creating jobs within volatile markets (CDC, 2017). Moreover, the document invoked a wider British 'securitisation' discourse about the need for UK aid to bring 'stability':

> CDC is one of only a few investors in the world with the skills and risk appetite to create jobs and opportunities in the most difficult markets, where private investors won't often go. Yet it is these same places where jobs and economic opportunities are most desperately needed to help bring stability and give people a stake in the future. It is here that CDC uses its expertise and capital to support businesses to create jobs, and to demonstrate to private investors that responsible investments in difficult markets can be viable. (ibid)

Through this securitised 'development' rhetoric—as well as its rebranding to BII—the organisation has sought to distance itself from past damage to its reputation from investments in companies such as Feronia Inc. and its palm oil subsidiary in the DRC.

Nevertheless, even in the Brexit era, CDC/BII has continued to be subject of numerous complaints from UK civil society groups and African communities concerned about the predatory nature of its investments. The case of Feronia Inc. again has recently come again to the fore as the UK government augmented its previous 2013 and 2015 injections into these DRC palm oil plantations, with an additional loan of £11 million in 2019 (FMO, 2023). This enhanced total CDC/BII investments which had already stood at USD $43 million in 2017 (Arsenault, 2017). However, the 2019 investment coincided with the murder of a Congolese community activist, allegedly by a security guard employed on the Feronia Inc. subsidiary's plantation (McVeigh, 2019). The Congolese activist had been contesting the palm oil operation on the basis that the land had been illegally taken from local communities during the colonial era. This grievous episode brought renewed notoriety to this CDC/BII investment, following on as it did from the 2015 death of a plantation worker in police custody after he had been accused of stealing palm nuts (RIAO-RDC, 2021: 19).

The 2019 murder of a Congolese activist, meanwhile, was compounded by accusations that CDC/BII did not act to redress the potential intimidation of local communities. In response to the 2019 homicide, they hired an independent investigator who concluded that the security guard's actions were not related to his employment on the plantation. This CDC/BII action did not satisfy civil society groups such as Human Rights Watch (2019) and Global Justice Now (2020) who criticised the human rights violations and alleged land grabs surrounding CDC/BII investments. This echoed the concerns of the Labour Party under the then leader Jeremy Corbyn—prior to its relaunch as a New Labour vehicle under Sir Keir Starmer. Labour's then shadow minister for development criticised CDC, and the UK government, in stringent language in the aftermath of the 2019 killing:

> This latest set of allegations against Feronia suggest horrific violations of workers' rights and the environment are taking place in the DRC – by a company which this country's development bank is a major shareholder in. We urgently need detailed answers to what has happened. If these latest reports are true, it is utterly disgraceful that under Tory leadership, the CDC has financed abuse through precious taxpayer money earmarked to support international development worldwide. (Labour Party, 2019)

The shadow minister explained that the Labour Party would transform CDC/BII into a green climate bank—albeit it is now unclear whether a (New) Labour government under Sir Keir Starmer would honour this pledge (Mitchell, 2023). This is evidenced by recent tensions within the Labour shadow cabinet between Shadow Chancellor, Rachel Reeves, and Environment Shadow Minister, Ed Miliband, about the financing of the party's promised 'green transition' (ibid). Also by tensions between Starmer and the Mayor of London, Sadiq Khan, on the latter's environmental initiatives. It is also brought into question by Labour officials' favouring of PSD strategies, Starmer's backtracking on his previous pledge to reconstitute DfID as an independent department, and the shift to CDC channelling of finance to private equity funds during the Blair era itself (Stacey, 2023). It would seem highly likely therefore that such dubious investments under BII would continue under a Starmer premiership given his embeddedness within the New Labour project, notably his apparent tutelage under Peter Mandelson (Savage, 2021).

The 2019 murder in the DRC was followed by the alleged murders of two villagers in 2021, apparently committed by security guards employed by Feronia Inc.'s subsidiary (World Rainforest Alliance, 2022). This included a twenty-year-old man who was reportedly killed after being wrongly thought to have stolen a plastic chair from the company (RIAO-RDC & GRAIN, 2021). After such scandals, CDC/BII divested in 2022 (World Rainforest Alliance, 2022). Soon after, Feronia Inc. filed for bankruptcy and its DRC subsidiary was 'essentially gifted to the private equity firm Kuramo Capital' (ibid). In this context, CDC/BII was criticised for its lack of an appropriate exit strategy. Civil society stakeholders claim that it divested without providing a clear route for workers and local communities to seek redress for labour and environmental abuses allegedly committed during the time of the CDC/BII group's financial involvement. As mentioned earlier, the fragmentation of land tenure titles during Western DFIs' involvement has also complicated the efforts of local communities to have their land restored to them—a problem that will remain long after CDC/BII's divestment.

Criticisms of the CDC/BII group during the lifetime of the Global Britain project have also been seen in terms of its decision to (re)invest within the Zambian agribusiness sector following on from its earlier divestment in 2006 from MDC. The CDC group announced in 2016 that it had invested USD $65 million in Zambeef Products plc to gain a 17.5% stake—a company that now owns the farms once operated by MDC. The UK's CDC (2017) group explained this decision in terms of food security and jobs for African citizenries:

> Zambeef directly employs over 6,200 people and generates significant further indirect employment… the company buys products from over 10,000 small-scale farmers, connecting them to an efficient supply chain

and providing them access to the market, thereby enhancing their livelihoods… Zambeef's chain of retail outlets contributes to increasing the availability and affordability of protein for Zambian, Ghanaian and Nigerian consumers.

However, this British investment is seemingly politicised given Zambeef's alleged connections to prominent politicians within Zambia. Zambeef's decision to issue redundancy to approximately 1,500 workers in 2013 was linked to alleged political retaliation from the Patriotic Front (PF) in terms of the company's suspected support for a rival politician (Zambia Reports, 2013). Indeed, the redundancies were blamed on politically motivated smears emanating from the PF in relation to alleged health hazards with the company's imported beef (ibid). This situation was despite the company's previous support to the PF leader, Michael Sata. Zambeef had assisted Sata's presidential campaigns in 2006 and 2011 through provision of air transportation (ibid). Nevertheless, the PF appears to have suspected that the company then switched allegiances and later played a role in assisting the rival United Party for National Development (UPND). The UPND are now the governing party of Zambia, following on from its presidential and parliamentary successes in 2021 (Resnick, 2022).

In this highly politicised context—with Zambeef's apparent strategic and shifting assistance to prominent politicians—the 2016 investment appears as an indirect favour towards those politicians assisted by the company. The seeming political orientation of CDC/BII investments is also heightened by the fact that in the case of Feronia Inc. in the DRC, 'a substantial part of the money that the development banks paid out' went in part to apparently cover 'rental and other fees to a powerful Congolese politician' (RIAO-RDC et al., 2021: 13). It is further amplified by the history of CDC investments in Nigeria amid a corruption scandal involving the former regional governor of Delta State, James Ibori. Written evidence to a UK parliamentary enquiry on the CDC group in 2013 emphasised that DfID had invested into a Nigerian firm—Seven Energy—despite several 'red flags' about that company's connections to senior politicians in the Nigerian government:

> Seven Energy – has been named by… the former Governor of the Central Bank of Nigeria as one of the vehicles through which Nigerian government officials and their associates filched in excess of $6 billion in oil… The

principal beneficiaries are widely reported to have been former President Goodluck Jonathan and his former oil Minister, Mrs. Alison-Madueke. IFC invested in Seven after Mr Sanusi made his allegations, despite, as we shall see, numerous "red flags" surrounding the company. Nonetheless, DfID through PIDG, the CDC Group and the IFC remains invested in Seven Energy. (Hildyard & Oloko, 2015)

This seeming pattern of CDC/BII investing in companies reportedly linked to senior politicians within governments including Zambia, the DRC and Nigeria would imply that there is an underlying realpolitik to British investment of capital. Namely to provide the UK government with enhanced political leverage and influence within African administrations. While the UK government engages in veiled criticism of Chinese 'debt diplomacy' in relation to the Belt and Road Initiative, it appears that there is a form of UK 'investment influencing' taking place via the CDC/BII group (Parker, 2018). Such concerns about the political usages of CDC/BII have been noted by Christian Aid (2023) in a recent submission to a UK parliamentary enquiry on the role of DFIs:

> Christian Aid is concerned by the possibility of political interference in BII's strategic outlook. In announcing the release of the IDS, then Foreign Secretary Liz Truss argued that BII was an important tool to "[challenge] some of the geopolitical efforts by malign actors". She told the Financial Times that BII would prioritise infrastructure investment, offering low- and middle-income countries 'alternatives' to taking on 'strings-attached debt from autocratic regimes' and non-market economies. She signalled that using economics as a foreign policy tool to exert more global influence was a "core part of the Global Britain agenda".

Civil society stakeholders are concerned about the British government's political usages of CDC/BII amid a 'new scramble for Africa' (Carmody, 2016).

Meanwhile, the BII injection of capital into Zambeef is despite historical allegations relating to that company's treatment of workers. One Zambeef worker alleged that management reallocated the most educated agricultural workers to clerical office duties to ensure that they would not then mobilise their fellow agricultural workers to protest against low pay and lack of appropriate overtime payments (Lusaka Times, 2012). The worker also highlighted alleged racist treatment of labourers by white managers (ibid). These concerns are amplified by media reports since the CDC/BII investment that the company has failed to provide corporate social responsibility (CSR) benefits to surrounding communities (Fundanga, 2017). Interestingly, the CDC/BII group argues that its insertion of capital into enterprises allows it to have influence upon the creation of Economic, Social and Governance (ESG) policies (Dolma Impact Fund, 2023). However, an extensive survey of CDC/BII investments by the Centre for Development Studies found little concrete evidence that the group's involvement had been directly attributable to the formation and maintenance of corporate ESG policies (Kelk & Copestake, 2022: 18). The CDC/BII group's claims to augur meaningful ESG benefits via its investments are highly contestable.

Moreover, there are concerns that CDC/BII invests into projects that benefit a privileged urban minority. A recent report by Global Justice Now (2020: 7) points to BII investments within the private education sector where high fees ensure that the schools it funds are only available to local elites. It points to BII investments within Bridge International Academies which operates in countries including Kenya, Nigeria and Uganda. While such schools may be attractive for local officials—as well as for British expatriates—there is little evidence of wider societal benefit (ibid: 7). This coincides with recent reports that the CDC/BII group invested in a private hospital in Kenya which allegedly 'imprisoned' patients who could not pay exorbitant medical fees (Lovett, 2023). This apparently included a schoolboy with a medical bill of £20,500 as reported by Oxfam. This CDC/BII investment was also found to have been made via a private equity fund based in a secrecy jurisdiction (ibid). Additionally, Global Justice Now (2020) finds that CDC/BII continues to invest in fossil fuel industries, despite recent pledges that it would divest to meet UK climate change commitments. The civil society group highlights that CDC/BII has recently invested in coal-fired cement factories in East Africa, a company that owns an oil pipeline in Cameroon, as well as a 'heavy-fuel oil-burning plant' in Benin (ibid: 28). Environmental fears have been corroborated by Dimitriadis et al. (2019) who report that CDC/BII have invested in companies such as Nigerian firm, Dangote Industries, involved in cement production and coal mining. They explain that:

> In 2019, a report commissioned by the climate organisation 350.org alleged Dangote Cement had failed to conduct environmental impact assessments before carrying out mining work, as required under Nigerian law. It also raised concerns that the company's mining activities had led to

the contamination of soil and drinking water for local communities, while respiratory diseases had also reportedly increased.

Global Justice Now (2020) also reports that the CDC/BII group continues to utilise private equity funds amid concerns about the use of secrecy jurisdictions (ibid: 6).

Given the above concerns, it is not surprising that the ICAI (2019) found that the CDC/BII group had failed to evidence its tangible assistance to the poorest communities. The ICIA (2019) issued CDC/BII with an 'amber/red' rating meaning that there were concerns about whether the use of public 'aid' money was meeting the UK's commitments to poverty reduction. This is clearly problematic for the UK government given its legal requirement to prioritise poverty reduction in its allocation of aid as per the 2002 legislation discussed in the previous chapter (Ambreena, 2019). More broadly, it is clear that the BII group—despite its rebranding—is a liability in terms of Global Britain's image in Africa. Despite promises that investments in Africa will boost employment conducive to poverty reduction, it is evident that there are serious social and environmental hazards associated with CDC/BII sponsored projects. This lack of apparent 'development' impact is perhaps due to the organisation prioritising profitability with returns averaging at 10.3% between 2012 and 2016. This is despite an official set target of only 3.5% (National Audit Office, 2016). In this context, the warnings of both Nkrumah and Ndlovu-Gatsheni about neo-colonialism and global coloniality appear highly relevant for making sense of CDC/BII's role in Africa.

British Development Finance and Neo-Colonialism in Africa

Nkrumah—and other African liberation leaders—recognised that developmental plans for economic diversification away from colonial models of production and exchange might necessitate injections of foreign capital. Foreign investment would speed up processes of infrastructural upgrading and provide financing for new enterprises necessary for industrialisation. Crucially, however, Nkrumah (1963: 170, 1965: 9) emphasised that foreign investments would have to be directed towards initiatives that were endorsed within the government's own economic blueprint. Foreign investors would be compelled to pay appropriate taxation and to refrain from activism in domestic politics. Foreign investment—in this sense—would be wholly subordinated to the developmentalist strategies of national elites within African polities—or as Nkrumah hoped for, an eventual Union of African States.

In this context, Nkrumah (1963, 1965) warned that foreign investment would become a route for neo-colonial influence if not appropriately disciplined by African officialdom. He warned that foreign investors might utilise financial injections to sway government officials. Moreover, foreign investments might perpetuate colonial patterns of raw material production and export. Indeed, foreign investment into plantations and extractive industries might not necessarily correlate with economic diversification and industrialisation (Nkrumah cited in Obeng, 1979a: 254). In fact, they might 'lock in' African countries into a model of economic—and political—dependence upon the 'West' (ibid). Nkrumah was clear that while foreign investment would be welcomed within Ghana, that nonetheless, African officials had to remain cognisant about its dangers—including possible violations of sovereignty emanating from foreign powers' financial influence and asset ownership (ibid).

Given Nkrumah's extensive warnings about the Janus-faced nature of foreign investments, his work is highly relevant in the current dissection of CDC/BII activities. The group's involvement in palm oil plantations, agribusiness farms, private hospitals and private schools appears to uphold his fears that foreign capital—when insufficiently disciplined by African officialdom—would bolster colonial patterns of exchange conducive to Euro-American interests (and those of narrow local elites). Moreover, the apparent linkages of CDC/BII investments to senior politicians within African governments would also confirm his fears about the improper use of foreign finance to sway political favour within African executives. The involvement of companies in political campaigning—as noted in terms of allegations concerning Zambeef—opens up pressing questions of whether CDC/BII insists such politicking ceases during its period of investment. Or whether in fact its decision to invest is in fact guided by political connections. Nkrumah's warnings of neo-colonialism appear highly prescient since it does appear that the CDC/BII group is utilising UK taxpayers' monies for geopolitical ambitions in Africa, as Christian Aid (2023) rightly warns. Not only are Chinese 'debt diplomacy' investments problematic for African sovereignties. UK development finance contributions are likewise highly questionable.

Moreover, in terms of Nkrumah's (1963: 170, 1965: 9) emphasis on the need for developmental state strategies, the role of Western

DFIs—including the UK's CDC/BII group—is clearly problematic. As the case of Feronia Inc. demonstrates, DFIs can entrench dependency upon export of raw materials such as palm oil for the benefit of processors and multinational firms in the 'West'. In this sense, DFI investments may close down policy space for African governments to pursue alternative economic models of development by ensuring that land and labour resources go towards the maintenance of colonial era production and sectors (cf. Trelstad, 2016: 357, 434). Furthermore, the building of infrastructure projects does not necessarily work towards diversification along the lines of developmental state strategies if these assets facilitate exploitative models of exportation (Langan & Scott, 2011: 19). Environmental depletion and the loss of valuable minerals to Europe may retard longer-term development opportunities for the African states in question (Bond, 2006: 13).

Interestingly in relation to Brexit, Nkrumah's concerns about a collective colonialism perpetrated by European powers appear prescient. As the case of Feronia Inc. demonstrates, Brexit does not halt collaboration between the UK's own DFI and that of EU member states. UK involvement in the Congolese plantation leveraged other European DFIs' capital as they followed the British example and invested into the Congolese palm oil industry. As the company collapsed, these DFIs then collaborated to sell the plantation operations as a going concern to a new investor, and they collectively appear to have failed to consider an effective exit strategy conducive to land restitution and the wellbeing of workers (RIAO-RDC et al., 2021; Global Justice Now, 2020). The launch of the EU's Global Gateway initiative with its provision of finance for the European Investment Bank (EIB) and other EU member state DFIs, increases the 'opportunities' for further future collaborations between European DFIs and the UK's own development finance body in the 'new scramble' for African resources.

The work of Ndlovu-Gatsheni (2015) on global coloniality adds further depth to a critique of Global Britain's development finance. The financialisation of development and the entrenchment of DFI influence within the Wall Street Consensus clearly reflects the coloniality of knowledge entrenched within Western 'development' circles (Gabor, 2021). Western policy-makers—including UK officials within the FCDO—perpetuate discourse about DFIs leveraging in private capital conducive to job creation and 'social stability' within 'fragile' African countries (BII, 2021). Moreover, they emphasise that such interventions are necessary to stem flows of migration involving dangerous journeys by unemployed African youth through the Sahara Desert and the Mediterranean Sea (UK Government, 2018c). As a result, DFI interventions are normalised and presented as 'common sense' solutions to 'development' dilemmas and to the realisation of the UN SDGs. African officials subject to Western discourses are thus encouraged to allow DFI investments within their territories and to foster a laissez-faire business environment conducive to attracting yet more forms of unregulated foreign private capital into their economies. Western officials' epistemological influence here—in shaping African officials' potential imaginaries of economic development through a hegemonic discourse linked to the Wall Street Consensus—seeks to undermine alternative imaginings of how economic development might be brought about, for instance, in terms of the developmental state approach outlined by Nkrumah (1963, 1965).

While some African officials respond to Western pressures with measures designed to enhance and protect their own policy-making autonomy—for instance, via the African Continental Free Trade Agreement (AfCFTA)—nevertheless there are clear material incentives to acquiesce to the agendas of foreign DFIs. These incentives become clear in relation to the apparent political connections of companies receiving UK financial injections in countries such as Zambia. The dangers of neo-colonial relationships highlighted by Nkrumah link neatly here to Ndlovu-Gatsheni's (2015) discussion of the coloniality of power. It is evident that material 'aid' from the UK not only benefits certain elite African politicians, but also acts as a form of revolving credit for the British state itself. As the Public Accounts Committee highlighted, the CDC/BII group sits on vast profits accumulated from its portfolio in Africa (Gilbert, 2022: 307). In addition, staff of CDC/BII benefit from lucrative salaries in the process of 'creating' low paid jobs for workers on plantations and other intensive agribusiness operations. In 2018, the CDC group employed 235 staff and 'spent £30.1 million on wages and salaries' (Global Justice Now, 2020: 6). The coloniality of power is thus expressed in terms of how Western 'development' agencies use wealth disparities inherited from the colonial period to then propagate exploitative models of extraction in African countries. Inequalities between Euro-American elites and impoverished agricultural workers in African countries persist as DFIs enrich the former, and perpetuate the exploitation of the latter.

Conclusion

UK governments since the 2016 referendum have repeatedly highlighted the importance of British financial investments for private sector development, economic growth and job creation in Africa. As part of a Wall Street Consensus involving the financialisation of development and the 'blending' of public finances with private capital to 'de-risk' investments, the UK government views the CDC/BII group as central to its Global Britain project. 'Aid' in the form of BII investments—either directly or indirectly via private equity funds based in secrecy jurisdictions—will ensure that the 'trillions' necessary for attainment of the UN SDGs will be delivered in conjunction with the efforts of other Western DFIs. As part of this mission civilisatrice, the UK government has renamed its CDC group to BII to ensure that 'Global Britain' is projected more clearly and to distance the organisation from the reputational damage associated with the CDC brand.

Nevertheless, this 'development' discourse is highly problematic. This arm of the UK government was founded in the colonial period to guard against the demands of liberation movements (Bracking, 2009: 67). It sought to satiate demand for jobs, while bolstering colonial patterns of production (Gilbert, 2022: 307). It sought to bolster UK domestic finances via 'revolving' aid that brought increased profits to the British treasury via 'bankable' projects (ibid). Since its rebranding to the Commonwealth Development Corporation—and now to the BII—the organisation has facilitated a neo-colonial agenda based on incentivising colonial patterns of production and closing down policy space for African governments to pursue developmentalist alternatives. In the process, companies in which CDC/BII has invested have allegedly mistreated their impoverished workers and have apparently caused health and environmental harm (Open Democracy, 2019). This is a far cry from nominal pro-poor 'development' objectives.

As the work of Nkrumah (1963, 1965) and Ndlovu-Gatsheni (2015) conveys, it is useful to conceptualise such UK interventions in terms of neo-colonialism and global coloniality. The UK government via the CDC/BII group seeks to maintain political influence in relation to African executives, funding companies which appear to have close connections to senior politicians. It seeks to ensure that UK interests continue to be served in terms of the reliable supply of raw materials such as palm oil. It is willing in this process to help facilitate infrastructural developments conducive to extraction and export. Meanwhile, the use of private equity funds in secrecy jurisdictions restricts fair taxation revenues to African governments and perpetuates reliance upon 'aid' from foreign powers including the UK. African officials, in this scenario, not only have to contend with the sovereignty implications of China's 'debt diplomacy' but have to contend with the repercussions of Western DFIs' investments in terms of collapsing policy space and intrusive political leverage.

Bibliography

Alami, I., Dixon, A. D., & Mawdsley, E. (2021). State Capitalism and the New Global D/development Regime. *Antipode, 53*, 1294–1318.

Alem, C., Ferreira Madeira, R., & Agostini Martini, R. (2017). *National Systems of Development Finance Institutions: Comparative Experiences*. BNDES.

Ambreena, M. (2019). The Legal Framework for UK Aid After Brexit. *Current Legal Problems, 72*(1), 37–57.

Arsenault, C. (2017, February 28). Congo Plantation Firm Financed by UK Aid Accused of Breaking Promises to Help Workers. *Reuters*. https://www.reuters.com/article/us-africa-aid-landrights/congo-plantation-firm-financed-by-uk-aid-accused-of-breaking-promise-to-help-workers-idUSKBN1670PX. Accessed 30 May 2023.

Attridge, S. (2019). *The Impact of Development Finance Institutions*. ZBW.

Attridge, S., & Engen, L. (2019). *Blended Finance in the Poorest Countries: The Need for a Better Approach*. Overseas Development Institute.

Bond, P. (2006). Resource Extraction and African Underdevelopment. *Capitalism Nature Socialism, 17*(2), 5–25.

Bougrea, A., Orbie, J., & Vermeiren, M. (2022). The New European Financial Architecture for Development: Change or Continuity? *European Foreign Affairs Review, 27*(3), 337–360.

Bracking, S. (2009). *Money and Power: Great Predators in the Political Economy of Development*. Pluto Press.

Bracking, S. (2012). 'How do Investors Value Environmental Harm/Care? Private Equity Funds, Development Finance Institutions and the Partial Financialization of Nature-based Industries. *Development and Change, 43*, 271–293.

British International Investment. (2021). *G7 Development Finance Institutions Create Platform to Boost Investment in Fragile States*. https://www.bii.co.uk/en/news-insight/news/g7-development-finance-institutions-create-platform-to-boost-investment-in-fragile-states/. Accessed 30 May 2023.

British International Investment. (2023a). *What Impact Means to Us: An Overview of How We Manage Impact*. British International Investment.

British International Investment. (2023b). *Written Evidence Submitted to International Development Committee by British International Investment*. UK Parliament. https://committees.parliament.uk/writtenevidence/117564/pdf/. Accessed 30 May 2023.

Carmody, P. (2016). *The New Scramble for Africa*. Polity Press.

Cassimon, D., & Van Campenhout, B. (2007). Aid Effectiveness, Debt Relief and Public Finance Response: Evidence from a Panel of HIPC Countries. *Review of World Economics, 143*, 742–763.

CDC. (2017). *Investing to Transform Lives: Strategic Framework 2017–2021*. CDC.

Christian Aid. (2023). Written Evidence to the International Development Committee. UK Parliament. https://committees.parliament.uk/writtenevidence/117562/pdf/. Accessed 30 May 2023.

Daddow, O. (2018). Brexit and Britain's Role in the World. In P. Diamond, P. Nedergaard, & B. Rosamond (Eds.), *The Routledge Handbook of the Politics of Brexit* (pp. 208–222). Routledge.

Dimitriadis, D., Vetch, F., & Williams, M. (2019, 24 November). UK Overseas Aid Still Invested into Fossil Fuels—Two Years After Climate Pledge. *Open Democracy*. https://www.opendemocracy.net/en/british-international-investment-fossil-fuels-uk-aid-cash-divest/. Accessed 24 November 2023.

Dolma Impact Fund. (2023). *ESG Policies*. Dolma Impact Fund.

Eaton, M. Ø. (2020). We Are All Children of the Commonwealth': Political Myth, Metaphor and the Transnational Commonwealth 'Family of Nations' in Brexit Discourse. *British Politics, 15*, 326–348.

Edigheji, O. (2005). A Democratic Developmental State in Africa? A Concept Paper. Centre for Policy Studies Research Report, No. 105, May 2005. Centre for Policy Studies.

FMO. (2023). *Historic Timeline of Plantations et Huileries du Congo S.A. (PHC), a Palm Oil Business Founded by the Lever Brothers in 1911*. FMO. https://www.fmo.nl/timeline-feronia. Accessed 30 May 2023.

Fundanga, C. (2017, June 26). Zambeef Not Doing Enough Corporate Social Responsibility in Chisamba. *Zambian Eye*. https://zambia.co.zm/news/headlines/2017/06/26/comment-zambeef-not-doing-enough-corporate-social-responsibility-in-chisamba/. Accessed 30 May 2023.

Gabor, D. (2021). The Wall Street Consensus. *Development and Change, 52*(3), 429–459.

Gilbert, P. (2022). The Crown Agents and the CDC Group: Imperial Extraction and Development's "Private Sector Turn." In G. Bhambra & J. McClure (Eds.), *Imperial Inequalities* (pp. 299–318). Manchester University Press.

Giordano, T., & Ruiters, M. (2016). Closing the Development Finance Gap in Post-Conflict and Fragile Situations: What Role for Development Finance Institutions? *Development Southern Africa, 33*(4), 562–578.

Global Justice Now. (2020). *Doing More Harm than Good: Why CDC Must Reform for People and Planet*. Global Justice Now.

Goga, S., Bosiu, T., & Bell, J. (2019). The Role of Development Finance in the Industrialisation of the South African Economy. Jason Bell Centre for Competition, Regulation and Economic Development.

Hildyard, N., & Oloko, D. (2015). *Written Evidence Submitted by The Corner House and Oloko*. UK Parliament. https://committees.parliament.uk/writtenevidence/63904/html/. Accessed 28 May 2023.

Human Rights Watch. (2019). A Dirty Investment: European Development Banks' Links To Abuses in the Democratic Republic of the Congo's Palm Oil Industry. Human Rights Watch. https://www.hrw.org/sites/default/files/report_pdf/drc1119_web_0.pdf. Accessed 30 May 2023.

ICAI. (2019). Report: CDC's Investments in Low-Income and Fragile States. ICAI. https://icai.independent.gov.uk/html-version/cdc/. Accessed 30 May 2023.

International Development Committee. (2016). *Inquiry on Fragility and Development in the Democratic Republic of the Congo: Written Evidence Submitted by CDC*. UK Parliament. https://committees.parliament.uk/writtenevidence/68314/pdf/. Accessed 30 May 2023.

International Development Committee. (2023). Oral Evidence: Investment for Development the UK's Strategy Towards Development Finance Institutions. UK Parliament. https://committees.parliament.uk/oralevidence/13257/html/. Accessed 30 June 2023.

Kelk, S., & Copestake, J. (2022). *Afterglow? The Long-term Influence of Development Finance Institutions on Firms' Environmental, Social and Governance (ESG) Policies*. Bath Papers in International Development and Wellbeing, No. 68, pp. 1–33. Centre for Development Studies. University of Bath.

Labour Party. (2019). *Dan Carden Responds to Allegations of Abuse in a CDC-Backed Company*. Labour Party. https://labour.org.uk/press/dan-carden-responds-to-allegations-of-abuses-in-a-cdc-backed-company/. Accessed 30 May 2023.

Langan, M., & Scott, J. (2011). The False Promise of Aid for Trade. *Brooks World poverty Institute Working Paper*, No. 160, pp. 1–32.

Lazzarini, S. G., Musacchio, A., Bandeira-de-Mello, R., & Marcon, R. (2015). What Do State-Owned Development Banks Do? Evidence from BNDES, 2002–09. *World Development, 66*, 237–253.

Loft, P. (2022). *British International Investment: Aid and Trade*. UK Parliament. https://researchbriefings.files.parliament.uk/documents/CBP-9560/CBP-9560.pdf. Accessed 30 May 2023.

Lovett, S. (2023, January 24). British Taxpayers Funding Kenyan Hospital Accused of Imprisoning Patients. *The Telegraph.* https://www.telegraph.co.uk/global-health/climate-and-people/british-taxpayers-funding-kenyan-hospital-accused-imprisoning/. Accessed 30 May 2023.

Lusaka Times. (2012, June 26). Zambeef Mistreatment. *Lusaka Times.* https://landmatrix.org/media/uploads/zambia-_-zambeef-plc-mpongwe-farms-employees-complain-of-mistreatment-by-foreign-employers.pdf. Accessed 30 May 2023.

Mailafia, O. (1997). *Europe and Economic Reform in Africa: Structural Adjustment and Economic Diplomacy.* Routledge.

Mawdsley, E. (2015). DfID, the Private Sector and the Re-centring of an Economic Growth Agenda in International Development. *Global Society, 29*(3), 339–358.

Mawdsley, E. (2018). 'From Billions to Trillions': Financing the SDGs in a World 'Beyond Aid.' *Dialogues in Human Geography, 8*(2), 191–195.

McVeigh. (2019, September 27). UK Development Bank Launches Inquiry After Murder of Congolese Activist. *The Guardian.* https://www.theguardian.com/global-development/2019/sep/27/uk-development-bank-launches-inquiry-after-murder-of-congolese-activist-cdc. Accessed 10 September 2023.

Mitchell, A. (2023, June 9). Labour in Major Economic U-Turn as it Delays Flagship £28bn "Green Prosperity Plan". *The Independent.* https://www.independent.co.uk/news/uk/politics/labour-rachel-reeves-green-plan-b2354512.html. Accessed 30 June 2023.

Mkandawire, T. (2001). Thinking about Developmental States in Africa. *Cambridge Journal of Economics, 25*(3), 289–313.

Mujenja, F., & Wolani, C. (2012). *Long-Term Outcomes of Agricultural Investments: Lessons from Zambia.* International Institute for Environment and Development.

National Audit Office. (2016). *Department for International Development: Investing Through CDC.* National Audit Office.

Ndlovu-Gatsheni, S. J. (2014). Global Coloniality and the Challenges of Creating African Futures. *Strategic Review for Southern Africa, 36*(2), 181–202.

Ndlovu-Gatsheni, S. J. (2015). *Empire, Global Coloniality and African Subjectivity.* Berghahn Books.

Nkrumah, K. (1963). *Africa Must Unite.* Panaf Books.

Nkrumah, K. (1965). *Neo-Colonialism: The Last Stage of Imperialism.* Panaf Books.

Noer, T. J. (1984). The New Frontier and African Neutralism: Kennedy, Nkrumah, and the Volta River Project. *Diplomatic History, 8*(1), 61–79.

Obeng, S. (1979a). *Selected Speeches of Kwame Nkrumah* (Vol. 1). Afram Publications.

Obeng, S. (1979b). *Selected Speeches of Kwame Nkrumah* (Vol. 2). Afram Publishers.
Öniş, Z., & Şenses, F. (2005). Rethinking the Emerging Post-Washington Consensus. *Development and Change, 36*(2), 263–290.
Parker, G. (2018, January 29). Theresa May Refuses to Endorse China's Belt and Road Initiative. *The Financial Times.* https://www.ft.com/content/6e3 9fd0e-0517-11e8-9650-9c0ad2d7c5b5. Accessed 30 May 2023.
Połońska-Kimunguyi, E., & Kimunguyi, P. (2017). Gunboats of Soft Power: Boris on Africa and Post-Brexit 'Global Britain'. *Cambridge Review of International Affairs, 30*(4), 325–349.
Public Bill Committee. (2016). *Commonwealth Development Corporation Bill – Written Evidence Submitted by Zambeef Products PLC.* UK Parliament. https://publications.parliament.uk/pa/cm201617/cmpublic/Commonwea lthDevelopmentCorporation/memo/CDCB06.htm. Accessed 30 May 2023.
Resnick, D. (2022). How Zambia's Opposition Won. *Journal of Democracy, 33*(1), 70–84.
RIAO-RDC and GRAIN. (2021, April 30). Interview with Mrs. Augin Nolofana, the Mother of a Young Villager from Mwingi, Killed by Agents of the PHC/KKM Company. *Farmlandgrab.org.* https://www.farmlandgrab.org/post/view/30275-rdc-entretien-avec-mme-augin-nolofana-la-maman-d-un-jeune-villageois-de-mwingi-qui-aurait-ete-tue-par-les-agents-de-la-societe-phc-kkm. Accessed 30 May 2023.
RIAO-RDC, FIAN Belgium, Entraide et Fraternité, CCFD-Terre Solidaire, FIAN Germany, urgewald, Milieudefensie, The Corner House, Global Justice Now, World Rainforest Movement and GRAIN. (2021). *Development Finance as Agro-Colonialism: European Development Bank Funding of Feronia-PHC Oil Palm Plantations in the Democratic Republic of the Congo.* RIAO-RDC. https://www.cidse.org/wp-content/uploads/2021/02/EN-Development_Finance_as_Agro_Colonialism_Feronia_PHC.pdf. Accessed 29 May 2023.
Savage, M. (2021, September 26). Old Faces of New Labour in Keir Starmer's Inner Circle. *The Guardian.* https://www.theguardian.com/politics/2021/sep/26/old-faces-of-new-labour-in-keir-starmers-inner-circle. Accessed 30 June 2023.
Stacey, K. (2023, June 28). Keir Starmer Considers Ditching Labour Pledge to Reinstate DfID. *The Guardian.* https://www.theguardian.com/politics/2023/jun/28/keir-starmer-considers-ditching-labour-pledge-to-reinstate-dfid-international-development. Accessed 30 June 2023.
Talani, L. S. (2017a). *The Political Economy of Italy in the Euro Between Credibility and Competitiveness.* Palgrave
Talani, L. S. (2017b). The ECB and the Quest for Competitiveness of the Eurozone: From the Competitive Devaluation of the Euro to QE. *Journal of Balkan and Near Eastern Studies, 19*(4), 351–365.

Thorne, J., & Du Toit, C. (2009). A Macro-Framework for Successful Development Banks. *Development Southern Africa, 26*(5), 677–694.

Trelstad, B. (2016). Impact Investing: A Brief History. *Capitalism and Society, 11*(2), 1–14.

UK Government. (2018a). PM Speech at the Africa "Call to Invest" UNGA Event. UK Government Online. https://www.gov.uk/government/speeches/pm-speech-at-the-africa-call-to-invest-unga-event. Accessed 30 May 2023.

UK Government. (2018b). UK Launches Ambition to Generate Billions More Investment in Africa to Trigger Transformational Growth. UK Government Online. https://www.gov.uk/government/news/uk-launches-ambition-to-generate-billions-more-investment-in-africa-to-trigger-transformational-growth. Accessed 30 May 2023.

UK Government. (2018c, August 28). PM's Speech in Cape Town: 28 August 2018. *UK Government*. https://www.gov.uk/government/speeches/pms-speech-in-cape-town-28-august-2018. Accessed 6 March 2023.

UK Government. (2020). *PM Hosts First Ever UK-Africa Investment Summit in London*. UK Government Online. https://www.gov.uk/government/news/pm-hosts-first-ever-uk-africa-investment-summit-in-london. Accessed 30 May 2023.

UK Government. (2021). *Global Britain in a Competitive Age: The Integrated Review of Security, Defence, Development and Foreign Policy*. HM Stationery Office.

UK Government. (2023). *UK to Host African Investment Summit in April 2024*. UK Government Online. https://www.gov.uk/government/news/uk-to-host-african-investment-summit-in-april-2024. Accessed 30 May 2023.

Ungoed-Thomas, J. (2009, May 3). Poverty Staff Share £65m Bonuses. *The Times*. https://www.thetimes.co.uk/article/poverty-staff-share-65m-bonuses-z86dlm2px0k. Accessed 28 May 2023.

War on Want. (2006). *Globeleq: The Alternative Report*. War on Want. https://www.waronwant.org/sites/default/files/Globeleq%20-%20The%20Alternative%20Report.pdf. Accessed 30 May 2023.

White, M. (2010, September 13). Anti-Poverty Quango Row: Look at Salaries, Not Expenses Claims. *The Guardian*. https://www.theguardian.com/politics/blog/2010/sep/13/anti-poverty-quango-expenses. Accessed 28 May 2023.

World Bank. (2009). *IFC and the Millennium Development Goals*. World Bank.

World Rainforest Alliance. (2022). *Collective Statement – Development Banks Make Shameless Exit from a Colonial Land Grab in the Congo*. Uruguay. https://www.wrm.org.uy/node/20351. Accessed 30 May 2023.

Zambia Reports. (2013). Zambeef to Lay Off 1,500 Workers. *Zambia Online*. https://zambia.co.zm/news/headlines/2013/06/24/zambeef-to-lay-off-1500-employees/. Accessed 30 May 2023.

CHAPTER 6

UK Corporate Interests and Neo-colonialism in Africa

INTRODUCTION

Since the Brexit referendum, UK officials have emphasised that corporate investment into Africa will bring dividends for British entrepreneurs and for African citizenries as part of the Global Britain project (UK Government, 2017, 2018, 2022a). Embracing the private sector development (PSD) rhetoric espoused by the Organisation for Economic Development and Cooperation (OECD) since the late 1990s, the UK government promises that its businesses' investments are a 'win-win' opportunity for development (Langan, 2011; Mawdsley, 2015). UK corporations through their willingness to engage in 'risky' markets in Africa—supported with British export credits—will ostensibly ensure that 'globalisation works for the poor'. This reflects a Post-Washington Consensus (PWC) in which relaxation of business regulations to create an 'enabling environment' for foreign investment, will nominally ensure that the free market serves social interests (Öniş & Şenses, 2005). Such language emanated from the 'Third Way' politics of Western politicians such as President Bill Clinton and Prime Minister Tony Blair (cf. Stiglitz, 1997, 2002). As such, the Blair government in the 2000s was a strong proponent of the need for British businesses to invest in Africa (Taylor, 2012: 454). Blair and the Department for International Development (DfID) framed this in terms of private sector contributions towards the UN Millennium Development Goals (MDGs) (DfID, 2009: 42).

© The Author(s), under exclusive license to Springer Nature Switzerland AG 2023
M. Langan, *Global Britain and Neo-colonialism in Africa*,
https://doi.org/10.1007/978-3-031-42482-3_6

This PWC discourse is amplified by the corporate sector's own embrace of corporate social responsibility (CSR) and Environmental, Social and Governance (ESG) language (Michael, 2003). Owing to consumer backlashes against sweatshop labour and environmental degradation—and the risk to profits that this entails—multinational corporations (MNCs) have sought to insulate themselves from boycotts and brand risk (Heal, 2008). This applies not only to famous household names where companies such as Nike have sought to defend themselves against civil society criticisms (Amazeen, 2011; Knight & Greenberg, 2002). Interestingly, it also applies to lesser known companies such as energy and mining conglomerates, including Glencore (2023)—with its British subsidiary, Glencore Energy UK. It also applies to British agribusiness companies such as Unilever (2023) and Associated British Foods (ABF, 2023) in terms of their operations in Africa. The websites of almost all major UK corporations contain CSR and ESG pledges that echo the 'pro-poor' rhetoric of the British government's own PSD pledges.

In this context, the chapter examines the implications of the Brexit referendum in terms of UK corporate activities in Africa, and whether 'pro-poor' outcomes are being delivered. The discussion first draws attention to the discursive significance of donor PSD narratives. The second section highlights the rhetoric of UK elites since the 2016 Brexit referendum about the need to enhance Africa-UK commerce. It highlights material changes to UK policies, including financial injections into UK Export Finance (UKEF)—an agency attached to the Department for International Trade (DIT) (recently renamed the Department for Business and Trade [DBT]). The third section considers recent examples of UK corporate activities in Africa in relation to the oil, minerals and land. This covers both the pre-referendum period of New Labour and Cameron, as well as the post-referendum context. It underscores that there are consistent problems associated with British corporate activities in Africa in terms of alleged labour and human rights abuses, as well as environmental degradation. The fourth section argues that the warnings of Nkrumah (1965) and Ndlovu-Gatsheni (2015) are relevant for an assessment of UK corporate activities in Africa in terms of the concepts of neo-colonialism and global coloniality.

Private Sector Development and Poverty Reduction in Africa: From Blair to Cameron

The ostensible contributions of MNCs to poverty reduction in the 'Global South' have long been underscored by the Western donor community, especially since the rise of 'Third Way' politics (cf. Stiglitz, 1997, 2002). Notably, the Clinton administration emphasised the compatibility of free markets with the creation of an 'efficient' welfare model (Peck & Theodore, 2001). A thriving private sector was envisaged as a vehicle for growth contributing to enhanced taxation revenues, the creation of jobs and social progress through CSR (cf. Hemphill, 1997; Jaenicke, 2000: 35–36). This pro-poor rhetoric was translated at the international level within a PWC discourse that emphasised the contributions of Western private sector engagement in Africa, Asia and Latin America to poverty reduction.

The PWC agenda was solidified in the aftermath of the East Asian Financial Crisis amid the contributions of Joseph Stiglitz who had been an advisor to Clinton (Fine & Waeyenberge, 2009). Stiglitz (1998) emphasised the importance of a business 'enabling environment' for foreign direct investment (FDI) into developing countries. Investments would create higher taxations revenues, employment, and infrastructural upgrades conducive to wider prosperity (Öniş & Şenses, 2005). Key development agencies such as the OECD embraced PSD statements in their presentation of the need for business entrepreneurs in donor nations to engage in 'risky' markets in Africa. For example, the OECD (2007) publication *Business for Development: Fostering the Private Sector* explained the significance of the private sector as the 'engine' of growth in developing countries:

> Over the years different paradigms have prevailed in development emphasis has shifted from basic needs, to capabilities, to structural programmes and the provision of a market-friendly business environment... nowadays the development of the private sector is regarded as essential. The logic behind this statement is simple: poverty reduction is the main objective of development co-operation ... economic growth is essential for development, and growth is best achieved through the private sector, which in turn needs to be promoted.

Coalitions of corporations in the UN Global Compact similarly embraced donor PSD narratives, which was soon reflected in the transition to the United Nations (UN) Sustainable Development Goals (SDGs) (Mawdsley, 2014). Goal 8 of the UN SDGs highlights the need to attain 'Decent Work and Economic Growth'—highlighting the centrality of the private sector to 'decent jobs'.

The inclusion of a central PSD discourse within the PWC coincided with the corporate sector's embrace of CSR and ESG narratives. Civil society campaigns involving consumer boycotts of MNCs motivated the rise of a protective CSR and ESG discourse (Amazeen, 2011; Knight & Greenberg 2002). Presenting themselves as ethical 'corporate citizens', MNCs could protect their profits and perhaps even win new consumers via moralised advertising campaigns (Willmott, 2003). Global governance organisations, such as the World Bank, soon also highlighted the benefits of CSR for poverty reduction (Michael, 2003: 117). As Michael (2003) notes though, this CSR rhetoric tied into a neoliberal model of development in which social functions previously undertaken by the state would ostensibly be enacted by the business community. This reflected the realities of structural adjustment programmes (SAPs) enacted in Africa in the 1980s and the 1990s as a result of conditionalities imposed by the World Bank and the International Monetary Fund (IMF). Austerity agendas imposed under SAPs limited the ability of many African governments to make necessary social investments, leaving an opening for the private sector to act as the 'engine' of progress (Dembele, 2007). World Bank and IMF conditionalities, meanwhile, also meant developing countries opening up their markets to MNCs from the West (Boussebaa, 2023: 558).

In terms of the UK, it is not surprising therefore that the government of Tony Blair embraced PSD discourse regarding 'development' in Africa. Highly influenced by the New Democrats and Bill Clinton, Blair promised at home—and abroad—that the private sector would be a partner for progressivism (Cammack et al., 2004: 161; Driver et al., 2004: 31). Whereas traditional Labour politicians had been sceptical about corporate profiteering, New Labour embraced the business community as an agent for change. As a result, DfID (2009) quickly became a chief proponent of PSD strategies and Aid for Trade (AfT) in Africa. The latter—spending UK aid monies on the business 'enabling environment'—was seen as key to levering in more FDI into Africa (Langan & Scott, 2014). Improvements to roads, ports, electricity supply, customs regulations, border controls and investments into facilities such as cold storage (for agricultural exporters) would ensure that AfT monies translated into poverty reduction (ibid.).

However, New Labour's PSD discourse also promised 'win-win' benefits for British commerce in terms of access to African markets. Prime Minister Blair and DfID, for example, were vocal supporters of the African Development Bank's (AfDB) Investment Climate Facility (ICF) (War on Want, 2007: 4). Launched in Tanzania in 2008, the ICF is a public-private initiative which brings together corporations, non-governmental organisations (NGOs), external donors and African governments to improve the business 'enabling environment'. The AfDB (2023) explains the ICF's objectives in terms that wholly align with the PSD narratives espoused by the OECD:

> ICF focuses on building the environment for investment by encouraging, developing, and working with coalitions for investment climate reform and supporting business community-government dialogue. Getting the investment climate right and supporting governments in creating a legal, regulatory and administrative environment that encourages businesses at all levels to invest, grow and create jobs will lead to improving Africa's image as an investment destination.

Critics of the initiative, however, argue that it has pursued a neoliberal 'small state' model of development that has encouraged laissez-faire approaches to corporate regulation. The Blair government's support for the initiative is, accordingly, seen in terms of the commercial interests of UK firms. For instance, Anglo-American—a British mining conglomerate—was the first private sector investor within the ICF, pledging USD $2.5 million. The UK meanwhile was the first government to contribute, pledging USD $30 million over a three-year timeframe (War on Want, 2007: 4). PSD objectives associated with the creation of a favourable investment climate is linked not only to ostensible 'pro-poor' goals but to the interests of UK corporations that benefit from 'smoother' access to Africa's primary resources via regulatory reforms. This was confirmed by DfID, emphasising that the ICF would 'support projects such as streamlining business regulation' and 'reforming customs administration and taxation and removing barriers to competition' (ibid.). Anglo-American, meanwhile, stated that the ICF would make investments more attractive within Africa (ibid.).

UK elites' embrace of corporate-led 'development' in Africa was also seen in terms of Prime Minister David Cameron. His coalition government launched so-called High Level Prosperity Partnerships (HLPPs) in the continent. The HLPPs emphasised the need for closer commercial linkages between the UK and the countries of Angola, Cote d'Ivoire, Ghana, Mozambique and Tanzania (War on Want, 2016: 12). These initiatives emphasised the 'African growth story' and the contributions that UK businesses could make to the continent's development (UK Government, 2013). Cameron's coalition utilised HLPPs to pursue commercial advantages in priority sectors. These were identified as extractives, agriculture, business environment, financial services, education, energy, infrastructure and the environment (War on Want, 2007: 12).

However, according to the UK Government (2013) website, only extractives and business environment initiatives were pursued in all five of the targeted countries. The UK government explained this focus on extractives in terms of aligning with G8 initiatives, which also conformed to the interests of UK mining companies such as Anglo-American (ibid.). The coalition government also appointed twenty 'prosperity officers' employed by the Foreign and Commonwealth Office (FCO) to 'complement fourteen existing UK trade and investment officers in the continent' (Vines, 2019: 24). It further established prime ministerial trade envoys to Angola, Nigeria and South Africa. Vines (2019: 24) explains these UK government initiatives in terms of the budget deficit in the UK. Enhanced profits for British businesses in Africa would benefit the UK economic base. This PSD focus on Africa for enhanced UK profitability, however, has found even further momentum in the wake of the 2016 referendum.

The 'New Scramble' for Africa: Brexit and PSD

The 2016 referendum gave further momentum to UK government focus upon PSD activities. The uncertainty caused by the UK's withdrawal from the EU necessitated diversification of UK commercial activities beyond Europe. This incentivised post-referendum governments to emphasise the need for enhanced commercial ties between UK businesses and African economies. Notably, Prime Minister Theresa May's official tour of South Africa, Kenya and Nigeria in 2018 included not only senior ministers from her cabinet, but a convoy of business delegates. This included representatives from Bechtel UK, Bombardier Transportation UK, the CDC group (covered in Chapter 5), JCB manufacturing and UK Export

Finance (UKEF). In her Cape Town speech, May reinforced PSD narratives. In language similar to DfID's embrace of the ICF under Blair, she emphasised the need for an attractive investment climate:

> As a Prime Minister who believes both in free markets and in nations and businesses acting in line with well-established rules and principles of conduct, I want to demonstrate to young Africans that their brightest future lies in a free and thriving private sector. One driven and underpinned by transparency, high standards, the rule of law and fairness. Only in such circumstances can innovation truly be rewarded, the potential of individuals unleashed, and societies provided with the opportunities they want, need and deserve. (UK Government, 2018)

May emphasised that British businesses would play a key role in driving forward development opportunities in Africa (ibid.). And—again with parallels to Blair and Cameron—her inclusion of UK business leaders underlined that there would be a profit motive for British companies.

The launch of the UK-African Investment Summit (UKAIS) under her successor, Boris Johnson, solidified this direction of travel. The first summit held in London in 2020 symbolised the British government's commitment to corporate partnerships and investments. This aligned not only to the pursuit of Brexit trade deals discussed in Chapter 3, but to exploring new contracts that British businesses might pursue through networking with African dignitaries and entrepreneurs. The UK Government (2020a) statement issued after the summit highlighted the opportunities provided by the African Union's new African Continental Free Trade Area (AfCFTA) for attracting British investments. It underscored the importance of Brexit trade deals for maintaining market access. Moreover, it emphasised the 'development' benefits that UK businesses could bring in terms of African livelihoods and wellbeing (UK Government, 2020a). Interestingly, the UK government also highlighted its apparent commitment to clean energy and infrastructure projects (ibid.). However, one UK civil society complaint emanating from the summit was that 'fossil fuel deals' had constituted 90% of the commercial agreements in the energy sector (Carrington, 2020). This included Tullow Oil's announcement of its enhanced investment within a controversial project in northern Kenya, which is discussed in the next section of the chapter.

In addition, to UK-African Investment Summits (with the second meeting due in April 2024), Johnson's government also announced increased finances for the UK Export Facility (UKEF). Attached to the Department for Business and Trade (DBT, previously DIT), UKEF focuses upon 'de-risking' projects in Africa. In January 2022, it was announced that it had tripled its investments in Africa to £2.3 billion (Tibke, 2022). Tibke (2022) explains that 'from approximately £600 million in 2018–19, UKEF's total investment in Africa has risen exponentially in the last four years, thanks to projects in countries such as Ghana, Ivory Coast, Egypt, Cameroon, and Tunisia'. Soon after this announcement, the UK Government (2022b) boasted that up to £4 billion would be available to finance projects undertaken by UK firms in Morocco. The UK Government (2022b) explained the significance of Morocco for British businesses:

> [UK] financing will promote investment between the two nations by helping Moroccan buyers access support to deliver projects, provided that at least 20% of the overall contract value is sourced from UK suppliers. Morocco offers a range of opportunities for UK businesses, such as potential projects in energy transition, water desalination, and infrastructure, including rail, roads, ports and airports.

UKEF's provision of credit, loans and guarantees to UK firms and to their clients is meant to ensure that British businesses capitalise upon opportunities within emerging markets amid a 'new scramble' (cf. Carmody, 2016). Infrastructural projects—rails, roads, ports and airports—not only have the advantage of creating profits for UK manufacturing firms but facilitate the extraction of raw materials and primary commodities to the benefit of processors in the UK (cf. Langan & Scott, 2014). Infrastructure projects facilitate and intensify the 'new scramble' for African resources by making extractive activities more feasible and profitable.

Interestingly, this investment in Morocco-UK trade cements the UKEF's interest in expanding a UK commercial footprint within Francophone Africa. UKEF, for example, has highlighted its funding of £236 million for the construction of six new hospitals in Cote d'Ivoire (UK Government, 2022c). The UK government's Trade Commissioner to Africa—a role created in 2018 to fulfil a post-Brexit referendum pledge by the Conservatives to capitalise on emerging markets—boasted of growing ties with Francophone Africa (Saigal, 2022). Speaking at the inaugural

UK-Francophone West Africa Trade and Investment Forum in October 2022 (during the short premiership of Liz Truss), he noted that Togo and Gabon had chosen to join the British Commonwealth as of June 2022 (ibid.). He praised British investments, with UKEF pledging £170 million towards construction of a new Ministerial City in Benin, and a new road between Benin and Togo. Furthermore, he explained his role (and that of the UKEF) in terms of trying to persuade British businesses to engage with 'risky' African markets:

> Someone once told me the price of risk in Africa is overpriced, and under-priced in other parts of the world," says Humphrey. "I think a large part of my job is selling Africa and its potential to investors and UK firms, which of course is a challenge in most circumstances… While companies will always have the final say in how and where they deploy their investments, there are tools we can use to de-risk projects. (ibid.)

This Franco-British commercial rivalry reflected a fractious relationship between the two countries under Boris Johnson and Liz Truss—note Truss' comments during her election campaign that 'the jury is still out' on whether French President Macron was a 'friend or foe' (Henley, 2022). The UK Trade Commissioner's use of the language of 'de-risking' also reflects the Wall Street Consensus highlighted in Chapter 5 in the context of the CDC/BII group (Gabor, 2021).

Despite PSD discourse, there are a multitude of concerns expressed by workers and civil society about British business behaviours. In particular, there are concerns that UK government prioritisation of activities in the extractive industries—especially in oil and minerals—is not commensurate with poverty reduction pledges. Rather than create decent jobs, there is concern that such investments exploit low paid workers, create health and environmental hazards and exacerbate climate change (War on Want, 2016). Moreover, in the agribusiness sector, in which British firms such as Unilever and Associated British Foods (ABF) operate, there are multiple concerns surrounding alleged 'land grabs' in which subsistence farmers are forcibly removed to the benefit of intensive commercial activities (Action Aid, 2015; Oxfam, 2013). British commercial activities in the oil, minerals and agribusiness sectors are therefore explored in more detail below vis-à-vis Global Britain's ostensible development goals in Africa.

UK Corporations for 'Development'? Oil, Minerals and Land

UK government discourse surrounding PSD has consistently emphasised the progressive nature of corporate investments in Africa. In keeping with 'Third Way' PSD rhetoric, businesses are viewed as partners for development. However, when cases of UK investment in key sectors—oil, minerals, and agribusiness—are examined, it is clear that there are a number of barriers to achieving such 'pro-poor' PSD goals. The behaviour of UK corporations in Africa in these essential sectors would appear to indicate that commercial operations denude human development outcomes. Namely, that business activities pose a challenge not only in terms of pollution, environmental degradation and climate change but also to the health and wellbeing of workers and host communities (War on Want, 2016).

Focusing upon the oil sector, there are serious concerns surrounding UK commercial involvement. One of the most glaring examples of UK corporate activity departing from PSD rhetoric is that of Glencore Energy UK Ltd. The company—a subsidiary of Glencore, a conglomerate based in Switzerland—has been found guilty by the Serious Fraud Office (SFO) of bribery in terms of its dealing in multiple African countries including Nigeria and Cameroon. The SFO (2022) reported that the UK firm had been fined approximately £280 million as a penalty for its use of bribery 'to gain preferential access to oil in Africa'. Outlining the legal judgement, the SFO (2022) explained that:

> Mr Justice Fraser, reflected in his judgement that "the facts demonstrate not only significant criminality but sophisticated devices to disguise it" before sentencing the commodities trading giant to pay a financial penalty in response to the seven charges of bribery that "represent sophisticated offending that was sustained over prolonged periods of time"… Mr Justice Fraser remarked on the culture that developed at Glencore "in which bribery was accepted as part of the West Africa desk's way of doing business…".

The SFO (2022) stated that the bribes had amounted to USD $29 million and had been distributed in Cameroon, Equatorial Guinea, Cote d'Ivoire, Nigeria and South Sudan.

Perversely, it appears that this penalty will not be used to compensate the African citizenries affected. The Nigerian state applied to the British court system to insist that a compensation order be confirmed in its favour in the context of the bribery. It believed that it had been damaged by Glencore Energy UK's actions in the following terms:

> The FRN [Federal Republic of Nigeria] considered itself to be a victim of Glencore's offending because, in summary, Glencore had effectively tried to control the Nigerian oil market through its bribes, skewing the market and creating a less competitive environment which in turn led to reduced prices and economic and reputational damage to a developing economy. It followed that the FRN's position was that it ought to be a candidate for a compensation order under the provisions of the *Sentencing Act 2020* ('the Act'). (Bunyan, 2023)

However, this appeal was denied by the British court. Bunyan (2023), who had been involved in the appeals case, reflected on the ruling in the following terms:

> So, the FRN's bold attempt to go directly to the court… failed to trigger a compensation order in its favour… the inescapable fact is that at this point Glenore's very significant financial penalties will provide a much-needed boost to the UK Consolidated Fund, but will do nothing to compensate Nigeria and its citizens for yet another egregious example of corruption visited upon them.

As a result, Nigeria's citizens will not see any immediate benefit. This is despite that the impact of the bribery may have denied the Nigerian state significant revenues. It is instead the British state that will benefit from the corporate penalty. The Consolidated Fund referred to by Bunyan (2023) above is the UK government's 'general bank account' (UK Parliament, 2023). As a result, British taxpayers will seemingly benefit from corruption in terms of the penalty being used to enrich the UK state.

Moreover, the activities of Glencore UK have been challenged in Chad in terms of their alleged health impact. In 2012, Glencore UK acquired a 35% interest in the Badila and Mangara oilfields in southwestern Chad (RAID, 2020: 7). In July 2014, this interest increased to 85% upon the company's purchase of another operator. However, a report issued in March 2020 by Rights and Accountability in Development (RAID) states that in September 2018, there was an apparent wastewater spill and crude oil leak associated with the Badila oil concession. RAID reports that in the days and weeks after these alleged incidents, 'dozens of local residents' surrounding the operations suffered severe health problems:

> dozens of local residents suffered physical injuries including burns, skin lesions, and pustules on the skin. Others complained of blurred vision, stomach aches, internal pains, vomiting and diarrhoea after using, and sometimes drinking, the water from the river. Some required hospitalization, including at least two children who suffered serious skin lesions and pustules after bathing in the water. (RAID, 2020: 4)

The NGO reports that the livelihoods of local farmers suffered around this same time, owing to the death of livestock (ibid.: 4). The report states that while Glencore has 'appointed an independent consultant' and has commissioned an 'independent Health Impact Risk Assessment' that the local residents interviewed 'were very clear: an unknown toxic substance in the water from Glencore's Badila oilfield caused their injuries' (ibid.: 5).

RAID alongside the Public Interest Law Centre (PILC) and a Chadian association—Jeunes Tchadiens de la Zone Petroliere (AJTPZ)—took these allegations to the UK's National Contact Point (NCP) for the OECD guidelines on multinational enterprises (UK Government, 2021a). The OECD (2023) explains its guidelines in the following terms:

> [they are] recommendations addressed by governments to multinational enterprises. They aim to encourage positive contributions enterprises can make to economic, environmental and social progress, and to minimise adverse impacts on matters covered by the Guidelines that may be associated with an enterprise's operations, products and services. The Guidelines cover all key areas of business responsibility, including human rights, labour rights, environment, bribery, consumer interests, disclosure, science and technology, competition, and taxation.

The UK NCP—part of the Department for Business and Trade (DBT)—is responsible for implementing the complaints mechanism under the guidelines. The UK NCP stated that it has decided 'that issues relating to the 2018 wastewater spill and subsequent alleged oil leak merit further examination' (UK Government, 2021a). Interestingly, the NCP reports that it also received allegations surrounding another, smaller wastewater spill that apparently occurred in 2020. It has decided not to currently investigate that episode, only the alleged events of 2018.

It notes, however, that the 2020 incident apparently involved 'wastewater spilling into Melom village, flooding farmland and allegedly flooding houses and contaminating the village well' (ibid.).

Concerns about the impact of UK oil companies in Africa are not, however, confined to Glencore UK. For instance, an Anglo-Irish firm, Tullow Oil, has received criticism for alleged wrongdoings in Kenya, Uganda and Ghana. As of 2016, the company operated in twelve African states south of the Sahara and described itself as 'Africa's leading independent oil company' (War on Want, 2016: 3). In Kenya, Tullow's investments were heralded in the wake of the first UK-African Investment Summit (UK Government, 2020a). The UK Government (2020b) boasted that the company was investing £1,200 million in continued oil production in Kenya, to the chagrin of environmental campaigners (Carrington, 2020). The summit deal reflects Tullow Oil's activities which began in Kenya in 2010, followed by its discovery of oil in 2012, and its operation of five oil blocks in the west and north-west of the country (Nanok & Onyango, 2017: 145). These blocks reportedly hold 600 million barrels of oil with an estimated value of USD $25 billion and cover an area 'equivalent to two-thirds the size of Scotland' (Nanok & Onyango, 2017: 145; War on Want, 2016: 8). The company's activities are focused on Turkana county, which is the country's largest and poorest region. Kenyans initially welcomed the oil discovery in alignment with the UK government's own optimistic discourse concerning 'pro-poor' PSD in Africa (Agade, 2014: 497).

However, there are allegations of forcible displacement to make way for oil drilling 'without adequate and timely compensation' (ibid.: 506–507). Moreover, Tullow Oil engaged in community consultations in 2016 to gain informed consent to access to land for exploration purposes, but an Oxfam report stated that company staff were unwilling to make the 'documentation of the consultations and of the agreement' available for review (Mullins & Wambayi, 2017: 30). Referring to the World Banks's International Finance Corporation (IFC)—which partly financed one of Tullow's partners in Turkana—the Oxfam report found that 'the lack of ready access by community members to the documentation required by IFC, combined with inconsistent understandings of what was agreed, means that "consent" to the access to land has not met FPIC standards' (ibid.: 30). Combined to this, there were concerns about the company's apparent failure to make Environmental Impact Assessments (EIAs) readily accessible to the local community (Agade, 2014: 507). This is compounded by low literacy rates and the reported lack of 'popular versions' of the EIAs being provided (ibid.: 507). As a result of these alleged failings—including allegations surrounding the accidental death of child—the local community appeared to be very worried about Tullow's oil operations:

> At present, the community is very concerned about the destruction of community vegetation and cultural sites such as graves and shrines by Tullow trucks and large-scale equipment, and the noise, dust and pollution of the machinery that has displaced them. There are also concerns raised by community members about waste disposal and the toxic chemicals used in the extraction process and whether or not they are disposed of safely. Vehicles have knocked cattle and a young boy was hit and killed, but the community complains that there has been no compensation for these events. (ibid.: 507)

The results of a survey of 426 households in the vicinity of the oil operations published in 2022 further underscores concerns about the impact on local peoples (Kirui, 2022). The survey found that 78% of households had 'experienced varied levels of excised (surrendered) land in which 28% experienced extensive excised or reduced land and 25% experienced severe excised or reduction of land' (ibid.: 47). The study also found that displacement had not only impacted upon livelihoods but had led to greater social precarity amid reduced access to social services and a decrease in social cohesion (ibid.: 48). It also found that food insecurity had increased as a result of the displacements due to oil activities (ibid.: 48). In terms of environmental impacts, meanwhile, the survey found that '64% of households experienced varied levels of the degradation (contamination) of land, in 37% experienced extensive to severely contaminated land' (ibid.: 48). A key informant to the study also reported that:

> a considerable number of households witnessed various land contamination from blasting to extraction and disposal of the wastes, as well as some unpleasant and/or poisonous chemicals. Consequently, they lost some of their livestock and access to land adjacent to the extraction sites as well as dumping sites. (ibid.: 48)

The research also found that while Tullow Oil had built wells for the community to access water, that this provision only lasted for a short period because, when extractive operations began, the wells became inaccessible (ibid.: 50). As a result, local community members had to move to find water supplies for themselves and their livestock. Related to this, '38% of households reported an extensive and severe reduction of access to water sources' (ibid.: 49).

Moreover, Nanok and Onyango (2017: 147) found that local citizens from Turkana only filled 1276 posts out of 2155 employees at Tullow Oil and 'its business contracted companies'. Meanwhile, 83% of the jobs filled by local Turkana citizens were semi or un-skilled posts, with only 2% constituting management positions (ibid.: 147). There are also allegations that white employees in Tullow's Kenyan operations have engaged in racist workplace behaviour amid a 'salary row' (Kamaris, 2019). Meanwhile, it is reported that Tullow's expenditure on CSR initiatives in Turkana has amounted to only 4% of its total investment (Nanok & Onyango, 2017: 146). One of these CSR schemes—the company's investment of USD $2.5 million into a Light Vehicles Scheme to lease 36 vehicles to local community members—was seen by local citizens to fall short of their expectations (ibid.: 147). As a result of such disappointments, Kenya's *Daily Nation* (2020) reported in 2020 that residents in Turkana were dissatisfied with the lack of benefits accruing to them. The newspaper quoted a Tullow Oil manager as acknowledging community unhappiness within the town of Lokichar:

> Tullow Kenya Managing Director Martin Mbogo admitted that the feeling in Lokichar was that Tullow had not really met the residents' expectations… in the eight years the company has been there "We always ask ourselves how much is enough, and the answer is dependent on whom we ask. We have to understand that it is not our intent to replace government. We will never meet the needs of everyone… We may provide infrastructure for schools and hospitals but furnishing them is the function of either the county or national government. But you see, the community will judge us on that".

The manager's reported remarks, however, do not sufficiently acknowledge that the community's views of private sector-led social provision is in large part a reflection of donors' and corporations' own PSD/CSR discourse. In the aftermath of SAPs and austerity agendas, communities have been led to believe by donors—and by corporations—that social progress will be forthcoming as a result of commercial operations. It is perhaps no surprise therefore that the community members of Turkana province are expecting 'PSD' largesse from oil discoveries.

Furthermore, there are concerns about whether the company is generating sufficient oil revenues as part of an opaque Production Sharing Agreement (PSA) with the Kenyan government (*The Nation*, 2020). There have also been intense internal Kenyan debates about how best to share oil monies (Wesangula, 2017). These internal debates have been complicated by concerns that Tullow Oil has apparently failed to consistently submit quarterly reports on time for each oil block during an Early Pilot Scheme in 2017 to sell the oil. Critics claimed that this meant that there was insufficient government scrutiny of company expenditure (Odhiambo, 2022). The Kenyan Petroleum Department's reported inability to properly audit the company's expenditure then appeared to have a negative impact upon the revenue share that accrued to the Kenyan government (ibid.). Lack of staff within the Petroleum Department also contributed to this problem, meaning that 'IOCs [International Oil Companies] are likely to recover non-allowable costs that would have been recovered if monitoring was carried out' (ibid.). The proportion of oil wealth accruing to the Kenyan state was lower than what many had anticipated. During the Early Pilot Scheme, the government earned the equivalent of approximately USD $10.4 million dollars (ibid.). A Turkana MP, James Lomenen, also raised questions about Tullow Oil's apparent use of a National Oil gas station for its trucks transporting oil to Mombasa's port (*The Nation*, 2020). The MP queried whether any conflict of interests had been resolved, since the head of National Oil was apparently the wife of a Tullow Oil employee (ibid.). National Oil, in turn, is owned by the Kenyan state.

Related to these concerns about a fair share of oil proceeds accruing to Kenya, the Governor of Turkana engaged in a verbal dispute with the then President of Kenya, Uhuru Kenyatta, about the revenues accruing to his region (Wesangula, 2017). This reflects one of the features of the 'resource curse' afflicting countries with oil discoveries in terms of increased political tension that in some situations have led to secessionism (Agade, 2014: 497). Note, for example, the Biafra conflict in Nigeria in the late 1960s. The Kenyan government has since agreed that 75% of the revenues will accrue to the central treasury, with 20% for Turkana county, and 5% for the communities immediately surrounding the extractive operations (Okolla, 2021). Nevertheless, despite this, a '2018 report put the poverty incidence at 756,000 of the 1.2 million residents [of

Turkana], and the illiteracy rate at 80%' (ibid.). There are also concerns that the oil industry is now 'crowding out' other economic sectors in the county including tourism and pastoralism, amid a boom in local land prices (ibid.). This is yet another feature of the so-called 'curse' which appears to have befallen the region.

Tullow Oil's activities in Uganda, meanwhile, have also led to criticisms. In 2009, the company began well testing. An international NGO, FIDH (2020: 83), reports that the testing 'produced emissions and the burning of gases, loud noises and disruptive lights'. Residents within 300 metres of the well were asked to leave for four days but reportedly received compensation only per household, not per person as they had requested (ibid.: 83). The testing also apparently led to loss of livelihoods for residents beyond 300 metres since the noises scared away their cattle (ibid.: 85). FIDH reports that this has had a lasting impact:

> Women explained that… to this day, [they] have not been able to fully recover from the economic impact… After the gas-flaring… soldiers in uniform were posted in the area… the limitation on movement impacted their capacity to bring food home. Residents reported being beaten up very badly by the soldiers, who were finally removed a few years ago. While Tullow provided partial compensation to the families within the 300-meter radius, communities explained that Tullow refused to provide compensation… for any impact caused beyond the 300 meter radius. (ibid.: 85)

The company's 2012 CSR report meekly noted that there were 'ongoing social and environmental challenges' in Uganda referring to crop damage (International Alert, 2014: 23).

Moreover, there have been criticisms that Tullow Oil's CSR investments (for example, into the building of a hospital) have provided short-term gains but have failed to address the long-term consequences of food insecurity, loss of livelihoods, as well as alleged negative health impacts deriving from its extractive activities. In terms of health, FIDH (2020: 106–107) raises concerns that gas flaring has apparently led to an increase in miscarriages and respiratory diseases:

> Hospital records showed an increasing number of miscarriages from six in 2014 to 145 in 2019. The hospital also documented an increase in the amount of respiratory diseases in Buliisa, from 2,118 cases in 2014 to 4,401 in 2019. Flaring, but also a number of gas emissions linked to

petroleum extraction, are known to increase the prevalence of miscarriages, according to scientific research.

Compensation offered to locals for displacement is also seen to have led to social tensions, not least in terms of domestic violence towards women who have received monies (International Alert, 2014: 20). There are also criticisms that those in receipt of compensation were not given proper advice as to how to wisely use the monies. Some reported that they did not even have bank accounts (ibid.: 23).

The company has also faced criticism relating to alleged bribery in Uganda. The Ugandan newspaper, *The Independent* (2013), reported a legal proceeding involving another oil operator, Heritage Oil, in which it was alleged in court that Tullow had considered bribing Ugandan authorities. Tullow denied this accusation but, according to the UK's *The Telegraph*, apologised to President Museveni for any embarrassment caused by the allegation (Dennys, 2013). Interestingly, it was reported that then UK Foreign Secretary, William Hague, had telephoned President Museveni to ask him not to hold Tullow liable for a USD $404 tax bill that had accrued under Heritage Oil, prior to Tullow's purchase of the latter's oil stake (ibid.).

Furthermore, Tullow's activities in Ghana's offshore Jubilee oilfield have also led to criticisms. There are concerns that local fishers have lost access to waters now occupied by operators including Tullow (Ovadia et al., 2020: 414–415). While the company has sought to provide community liaison officers to respond to concerns, these staff appear not to be easily found in the locales (ibid.: 409). Company CSR provision of scholarships are also said to go towards young persons with powerful family connections, not to local youth (Moses, 2021: 6). Training offered to young people to diversify local employment away from reliance upon fishing has also apparently lacked follow-on start-up capital to enable young people to utilise new skills (Ovadia et al., 2020: 412–413). Local discontent also raises the prospect of social unrest. One fisher interviewed as part of research by Ovadia et al. (2020: 414–415) raised the prospect of kidnappings if livelihoods continued to be destroyed:

> The operations of the oil and gas companies are affecting us a lot now, we catch less fish. Fishing is the only source of our livelihood and if we are out of business what shall we do? The fishing companies better address the issues we put before them because if they don't they will be treading on

dangerous grounds. Look!!!!! That's all we know how to do (fish). I am telling you if we lose it we will start kidnapping some of the children and workers of the oil companies so they can pay us ransom to release them.

Meanwhile, it was reported in 2023 that Ghana's government was seeking to impose a tax bill amounting to USD $387 million upon Tullow, which the company is disputing (Burkhardt, 2023). These issues cumulatively raise the question of whether citizens in Kenya, Uganda and Ghana are benefitting from the operation of British companies such as Tullow Oil in extractive processes. Or whether such companies stand to accrue massive profits at the expense of the health, livelihoods and environmental integrity of workers and host communities. The Serious Fraud Office's (2022) recent case of successfully pursuing Glencore Energy UK for bribery in African contexts also raises deep concerns about the subversion of sovereign states.

These worrying situations are not confined to British companies in the oil sector. The minerals sector is also a key site of conflictual relations between corporations keen to extract lucrative commodities such as gold—as well as critical minerals—and local workers and communities. For instance, British company Lonmin was implicated in the deaths of thirty-four workers in 2012 at its Marikana platinum mine in South Africa, as police fired upon strike action (War on Want, 2016: 26). Workers had been dissatisfied by the company's failure to build residential accommodation. This was despite Lonmin having promised in 2006 that it would build 5,500 houses for staff by 2011 (Amnesty International, 2016: 3). By 2016, in a letter from the company to Amnesty International, it noted that 13,500 of its employees were 'in need of formal accommodation' (ibid.: 4). South Africa's Department of Mineral Resources, meanwhile, appeared unwilling or unable to hold the company to account (ibid.: 6). The future President of South Africa, Cyril Ramaphosa, joined the Lonmin board in 2010 and stated in testimony to the Farlam Commission (investigating the deaths) that 'he had no real idea why the alleged financial constraints to building these [social housing for Lonmin workers] had risen in 2006-08, before the advent of the world financial crisis' (Bond, 2019a).

Furthermore, Lonmin's ostensible marketing operations in Bermuda were deemed to have facilitated 'at least $100 million in capital flight from South Africa to Bermuda using a classical transfer pricing tax dodge' (ibid.). Lonmin also engaged in a rapid round of worker redundancies prior to being bought out by another company in 2019:

> Already in 2016, Lonmin's workforce shrunk dramatically, from 40 000 to 33 000 employees, with another 8000 workers fired in 2018 and 4100 in mid-2019. Sibanye's takeover plan projected the firing of a further 12 600 Lonmin workers within three years. (Bond, 2019b)

The Marikana massacre has also led to ongoing political tensions—and disillusionment among the citizenry—within South Africa:

> Dissatisfaction with the ANC's [African National Congress] neo-liberal economic policy and the failure to transform the mining sector is also fuelled by recurring scandals involving both the ruling party and the mining industry. Cyril Ramaphosa… was accused of calling for police repression in Marikana, with a visible conflict of interest since he was both a leader in the ANC and a shareholder in Lonmin. More recently still, ANC Chairperson Baleka Mbete was accused of having received bribes from Gold Fields. (Botiveau, 2014: 136)

Close connections between the South African elite and Lonmin has had long repercussions for the trajectory of the country's domestic politics.

Furthermore, concerns about British firms' involvement in African mining is underscored in the case of a Madagascan operation—QMM. QMM is focused on ilmenite extraction (used in titanium) and is 80% owned by Britain's Rio Tinto. War on Want (2016: 15) documents the alleged problems surrounding this British-backed venture:

> Thousands of people have already been affected through displacement and associated loss of land, disruption to fishing, flooding of agricultural areas and dust pollution over food growing areas and pastures, affecting livelihoods and food production. Around 6,000 people live in rural villages in and around the forest and heathland area. Much of the forest, vegetation cover and topsoil have been removed to make room for the mine.

Allegations of predatory behaviour by UK firms also extends to the area of agribusiness. Associated British Foods (ABF), for example, has been accused of land-grabbing by Oxfam (2013) in relation to sugar production. ABF owns AB Sugar as well as the 'largest sugar company in Africa, Ilovo'. Oxfam (2013) explains that there have been land-grab concerns in relation to Ilovo in Zambia, Malawi and Mali. For example, the company was reportedly forced to abandon plans to create a large sugar plantation in Mali due to protests from the local community (ibid.). While ABF denies the various claims, Oxfam (2013) laments that the company has failed to create 'clear guidelines' to prevent land controversies from arising. These concerns about land-grabbing are amplified by the UK government's support for the G8 New Alliance for Food Security and Nutrition (NAFSN). The NAFSN was launched in 2012 with a view to improving agricultural production in the wake of global food crisis. Key donors including the UK, USA and France—as well as British companies such as Unilever and Diageo—supported the initiative alongside participating African governments such as Tanzania, Ghana and Nigeria (Action Aid, 2015: 5–7). The UK reported in 2013/2014 that it had pledged a total of USD $444 million to the NAFSN, a figure which increased to around USD $900 million (ibid.: 11). A NAFSN 2014–2015 progress report noted that public donors had released USD $3.2 billion of a total $6.2 billion pledged. Corporate partners, meanwhile, had released USD $684 million of a total $10.2 billion pledged (Barbiere, 2016).

However, the NAFSN was criticised for land-grabs in Africa to the benefit of Western multinationals. This became most apparent in NAFSN support for the Southern Agricultural Growth Corridor (SAGCOT) in Tanzania where investors stood to gain up to 80,000 hectares at very low prices of around USD $1 per year per hectare (De Schutter, 2015: 23). A report published by the European Parliament outlined the problems of such schemes in terms of loss of land use and water access, irrespective of the jobs that might be created (ibid.). The parliament's rapporteur on the NAFSN commented on the use of aid monies to subsidise corporations' access to cheap land:

> The big multinationals like Monsanto, Cargill and Unilever are very focussed on making a profit. It is hard to see how this kind of aid to multinationals through the New Alliance could be of benefit to local populations in terms of sustainable development. Especially when we know that family farms are largely excluded from the decision-making process linked to this initiative. (cited in Barbiere, 2016)

Resulting from these reputational risks to donors, the NAFSN has quietly faded from policy agendas, with France withdrawing in 2018 (Milerová Prášková & Novotný, 2021: 1753). Nevertheless, there are new schemes such as African Development Bank's (2023) Africa Adaptation Acceleration Programme (AAAP) with a similar focus on ostensible 'food security' objectives. In 2021, the government of Boris Johnson pledged USD $20 million to the AAAP (UK Government, 2021b). This is despite the fact that the AfDB has been linked to land-grabbing in Malawi, where AfDB's support to an outgrower sugar production scheme was criticised for the displacement of local villagers (Bae, 2019: 6). This outgrower initiative connected smallholders to large agro-corporations, including Ilovo, owned by Associated British Foods (ABF) (ibid.: 3). This British company remains central to sugar production in Malawi—namely 'all sugar products in Malawi are still sold under the name of Illovo and most locals in Dwangwa [where villagers have been displaced] have no knowledge of the existence of ABF' (ibid.: 3). While the benefits of such AfDB schemes for donors' home corporations are clear, the 'development' largesse for local communities is much less certain.

It is clear therefore that British companies operating in the areas of oil, mineral and intensive agribusiness have far from an unchallenged reputation. There are wide-ranging allegations of regressive health, labour rights, livelihoods and environmental impacts. As such, it is concerning that 'Global Britain' has trebled UKEF investments in Africa to £2.3 billion, as announced in 2022 (Tibke, 2022). As discussed, the UKEF seeks to incentivise UK investments via guarantees, insurance and loans assisting British firms and their clients. Given the allegations explored above in relation to many leading UK investors—including the recent SFO and NCP investigations into Glencore UK—the activities of UKEF are of highly dubious 'development' value. Moreover, amid the experience of the Marikana massacre and Lonmin, it is disturbing that the UKEF is highlighted in the UK Government's (2022c) post-Brexit 'critical minerals strategy'. The record of recent British investments in the mining sector does not bode well for human rights—or for the environment—amid a 'new scramble' for the continent.

Worryingly, despite recent pledges that the UKEF will not be used to facilitate fossil fuel deals, the history of the organisation would suggest that it has a clear preference for funding dirty extractive processes (UK Government, 2020b). This is underscored by the fact that by 2019 that UKEF had supported '£2.6 billion worth of fossil fuel projects over the previous five years' (UK Parliament, 2019). In addition, in July 2020, UKEF approved allocations of £900 million in loans and guarantees towards a liquid natural gas (LNG) mega-project in Mozambique

(Wright, 2022). Friends of the Earth (2023) took UKEF to the English courts for alleged breaches of UK climate change commitments under the Paris Agreement in relation to that deal. Nevertheless, the English courts rejected the case, and the UK Supreme Court refused an appeal (ibid.). Furthermore, concerns about UKEF's commitment to fossil fuels are underscored by its apparent 2015 discussions with Tullow Oil about potential support for its Ugandan oil operations. Greenpeace's *Unearthed* noted that 'the firm, whose chief executive is a major Conservative Party donor, has been in talks with officials over various schemes to back the production phase of the $8bn venture' (Carter et al. 2016). It remains to be seen therefore whether the pledge not to finance overseas fossil fuel extraction will be upheld, amid a lobbying campaign from UK energy firms, combined to the apparent reticence of both Prime Minister Sunak and Opposition Leader Starmer towards environmentalism (Observer Editorial, 2023; Lanktree, 2022; Wheeler & Nathan, 2023). In this context, the UK-African Investment Summit's heralding of investment from companies such as Tullow Oil also seems of doubtful value to poverty reduction (UK Government, 2020b). Instead, the summit (with the next due in April 2024) appears to promote British access to energy supplies ahead of a genuine concern for the UN SDGs.

Global Britain, UK Corporations and Neo-colonialism in Africa

It is clear from the above discussion that the work of Nkrumah (1965) and Ndlovu-Gatsheni (2015) on neo-colonialism and global coloniality is highly applicable to an understanding of UK commercial behaviour in Africa. Nkrumah warned that foreign corporations could continue to dominate African economies even after juridical independence. In relation to extractive processes, he warned that foreign entities would seek continued access to Africa's wealth and that this would have little benefit for ordinary citizens if oriented only towards external profit:

> When external capital is merely applied for the purpose of obtaining a quick profit, it more often impoverishes rather than enriches the country in which it is invested. For example, the extraction and exportation of mineral ores through the use of imported machinery and by the employment of low paid labour is of no material benefit to the people of the country concerned. (cited in Obeng, 1979: 222)

Nkrumah (1965) envisaged that Euro-American officials would utilise their corporate presence to wield political influence, as well as to gain continued access to vital raw materials. Western governments would utilise 'aid' monies to lubricate their corporations' access to African resources, not least through subsidising investments or by corrupting state officials. He explained that 'the economics of neo-colonialism is obvious. It gives fake aid to the newly independent country which makes that country virtually dependent economically on the colonial power' (Nkrumah cited in Obeng, 1979: 439). Nkrumah (1965: xv) noted that European aid monies might therefore serve as a 'revolving credit', with finance being levied towards African states and returning in greater quantities to the donor in terms of extractive profits in the longer term.

The example of Glencore Energy UK is perhaps the most obvious recent case in which Nkrumah's warnings have come to fruition. Not only did bribery undermine the sovereignty of the Nigerian state (among others) in terms of the organisation of its oil economy, but in keeping with Nkrumah's (1965: xv) concerns about 'revolving credit', such ill-won profits appear to then enriched the British state through the application of the corporate penalty (Bunyan, 2023). The fine placed upon Glencore Energy UK will not be used to compensate African welfare systems that appear to have lost legitimate revenues from oil. Instead, this money will be used to subsidise the UK taxpayer by being placed within the British government's Consolidated Fund (ibid.). In this sense, corporate corruption enacted by British firms in Africa appears to be a 'win-win' for the British state. If corporate activity is so egregious that, for the reputational protection of 'Global Britain', the British courts are forced to act, then the penalties applied anyway enrich British treasuries. If corporate corruption remains hidden, then British firms benefit from preferential access to raw material supplies, also benefitting the British state, not least in terms of taxation revenues levied upon headquarters back in London.

Nkrumah's warnings about the need for developmental state strategies overseen by African executives with the power to discipline, direct and regulate foreign corporate investments is also prescient in the examination of British investments. The lasting damage caused by Lonmin and the Marikana massacre upon the ANC underscores Nkrumah's argument that developmental state elites must ensure that foreign investments serve poverty reduction. The association between Cyril Ramaphosa and Lonmin illustrates the forms of relationships that Nkrumah explicitly warned against (cf. Bond, 2019a, 2019b). The co-optation of local elites—whether implicit or explicit—via corporate board positions leaves governments open to possible corporate pressures. Ramaphosa's reputational damage in the aftermath of the Marikana massacre also did much to add to social tension within the country (Botiveau, 2014: 136). Furthermore, in the situation of Uganda, the reported telephone call from then UK Foreign Secretary, William Hague to lobby the Ugandan President against the imposition of a tax bill upon Tullow Oil is yet another example of how corporate influence and political pressures merge together to close down developmentalism within a neo-colonial relationship (with UK aid-giving to Uganda as de facto leverage in this instance) (Dennys, 2013).

Ndlovu-Gatsheni's (2015) tripartite focus upon global coloniality also lends analytical weight. UK elites are cultivating the coloniality of knowledge in their articulation of 'pro-poor' PSD discourse to facilitate UK corporate involvement in Africa. The investments of Tullow Oil in Kenya, for example, are presented as a 'common sense' benefit for the Kenyan citizenry. Corporate CSR and ESG pledges also work to justify extractive activities as being a 'win–win' opportunity. These dominant discourses, espoused not only by UK officials and corporate partners but also by the wider donor community including the OECD (2007), strategically downplay the negative impact of such activities in terms of possible displacements, environmental hazards, health impacts and labour rights abuses. As a result, certain African officials attending the UKAIS in London may more easily justify lucrative deals that lead to enrichment of UK enterprise and a domestic elite, since they may legitimise such policies to their own electorates via recourse to donors' dominant PSD discourse. Indeed, the original discovery of oil in Turkana in 2012 was met with much jubilation by locals who took at face value PSD/CSR claims that wealth would 'trickle down'. And yet these same communities now fear the ongoing implications of the oil sector for their livelihoods, the environment and their health amid an apparent 'resource curse' (Agade, 2014: 497).

Ndlovu-Gatsheni (2015) focus upon the coloniality of being and the endurance of racialised power hierarchies also bears utility in making sense of how abuses of human rights and labour rights—such as the Marikana massacre—do not appear to embolden greater political action on the part of UK elites. Notwithstanding the investigation of the UK's NCP into Glencore UK's alleged wastewater spill and oil leaks in Chad, there appears to be a relative political tolerance within the Global Britain project for alleged human rights and labour abuses by British corporations in Africa. Otherwise, government statements emanating from the UKAIS, for example, would not effusively praise deals involving companies accused of exploiting local communities. Nor would UKEF have been used to historically assist oil and mineral extraction in Africa, given long-standing allegations in these sectors. It appears that, just as with UK officials' willingness to tolerate black migrants' deaths in the Mediterranean Sea as part of efforts to mitigate migration, so too are they willing to tolerate the suffering of predominantly black workers and communities amid a scramble for the African continent's wealth. The coloniality of being impacts upon UK officials' perspectives, wittingly or unwittingly, on British corporate investment in Africa.

Conclusion

UK officials have long espoused 'pro-poor' PSD narratives in their presentation of corporate investment into Africa as a 'win-win' opportunity. In alignment with a PWC influenced by Third Way politics, UK PSD narratives have emphasised that British enterprises can create jobs, enhance taxation revenues and assist infrastructure in the African continent. Meanwhile, UK corporations such as Unilever and ABF promise that they will act on CSR and ESG pledges. In the wake of the Brexit referendum, moreover, UK officials have emphasised that Global Britain should be a partner for choice for African countries, notably in terms of the launch of the 2020 (and soon to be 2024) UKAIS. Through the provision of enhanced guarantees, loans and insurance via UKEF in the post-referendum period, UK officials seek to secure new contracts outside of the European Single Market. By appointing a UK Trade Commissioner for Africa in 2018, UK officials also demonstrate that they are seeking new commercial alliances as part of their Global Britain project.

As this chapter has illustrated, however, that are worrying allegations associated with UK corporate behaviour in Africa. Notably, in the oil sector there are serious allegations about displacement of local communities, water loss and livelihoods loss. There are also serious concerns about the health implications of alleged wastewater spills for communities, notably in the case of Glencore UK in Chad that is currently being investigated by the UK NCP. In the case of Glencore UK, there are also ongoing concerns about the apparent lack of compensation for African citizenries affected by bribery, with the penalty imposed by UK courts appearing to enrich the British state. Moreover, in the minerals sector, the legacy of the Marikana massacre continues to loom over the ANC and reduce domestic confidence in its ability to manage the country's mineral wealth. And in the agribusiness sector, there are concerns about the UK government's support for the NAFSN as well as more recent schemes associated with the AfDB. British companies, such as ABF, are seen to benefit from donor support for schemes that have dubious benefit for 'development' in countries such as Malawi.

In this context, it is highly concerning that Global Britain has increased finance to subsidise British firms' activities in Africa via the UKEF, and that it unproblematically praises investment deals such as that of Tullow Oil in Kenya. Global Britain's behaviour in the continent bears out the concerns of Nkrumah regarding neo-colonial forms of corporate (and foreign government) exploitation. Rather than bring wealth creation and jobs, the examples of UK corporate involvement in land, minerals and oil illustrate that African workers and host communities may gain little prosperity while British firms (and local elites) are enriched. In terms of global coloniality, the dominance of donor PSD discourse—as evidenced by the UKAIS—belies the coloniality of knowledge. Hegemonic donor 'development' discourses not only impact how African officials engage with British counterparts at summits but also how local communities—at least initially—may welcome foreign investment. The coloniality of being, meanwhile, impacts upon UK officials' apparent willingness to turn a blind eye to alleged corporate wrongdoing in terms of Global Britain's highly problematic investments into Africa.

Bibliography

ABF. (2023). *Responsibility Governance*. ABF. https://www.abf.co.uk/responsibility/our-approach/responsibility-governance. Accessed 18 July 2023.

Aid, A. (2015). *New Alliance, New Risk of Land Grabs: Evidence from Malawi, Nigeria, Senegal and Tanzania*. Action Aid.

AfDB. (2003). *Investment Climate Facility*. AfDB. https://www.afdb.org/en/topics-and-sectors/initiatives-partnerships/investment-climate-facility/climate-change. Accessed 19 July 2023.

AfDB. (2023). *Africa Adaptation Acceleration Plan*. https://www.afdb.org/en/topics-and-sectors/initiatives-partnerships/africa-adaptation-acceleration-program. Accessed 19 July 2023.

Agade, K. M. (2014). "Ungoverned Space" and the Oil Find in Turkana, Kenya. *The Round Table, 103*(5), 497–515.

Amazeen, M. (2011). Gap (RED): Social Responsibility Campaign or Window Dressing? *Journal of Business Ethics, 99*, 167–182.
Amnesty International. (2016). *Smoke and Mirrors: Lonmin's Failure to Address Housing Conditions at Marikana, South Africa*. Amnesty International.
Bae, Y. J. (2019). A Displaced Community's Perspective on Land-Grabbing in Africa: The Case of the Kalimkhola Community in Dwangwa, Malawi. *Land, 8*(187), 1–16.
Barbiere, C. (2016, April 22). *MEPs Speak Out Against GMOs in "New Alliance" Food Strategy for Africa*. EurActiv.fr (S. White, Trans.). https://www.euractiv.com/section/development-policy/news/meps-speak-out-against-gmos-for-development-in-africa/. Accessed 22 July 2023.
Bond, P. (2019a, June 6). *Lonmin's Murder by Money*. CADTM. https://www.cadtm.org/Lonmin-s-murder-by-money. Accessed 22 July 2023.
Bond, P. (2019b, May 29). *Does Lonmin's Inclement Death Resolve—Or Reload—The Marikana Massacre?* Pambazuka.org. https://www.pambazuka.org/economics/does-lonmin%E2%80%99s-inclement-death-resolve-%E2%80%93-or-reload-%E2%80%93-marikana-massacre. Accessed 22 July 2023.
Botiveau, R. (2014). Briefing: The Politics of Marikana and South Africa's Changing Labour Relations. *African Affairs, 113*(450), 128–137.
Boussebaa, M. (2023). Decolonizing International Business. *Critical Perspectives on International Business, 19*(4), 550–565.
Bunyan, A. (2023, February 22). *Oiling the Wheels*. 2 Hare Court Blog. https://www.2harecourt.com/training-knowledge/oiling-the-wheels/. Accessed 22 July 2023.
Burkhardt, P. (2023, February 14). *Tullow Oil Disputes $387 Million of Ghana Tax Assessments*. BNN Bloomberg. https://www.bnnbloomberg.ca/tullow-oil-disputes-387-million-of-ghana-tax-assessments-1.1883529. Accessed 22 July 2023.
Cammack, P. (2004). Gidden's Way with Words. In S. Hale, W. Leggett, & L. Martell (Eds.), *The Third Way and Beyond: Criticisms, Futures, Alternatives* (pp. 151–166). Manchester University Press.
Carmody, P. (2016). *The New Scramble for Africa*. Polity Press.
Carrington, D. (2020, January 24). *"Hypocrisy": 90% of UK-Africa Summit's Energy Deals Were in Fossil Fuels*. The Guardian. https://www.theguardian.com/environment/2020/jan/24/90-pe-cent-uk-africa-energy-deals-fossil-fuels. Accessed 22 June 2023.
Carter, L., McClenaghan, M., & Clarke, J. (2016, September 25). *Oil Frontiers: Government Backs Oil Firm's Drive into African National Park*. Unearthed.. https://unearthed.greenpeace.org/2016/09/25/revealed-british-oil-firms-africa-national-parks/. Accessed 10 September 2023.
De Schutter, O. (2015). *The New Alliance for Food Security and Nutrition in Africa*. European Parliament.

Dembele, D. (2007). The International Monetary Fund and World Bank in Africa: A "Disastrous" Record. In V. Navarro (Ed.), *Neoliberalism, Globalization, and Inequalities* (pp. 369–377). Routledge.

Dennys. (2013, March 22). Tullow Oil Apologises to Ugandan Government Over Bribery Allegations. *The Telegraph*. https://www.telegraph.co.uk/finance/newsbysector/energy/oilandgas/9949319/Tullow-Oil-apologises-to-Ugandan-government-over-bribery-allegations.html. Accessed 22 July 2023.

DfID. (2009). *DfID in 2009–10: Response to the International Development (Reporting and Transparency) Act 2006*. DfID. https://assets.publishing.service.gov.uk/government/uploads/system/uploads/attachment_data/file/67675/dfid-in-2009-10-revised-6-sept-2010.pdf. Accessed 31 June 2023.

DfID. (2013). *The Investment Climate for Africa*. London: DfID. https://www.gov.uk/guidance/the-investment-climate-facility-for-africa-icf. Accessed 31 June 2023.

Driver, S. (2004). North Atlantic Drift: Welfare Reform and the "Third Way" Politics of New Labour and the New Democrats. In S. Hale, W. Leggett, & L. Martell (Eds.), *The Third Way and Beyond: Criticisms, Futures, Alternatives* (pp. 31–47). Manchester University Press.

FIDH. (2020). *New Oil, Same Business? At a Crossroads to Avert Catastrophe in Uganda*. FIDH.

Fine, B., & Van Waeyenberge, E. (2009). Correcting Stiglitz: From Information to Power in the World of Development. *Socialist Register, 42*, 146–168.

Friends of the Earth. (2023, June 21). *Friends of the Earth vs UK Export Finance: Case Documents*. Friends of the Earth Policy. https://policy.friendsoftheearth.uk/reports/friends-earth-vs-uk-export-finance-case-documents. Accessed 23 July 2023.

Gabor, D. (2021). The Wall Street Consensus. *Development and Change, 52*(3), 429–459.

Glencore. (2023). *Sustainability: The Pillars of Our Sustainability Strategy*. Glencore. https://www.glencore.com/sustainability. Accessed 18 July 2023.

Heal, G. (2008). *When Principles Pay: Corporate Social Responsibility and the Bottom Line*. Columbia University Press.

Hemphill, T. A. (1997). Legislating Corporate Social Responsibility. *Business Horizons, 40*(2), 53–59.

Henley, J. (2022, August 26). "Serious Problem" If France and UK Can't Tell If They're Friends or Enemies, Says Maron. *The Guardian*. https://www.theguardian.com/world/2022/aug/26/serious-problem-if-france-and-uk-cant-tell-if-they-are-friends-or-enemies-says-macron-liz-truss. Accessed 20 June 2023.

International Alert. (2014). *What's in It for Us? Gender Issues in Uganda's Oil and Gas Sector*. International Alert. https://www.international-alert.org/wp-content/uploads/2021/08/Uganda-Gender-Oil-Gas-EN-2014.pdf.

Accessed 23 July 2023.
Jaenicke, D. (2000). New Labour and the Clinton Presidency. In D. Coates & P. Lawler (Eds.), *New Labour in Power*. Manchester University Press.
Kamaris, K. (2019, March 8). *Labour Malpractices: Racism and Salary Row at Tullow Oil, Turkana*. Cnyakundi.com. https://cnyakundi.com/labour-malpractices-racism-and-salary-row-at-tullow-oil-turkana/. Accessed 22 July 2023.
Kirui, A. C. (2022). Displacement for Development: The Nature of Oil-Induced Displacement of Households in Turkana County. *Journal of Humanities and Social Sciences*, 1(1), 41–53.
Knight, G., & Greenberg, J. (2002). Promotionalism and Subpolitics: Nike and Its Labor Critic. *Management Communication Quarterly*, 15(4), 541–570.
Langan, M. (2011). Private Sector Development as Poverty and Strategic Discourse: PSD in the Political Economy of EU–Africa Trade Relations. *The Journal of Modern African Studies*, 49(1), 83–113.
Langan, M., & Scott, J. (2014). The Aid for Trade Charade. *Cooperation and Conflict*, 49(2), 143–161.
Lanktree, G. (2022, February 21) Boris Johnson's Ban on State Help for Fossil Fuel Exports Sparks Furious Lobbying. *The Independent*. https://www.politico.eu/article/boris-johnson-uk-ban-fossil-fuel-project-industry-lobbying/. Accessed 23 July 2023.
Mawdsley, E. (2014, September). A New Development Era? The Private Sector Moves to the Centre. In *Norwegian Peacebuilding Resource Centre Report*. NOREF.
Mawdsley, E. (2015). DfID, the Private Sector and the Re-centring of an Economic Growth Agenda in International Development. *Global Society*, 29(3), 339–358.
Michael, B. (2003). Corporate Social Responsibility in International Development: An Overview and Critique. *Corporate Social Responsibility Environmental Management*, 10, 115–128.
Milerová Prášková, D., & Novotný, J. (2021). The Rise and Fall of the New Alliance for Food Security and Nutrition: A Tale of Two Discourses. *Third World Quarterly*, 42(8), 1751–1769.
Moses, A. (2021). Dealing with Social Acceptance: The Strategies of Offshore Petroleum Extraction Companies and Stakeholder Attitudes in Ghana. *The Extractive Industries and Society*, 8(3), 1–10.
Mullins, D., & Wambayi, J. (2017). *Testing Community Consent: Tullow Oil Project in Kenya*. Oxfam.
Nanok, J. K., & Onyango, C. O. (2017). A Socioeconomic and Environmental Analysis of the Effects of Oil Exploration on the Local Community in Lokichar, Turkana County, Kenya. *International Journal of Management, Economics and Social Sciences*, 6(3), 144–156.

Ndlovu-Gatsheni, S. J. (2015). *Empire, Global Coloniality and African Subjectivity*. Berghahn Books.

Nkrumah, K. (1965). *Neo-Colonialism: The Last Stage of Imperialism*. Panaf Press.

Obeng, S. (1979). *Selected Speeches of Kwame Nkrumah*, (Vol. 1). Afram Publishers.

Observer Editorial. (2023, July 1). The Observer View on Rishi Sunak's Lack of Commitment to the Environment. The Observer. Available at: https://www.theguardian.com/commentisfree/2023/jul/01/observer-view-on-rishi-sunak-lack-of-commitment-to-environment. Accessed 10th August 2023.

Odhiambo, M. (2022, September 22). Why Kenyans Are Yet to Reap from Oil—Audits. *The Star*. https://www.the-star.co.ke/business/kenya/2022-09-22-why-kenyans-are-yet-to-reap-from-oil-audit/. Accessed 22 July 2023.

OECD. (2007). *Business for Development: Fostering the Private Sector*. OECD.

OECD. (2023). *OECD Guidelines for Multinational Enterprises on Responsible Business Conduct*. OECD.

Okolla, D. (2021, August 27). *Guns, Oil and Water in Turkana County: What Do the Stars Portend?* The Elephant. https://www.theelephant.info/features/2021/08/27/guns-oil-and-water-in-turkana-county-what-do-the-stars-portend/. Accessed 22 July 2023.

Öniş, Z., & Şenses, F. (2005). Rethinking the Emerging Post-Washington Consensus. *Development and Change, 36*(2), 263–290.

Ovadia, J., Ayelazuno, J., & Van Alstine, J. (2020). Ghana's Petroleum Industry: Expectations, Frustrations and Anger in Coastal Communities. *The Journal of Modern African Studies, 58*(3), 397–424.

Oxfam. (2013, October 2). *Nothing Sweet About It: How Sugar Fuels Land Grabs*. Oxfam Media Briefing. https://www.oxfam.ca/wp-content/uploads/2013/10/nothing-sweet-about-it-media-brief-2-october-2013.pdf. Accessed 30 June 2023.

Peck, J., & Theodore, N. (2001). Exporting Workfare/Importing Welfare-to-Work: Exploring the Politics of Third Way Policy Transfer. *Political Geography, 20*(4), 427–460.

RAID. (2020). *Glencore's Oil Operations in Chad: Local Residents Injured and Ignored*. RAID. https://www.raid-uk.org/sites/default/files/raid_report_glencore_chad.pdf. Accessed 22 July 2023.

Saigal, K. (2022, October 20). UK Export Finance Guarantees £170m Worth of Deals in Benin and Togo. The Africa Report. https://www.theafricareport.com/252314/uk-export-finance-guarantees-170m-worth-of-deals-in-benin-and-togo/. Accessed 28th June 2023.

SFO. (2022, November 3). *Glencore to Pay £280 Million for "Highly Corrosive" and "Endemic" Corruption.* News Releases. https://www.sfo.gov.uk/2022/11/03/glencore-energy-uk-ltd-will-pay-280965092-95-million-over-400-million-usd-after-an-sfo-investigation-revealed-it-paid-us-29-million-in-bribes-to-gain-preferential-access-to-oil-in-africa/. Accessed 22 July 2023.

Stiglitz, J. (1997). The Role of Government in Economic Development. In *Annual World Bank Conference on Development Economics* (Vol. 1996, pp. 11–23). World Bank.

Stiglitz, J. (1998, October 19). Towards a New Paradigm for Development. In *9th Raul Prebisch Lecture, Geneva.* United Nations Conference on Trade and Development.

Stiglitz, J. (2002). New Perspectives on Public Finance: Recent Achievements and Future Challenges. *Journal of Public Economics, 86*(3), 341–360.

Taylor, I. (2012). Spinderella on Safari: British Policies Toward Africa Under New Labour. *Global Governance, 18*(4), 449–460.

The Daily Nation. (2020, February 25). *Kenya: Locals in Oil-Ruch Turkana Claim Only the Elite Have Benefited from Tullow Oil's Operations; Company Comments.* Business and Human Rights Resource Centre—*The Daily Nation.* https://www.business-humanrights.org/en/latest-news/kenya-locals-in-oil-rich-turkana-claim-only-the-elite-have-benefited-from-tullow-oils-operations-company-comments/. Accessed 22 July 2023.

The Independent. (2013, March 22). Did Tullow Oil Bribe Museveni? *The Independent.* https://www.independent.co.ug/tullow-oil-bribe-museveni/. Accessed 22 July 2023.

The Nation. (2020). Tullow Oil Keeps Under Wraps All Its Trading Deals. *The Nation*, 4 August 2019, updated 28 June 2020. https://nation.africa/kenya/business/tullow-oil-keeps-under-wraps-all-its-trading-deals-191900. Accessed 22 July 2023.

Tibke, P. (2022, January 21). *UK Export Finance More Than Triples Its Investment in Africa to £2.3 Billion.* Trade Finance Global. https://www.tradefinanceglobal.com/wire/uk-export-finance-more-than-triples-its-investment-in-africa-to-2-3bn/. Accessed 30 June 2023.

UK Government. (2013, November 19). *High Level Prosperity Partnerships in Africa.* UK Government Online. https://www.gov.uk/government/publications/high-level-prosperity-partnerships-in-africa. Accessed 30 June 2023.

UK Government. (2017, March 9). *Commonwealth Trade Ministers Meeting: Towards a Free Trading Future.* UK Government Online. https://www.gov.uk/government/speeches/commonwealth-trade-ministers-meeting-towards-a-free-trading-future#:~:text=Liberation%20from%20poverty&text=I%20have%20long%20believed%20that,as%20a%20badge%20of%20honour. Accessed 6 March 2023.

UK Government. (2018, August 28). *PM's Speech in Cape Town: 28 August 2018*. UK Government Online. https://www.gov.uk/government/speeches/pms-speech-in-cape-town-28-august-2018. Accessed 6 March 2023.

UK Government. (2020a, January 20). *UK Government Statement: London 20th January 2020*. UK Government Online. https://assets.publishing.service.gov.uk/government/uploads/system/uploads/attachment_data/file/859314/2020_01_20_AIS_-_UK_Government_Statement_-_Final_Version.pdf. Accessed 30 June 2023.

UK Government. (2020b, December 12). *PM Announces the UK Will End Support for Fossil Fuel Sector Overseas*. UK Government Online. https://www.gov.uk/government/news/pm-announces-the-uk-will-end-support-for-fossil-fuel-sector-overseas. Accessed 23 July 2023.

UK Government. (2021a). Decision: Initial Assessment: AJTZP, RAID and PILC Complaint to the UK NCP About Glencore UK Ltd. *Statement Published on 15th January 2021 by UK National Contact Point (UK NCP) for the OECD Guidelines on Multinational Enterprises*. UK Government. https://www.gov.uk/government/publications/ajtzp-raid-pilc-complaint-to-the-uk-ncp-about-glencore-uk-ltd/initial-assessment-ajtzp-raid-pilc-complaint-to-the-uk-ncp-about-glencore-uk-ltd. Accessed 22 July 2023.

UK Government. (2021b). *UK Commits New Support to African-Led Projects to Protect Vulnerable Communities at the Frontline of Climate Change*. UK Government Online. https://www.gov.uk/government/news/uk-commits-new-support-to-african-led-projects-to-protect-vulnerable-communities-at-the-frontline-of-climate-change. Accessed 30 June 2023.

UK Government. (2022a, June 23). *PM Speech at the Commonwealth Business Forum*. UK Government. https://www.gov.uk/government/speeches/pm-speech-at-the-commonwealth-business-forum. Accessed 6 March 2023.

UK Government. (2022b, November 23). *UK Export Finance Commits Up to £4bn to Strengthen UK Morocco Trade Ties*. UK Government Online. https://www.gov.uk/government/news/uk-export-finance-commits-up-to-4bn-to-strengthen-uk-and-moroccan-trade-ties. Accessed 22 June 2023.

UK Government. (2022c, January 25). *UK Signals West Africa Expansion at Africa Investment Conference*. UK Government Online. https://www.gov.uk/government/news/uk-signals-west-african-expansion-at-africa-investment-conference. Accessed 18 July 2023.

UK Government. (2022d, July 22). *UK Critical Minerals Strategy*. UK Government Online. https://www.gov.uk/government/publications/uk-critical-mineral-strategy. Accessed 18 July 2023.

UK Parliament. (2019, June 10). *MP Calls for End of Taxpayer Support for Fossil Fuel Projects from 2021.* Environmental Audit Committee, UK Parliament. https://committees.parliament.uk/committee/62/environmental-audit-com mittee/news/100313/mps-call-for-end-of-taxpayer-support-for-fossil-fuel-projects-from-2021/. Accessed 23 July 2023.

UK Parliament. (2023). *Glossary—Consolidated Fund.* UK Parliament. https://www.parliament.uk/site-information/glossary/consolidated-fund/. Accessed 22 July 2023.

Unilever. (2023). *Planet and Society.* Unilever. https://www.unilever.com/planet-and-society/. Accessed 18 July 2023.

Vines, A. (2019). The Evolution of UK Policy to Sub-Saharan Africa, 1997–2019. In D. Beswick, J. Fisher & S. Hurt (Eds.) *Britain and Africa in the Twenty-First Century* (pp. 15–34). Manchester University Press.

War on Want. (2007). *Fanning the Flames: The Role of British Mining Companies in Conflict and Violating Human Rights.* War on Want.

War on Want. (2016). *The New Colonialism: Britain's Scramble for Africa's Energy and Mineral Resources.* War on Want.

Wesangula. (2017, June 30). *Tullow Oil Project in Drought-Hit Part of Kenya Suspended.* Climate Change News. https://climatechangenews.com/2017/06/30/tullow-oil-project-drought-hit-part-kenya-suspended/. Accessed 22 July 2023.

Wheeler, C., & Nathan, M. (2023, July 9). "I Hate Tree Huggers"—Keir Starmer Explodes Over Green Policy. *The Times.* https://www.thetimes.co.uk/article/i-hate-tree-huggers-keir-starmer-explodes-over-green-policy-6hhnj9r9x. Accessed 23 July 2023.

Willmott, M. (2003). Citizen Brands: Corporate Citizenship, Trust and Branding. *Journal of Brand Management, 10*(4), 362–369.

Wright, O. (2022, July 27). PM Cleans Up UK's Reputation on Environment by Defunding Global Oil Projects. *The Times.* https://www.thetimes.co.uk/article/pm-cleans-up-reputation-by-defunding-foreign-oil-projects-vt68ldlk8. Accessed 23 July 2023.

CHAPTER 7

UK Security Interests and Neo-colonialism in Africa

INTRODUCTION

The Brexit referendum result was based in large part upon perceived UK security interests regarding 'fragile states' in the 'Global South'. The notorious 'Breaking Point' poster unveiled by the United Kingdom Independence Party (UKIP) leader, Nigel Farage, showing predominantly non-white refugees transiting through Europe symbolised how migration galvanised the Leave campaign (Browning, 2019; Stewart & Mason, 2016). Brexiteer politicians argued that freedom of movement within Europe imperilled the security of British citizens (Browning, 2019: 1390). The securitisation of migration—often via right wing populist discourse linking refugees to alleged involvement in terrorism, drugs and sexual assaults—played a key role in securing the UK electorate's decision to withdraw from the European project (Browning, 2019: 234; Grinan-Moutinho, 2022).

UK elites, however, have long engaged in securitising discourse surrounding the ostensible risks emanating from the 'Global South'. UK officials within key agencies—the Foreign Commonwealth and Development Office (FCDO) and the Department for International Development (DfID) before it—have engaged in rhetoric surrounding British interventions in Africa to 'stabilise' former colonies. As discussed in Chapter 4, this has involved the mobilisation of British aid monies towards perceived UK security interests. For example, the use of British aid in terms of the externalisation of migration via the Rwandan deportation initiative (Gower et al., 2022). UK government policy has also involved the deployment of British security services. Recently, the UK National Crime Agency (NCA) has provided training to security counterparts in Tunisia and Algeria to harden their borders (Dathan, 2023). Furthermore, it has involved UK government encouragement of—and financing of—British private military companies (PMCs) to provide 'security' to African clients, as well as the sale of arms as part of 'security sector reforms' (Fisher & Anderson, 2015; Lazell & Petrikova, 2021). Moreover, as the cases of Sierra Leone and Libya illustrate, British military forces have been deployed in situations where UK officials perceive there to be security—and reputational—threats (Gegout, 2018: 239).

Accordingly, this chapter examines 'Global Britain's' pursuit of security interests in Africa, with a view to understanding trends since the Brexit referendum. It first provides context by assessing UK elites' pursuit of perceived security interests vis-à-vis African countries from Blair to Cameron. It underscores Blair's mix of humanitarian rhetoric and realpolitik, notably in terms of his support for British sales of armaments (Taylor, 2012: 452). It highlights how British discourse of 'responsible' arms sales—via the Arms Trade Treaty (ATT)—helps to legitimise the pursuit of British commercial interests (Stavrianakis, 2016: 841). The second section examines how the Leave campaign drew upon these pre-existing narratives surrounding the 'Global South' to capitalise upon British citizens' anxieties towards migration. The third section then examines trends in UK security approaches to Africa since the 2016 referendum. It highlights UK interventions to enhance border security and counter-terrorism policing. It explains assistance in these areas as part of populist efforts to mitigate conflict-driven migration. The section also raises concerns about human rights consequences, for example, in terms of UK assistance to Nigerian and Kenyan police. The fourth section assesses the UK's securitised approach to in terms of neo-colonialism and global coloniality. UK elites' securitisation of African countries is seen to have made them vulnerable to forms of British interventions that denude sovereignty and imperil human rights.

UK Security Interests in Africa: From Blair to Cameron

UK elites have pursued a securitised approach to the African continent long before the populist denigration of migrants as part of the Leave campaign. New Labour presented the continent not only as a 'scar upon the conscience' of the world in terms of humanitarian needs, but additionally presented poverty and instability in African contexts as a 'threat' to British citizens (Abrahamsen, 2004: 683; Porteous, 2005: 289). Blair especially advocated for a muscular liberalism in an era of 'globalisation' that viewed 'instability' in one regional context as a potential source of disorder in the West. Blair made clear as early as April 1999 that Western intervention would be justified in such situations to restore democracy, rule of law and international tranquillity (Sloboda & Abbot, 2004). Outlining his 'Chicago Doctrine' of liberal interventionism amid the Kosovo crisis, Blair argued that globalisation required international responses to countries, and regions, experiencing turmoil:

> Twenty years ago we would not have been fighting in Kosovo....[but] globalisation is not just economic. It is also a political and security phenomenon...Many of our domestic problems are caused on the other side of the world... Poverty in the Caribbean means more drugs on the streets in Washington and London. Conflict in the Balkans causes more refugees in Germany ...We are all internationalists now... We cannot turn our backs on conflicts and the violation of human rights within other countries if we want still to be secure. (cited in UK National Archives, 2010)

In such terms, Blair articulated a securitised approach to 'development' based not solely upon moral concerns but by a realpolitik aimed towards securing safety on British streets. Such rhetoric, of course, soon resurfaced in terms of Blair's discursive approach to the invasions of Afghanistan and Iraq after the 9/11 attacks (Haines, 2016).

Importantly in terms of UK relations with African countries, Blair's Chicago Doctrine extended to the African continent. Blair authorised UK military intervention in 2000 to safeguard the capital of Sierra Leone that faced seizure by a rebel militia. Sierra Leone had been experiencing civil war since 1991, with a 1996 peace accord that collapsed in 1997. The Canadian Government (2018) describes the UK's 2000 intervention in the following terms:

In April and May 2000, UN peacekeepers under UNAMSIL came under attack by rebel forces. The United Kingdom sent 1500 troops to evacuate its citizens and to support UNAMSIL. This intervention turned the tide and the rebels began to give ground and returned to the negotiation table. After the armed intervention, British troops stayed to train the Republic of Sierra Leone Armed Forces (RSLAF) so these forces could disarm the rebels themselves.

The New Labour government justified the UK's support to Sierra Leone in terms of democracy, rule of law and a global order based upon international responsibility for human rights (Harris, 2001: 28). This decision came not only in the aftermath of the Kosovo conflict. But importantly in terms of UK elites' mindsets—including Blair—it came in the recent memory of the 1994 Rwandan genocide. Bill Clinton— Blair's US counterpart—told Blair upon leaving office that he regretted not taking a greater interest in the continent (Porteous, 2005). Indeed, Clinton had been condemned for not taking more action to prevent the genocide amid the 'end of history' and the US unipolar moment in the 1990s (for example, see Burkhalter, 1994). Moreover, Blair's decision to assist the government of Sierra Leone apparently had a personal dynamic, since his father had spent time in that country as a university professor. Blair had memories of visiting Sierra Leone during his youth (Zack-Williams, 2016). His decision to assist United Nations (UN) and Sierra Leonean government forces against the RUF militia continues to be seen as one of the few foreign policy 'successes' of the Blair years amid the fallout of the Iraq War, and more recently, the return of Taliban rule in Afghanistan (Dorman, 2009).

UK elites' decision also reflected a concern to protect Britain's reputation (Gegout, 2018: 231). The 1998 'arms to Africa' affair had cast a shadow over New Labour's 'ethical foreign policy'. Civil servants in the Foreign Office had apparently endorsed the sale of USD $10 million worth of arms from a British PMC, Sandline International, to restore the government of Ahmed Tejan Kabbah in Sierra Leone, who had been ousted in a military coup in 1997. The sale had been done in contravention of an UN arms embargo with the apparent knowledge of Foreign Office officials, but without the authorisation of then Foreign Secretary, Robin Cook (Marsden, 1999; UK Parliament, 1999). This scandal was soon followed by a related scandal in which other British PMCs apparently armed rebels supporting the deposed military junta that had ousted

Kabbah (Watt & Norton-Taylor, 1999). Britain was therefore accused of arming both sides of the conflict. Blair himself denied that the rearming of the rebels could be attributed to the UK in terms derided as 'weasel words' by the Liberal Democrats, who explained that Blair's account was 'a legalistically accurate description of a transaction carried out by UK companies buying arms from a second country and transporting them to a third country. This means that British companies can get off scot-free' (ibid.).

These inter-linked scandals brought into question the 'ethical foreign policy' that had been announced by New Labour upon its assumption of office, as well as highlighting the ethically dubious behaviour of British PMCs. In this context, Britain's military intervention in 2000 has been interpreted as a means of restoring the UK's reputation by assisting the UN mission and thus diverting attention away from scandals. Gegout (2018: 239) explains here that:

> The [UK] government believed that a successful mission in Sierra Leone could redeem it and guarantee the United Kingdom's 'moral integrity'… This is important for the United Kingdom at the international level, as it helps strengthen its global role, and it shows African elites that it wants to undo the wrongs of imperialism.

In a similar vein, Ero (2001: 58) notes that the 2000 UK intervention in 'Sierra Leone represented a case of forced responsibility, following heavy criticism [of the Blair government] in the arms-to-Africa affair'. Britain as the coloniser of Sierra Leone also sought to demonstrate its continued influence within—and paternalistic responsibility for—its former colonial possession. Moreover, Blair sought to demonstrate his government's support for an international system underpinned by the UN. This was before his overriding of that system in the 2003 invasion of Iraq, condemned as 'illegal' by UN General Secretary, Kofi Annan (Tyler, 2004).

While Blair's approach to Sierra Leone continues to be viewed as an example of successful UK foreign policy, nevertheless, Amnesty International (2006: 17) underscores that the Sandline scandal demonstrated that the UK government had failed to provide proper oversight of how arms provided by UK PMCs were being used in conflict zones. They note that Nigerian troops under the UN umbrella allegedly committed human rights abuses with arms supplied by a British PMC in the effort to restore

Kabbah in the late 1990s (ibid.). Meanwhile, the behaviour of British PMCs after the 2000 intervention also posed a reputational risk to the UK. In September 2000, the Campaign Against the Arms Trade (CAAT 2000) drew attention to allegations that British mercenaries 'have been accused of killing civilians in a Russian-built Mi-24 attack helicopter'. It claimed that there was a direct link between British mercenaries and UK armed forces: 'working with British armed forces, these mercenaries are effectively being used as a tool of [UK] foreign policy. This shows quite explicitly why the UK government is no closer to legislating against human rights abusers' (ibid.).

Meanwhile, Ero (2001: 58) explains that Britain's close association with the Kabbah government posed a challenge to Britain's reputation, given that Kabbah was part of the pre-war order that had stoked conflict. Despite these criticisms, UK support continued throughout Blair's tenure in office. In 2007—the year of Blair's handover to Gordon Brown— and Kabbah's stepping down due to Presidential term limits—the UK provided USD $23.6 million to an internationally composed military training programme in the country (Reuters, 2007). The UK's intervention in Sierra Leone was accompanied by Blair's support for African Union (AU) peacekeeping initiatives in several conflicts, notably in terms of the Darfur crisis in Sudan. In 2005, the UK contributed £6.6 million in material support to AU peacekeepers including '600 vehicles, diverse equipment, and the airlift of Nigerian troops' in relation to that conflict (Apuuli, 2019: 59). In the years of the Brown government, the UK also supported AU efforts, notably within Somalia 'to the tune of £15 million, covering military equipment, logistics, and salaries for military personnel' (ibid.).

While Sierra Leone demonstrated the UK's 'hard power' in Africa, Blair's courting of the de facto leader of Libya, Muammar Gaddafi, in the aftermath of Iraq demonstrated an attempt to exercise 'soft power' (cf. Honeyman, 2017: 54). Blair visited Libya and met with Gaddafi in 2004 amid the announcement of the latter's willingness to dismantle Weapons of Mass Destruction (WMD) programmes (Jakobsen, 2012). The détente underscored UK commercial interests in Libya. For instance, Anglo-Dutch oil firm, Shell, thus agreed a £110 million deal for gas exploration off the Libyan coast (Oliver, 2004). The thawing of relations also facilitated the UK arms industries' profits through sale of lethal weapons to the Libyan state. As Hansen and Marsh (2015: 280) note, a

'UK Ministry of Defence report from late 2006 described Libya as a "priority area" for arms exports'. By the 2010 LibDex arms fair in the Libyan capital of Tripoli, half of the arms companies displaying their wares were from the UK (ibid.). High-level UK officials, including Blair, played a key role in promoting UK arms. In 2010, it was reported by British media that the UK government had approached Khamis Gaddafi, the son of the Libyan leader, in terms of possible arms for the 32nd Brigade. This regiment was later implicated in gross human rights abuses during the Libyan civil war, initiated one year later in 2011 (ibid.).

However, with the formation of the coalition government under David Cameron in 2010, UK policy towards Libya shifted. The Conservatives in opposition had made political capital in attacking New Labour for taking a 'soft' approach to one of Britain's erstwhile nemeses (Dawson, 2022: 369). Public memories concerning the murder of a police officer outside the Libyan Embassy in London in 1984, the Lockerbie bombing of 1988, as well as the more recent release of the Lockerbie bomber in 2009 combined to make the UK-Libya détente a subject of Conservative attacks on New Labour's foreign policy (ibid.: 370). Prime Minister Cameron, in this context, decided to engage in 'an arm-lengths regime change strategy' alongside France in terms of North Atlantic Treaty Organisation (NATO) intervention in the Libyan civil war (Pradella & Rad, 2017: 2421). Emboldened by Gaddafi's speech in which he threatened to go 'house by house' to root out rebel militias, Cameron worked alongside NATO allies to impose a no-fly zone (Dawson, 2022: 370; Reuters, 2011). This was soon extended into military action against the Libyan army following President Obama's call for air strikes in March 2011. As Zenko (2016) explains: 'decapitation strikes against Qaddafi were employed early and often... just hours into the intervention, Tomahawk cruise missiles launched from a British submarine... struck an administrative building... less than 50 yards away from the dictator's residence'.

The British decision was in large part driven by the coalition government's ontological (in)security in the sense of their perception of Britain's declining power status (Dawson, 2022: 357–358). With defence budget cuts necessitated by domestic austerity politics, Cameron viewed Libyan intervention as a means of enhancing Britain's global role. In addition, NATO intervention was viewed as a means of 'punishing Gaddafi for humiliating and painful terrorist violence' that occurred during the era of Prime Minister Margaret Thatcher (ibid.). Cameron also saw intervention as a means of drawing a line under New Labour's foreign policy. Political attacks on the Labour Party on the issue of Gaddafi. Intervention in Libya was further understood by Cameron as a means of minimising conflict-driven migration (Davidson, 2013: 323). The UK and other European states had resented the Gaddafi state for its leveraging of the migration issue, and its tolerance of smuggling gangs/This was despite a 2008 agreement between Libya and Italy to limit migrant flows, which did subsequently decline (Chothia, 2018). The overthrow of Gaddafi and a quick end to conflict were thus seen as strategic goals for the UK.

The consolidation of British corporate access to Libya's lucrative oil and gas reserves was a further motivating factor. The New Labour government met with Anglo-Dutch firm, Shell, on 'at least 11 occasions and perhaps as many as 26 times in less than four years' since its 2004 partnership with Libya's state-owned energy group (Mcalister, 2009). Gaddafi's erratic behaviour was deemed a threat to UK energy interests. Since Gaddafi's overthrow, British Petroleum (BP) has now resumed exploration of 54,000 square kilometres of onshore and offshore areas for oil and gas extraction (AFP, 2023; Ghaddar & Bousso, 2018). This is in partnership with Italy's ENI and relates to concessions gained via a 2007 deal with the Gaddafi state (Ghaddar & Bousso, 2018). Shell is also seeking to return to the country since its 2012 withdrawal (Bousso, 2021). British oil interests also apparently played a role in supporting the rebels during the conflict itself. Reuters reported that British oil trader, Vitol, had purchased naptha from 'the rebel-held port of Tobruk… providing the opposition with much needed funds to fight government forces' (Donati, 2011).

The violent demise of Gaddafi further opened-up lucrative opportunities for British PMCs. War on Want (2016: 7) reported that 'just days after Gaddafi's death, the UK company Trango Special Projects was touting for business among prospective investors'. British firm, G4S, also sought to capitalise on the regime change, employing the former British ambassador to Libya as an advisor. In 2012, it successfully won a £8 million contract to protect the EU delegation and its embassies in Tripoli and Benghazi. However, this contract was soon overturned upon the protest from Libya's National Transitional Council (NTC) (War on Want, 2016: 12). Other British PMCs have since had more success. For example, Vellichor Risk (2020) stated on social media on 28 January 2020 that it was 'proud to announce that we are now delivering services to one of the largest international oil & gas company in Libya'. On 14 March 2021, the company's social media account posted a piece about a 'business breakfast' which company representatives seem to have attended in Tripoli—an event hosted by the UK ambassador to Libya (Vellichor Risk, 2021). The social media post explains that 'the breakfast was organised by… [the] Country Director of the UK Department for International Trade' (ibid.).

Interestingly, given British sale of arms to the Gaddafi state (amid sales to many other African countries), the international Arms Trade Treaty (ATT) regulating the sale of conventional arms was brought into force in 2014 during the coalition government. This was championed by William Hague as the then Foreign Secretary. Hague warned other states that they would be judged 'harshly' if they failed to endorse the treaty (Stavrianakis, 2016: 840). This followed on from the Blair government's public support for the creation of such a treaty from 2005 onwards. Given Britain's role as one of the world's major arms exporters, this vocal support for the regulation of arms sales has been viewed as evidence of an ethical element within British decision-making. However, given how the ATT provides scope for discretionary judgement on the part of exporting states, Stavrianakis (2016) convincingly argues that the treaty in effect gives rhetorical cover for Western arms suppliers to continue to profit from their trade while appearing to abide by liberal norms. She explains that the ATT:

> introduces a balancing act in which states can weigh the risk of human rights violations against the interests of peace and security and justify exports in the name of the latter. With the effect of naturalising liberal states' practices and allowing them to evade scrutiny, create the impression of responsibility and morality, and effect leadership of a liberal international order that is nonetheless reliant on coercion and violence, the ATT takes on a rather different hue as a means for the reworking and re-legitimation of liberal forms of militarism. (2016: 841)

UK elites' support for the treaty should not be viewed as an ethical departure from realpolitik. Rather, it should be understood as legitimising continued UK arms sales to dubious regimes. This is anchored by a sanitising ATT narrative of respect for human rights.

The UK's leading role within the global arms trade—and the licensing of arms sales to governments with dubious human rights records in countries such as Uganda, Sudan, Kenya and Eritrea—continued throughout the New Labour years and the Cameron—led coalition government (Taylor, 2012: 452). Gegout (2018: 214) explains that:

the United Kingdom was the fourth main European exporter of arms to Africa between 2004 and 2012: it sold arms there to a value of €1.5 billion... The United Kingdom exported twice as many arms to sub-Saharan Africa than to North Africa. Most arms went to South Africa, but the United Kingdom also exported to Kenya, Botswana, Sierra Leone, Tanzania, Algeria and Morocco... British arms indirectly ended up in Sierra Leone, the DRC and the CAR.

The enthusiasm of Blair for support to the arms industry is seen as galling by both Porteous (2005) and Taylor (2012) given the 'ethical foreign policy' promised by New Labour. The scholars explain this in terms of Blair's concern for the arms industry's profitability and its employment of 400,000 workers in the UK (Porteous, 2005: 287; Taylor, 2012: 452). Moreover, Claire Short, the former Development Secretary, explained that 'my dear friend Tony Blair... absolutely, adamantly, favoured all proposals for arms deals' (cited in Taylor, 2012: 452). As a result, in the years 2001–2005 and 2006–2010, 'the volume of British arms exports orders increased by 67 per cent' (ibid.). Cameron continued this approach, especially in terms of arms sales to Libya after the torture and murder of Gaddafi. In 2013 alone, British arms sales to the war-torn country totalled £7.8 million (AOAV, 2023).

Cameron also followed Blair's securitised approach to the African continent on the subject of 'anti-terrorism'. As Abrahamsen (2004) explains, New Labour had depicted Africa not only as a humanitarian concern but as a potential source of 'risk' to UK citizens in the context of the US-led 'global war on terror':

> Blair's Africa may be a 'scar on the conscience of the world', but it is simultaneously a dangerous place that can impinge on 'our national security and wellbeing'... New Labour's policy discourses have placed the continent firmly within a logic of fear and linked its underdevelopment to a threat of terrorism....

Cameron and Hague similarly depicted the continent as a potential terror threat. In particular, they spoke of the grave dangers of Islamist groups such as Boko Haram for security on British streets (Apuuli, 2019; UK Government, 2014). The Chibok kidnapping of schoolgirls in 2014 by the militant group in northern Nigeria intensified UK elites' desire to utilise 'development' aid for 'stabilisation' vis-à-vis conflicts within Africa

(Lazell & Petrikova, 2021). UK offers to help find the missing schoolgirls also helped the coalition government to soften its own image. It enabled ministers to voice their concern about gendered violence and to associate themselves with the popular 'Bring Back Our Girls' campaign endorsed by US First Lady, Michelle Obama (Olutokunbo et al., 2015). With parallels to Sierra Leone, the coalition government also stepped-up military training for Nigerian armed forces, given UK concerns about the presence of Boko Haram in West Africa (Enayaba, 2021: 259).

Furthermore, Cameron placed significant emphasis on 'stabilisation' efforts in Somalia in relation to Al Shabaab. In 2012, the UK hosted an international conference on how to deal with the insurgency of the Islamist group (Apuuli, 2019: 61). In 2013, Cameron ordered the reopening of the British embassy in Somalia's capital of Mogadishu (ibid.). In 2015 after his re-election, he authorised a doubling of the UK's contributions to peacekeeping efforts in Africa, by deploying troops to Somalia and South Sudan (UK Government, 2015). This effort was presented by Cameron as a form of 'containment' (Apuuli, 2019: 61). Moreover, the UK government (2015) explained the deployments in terms of ending 'destabilising conflicts that are prompting mass migration'. Cameron stated that: 'our commitment to peacekeeping operations will help to alleviate serious humanitarian and security issues in Somalia and South Sudan, helping to bring stability to the region and preventing these challenges from spreading further afield' (cited in UK Government, 2015). As the next section makes clear, however, this securitised approach to Africa established fertile ground for the Leave campaign's populist appeals against migration during the 2016 Brexit referendum.

The Brexit Referendum and the Securitisation of Migration

The securitisation of 'development' and migration under Blair and Cameron laid the ground for the Leave campaign's populist appeals during the 2016 referendum. UK elites' portrayal of the African continent as not only a humanitarian 'scar' but as a possible source of terrorist threat entrenched British public fears concerning migration. Incidents such as the 2014 Chibok kidnapping—combined to rhetoric from DfID and the then Foreign and Commonwealth Office (FCO) about the dangers of 'fragile states'—heightened UK public anxieties about migration from the 'Global South' (Browning, 2019: 1390). This was amplified by terrorist events in France, such as the November 2015 Paris attacks which stoked British fears about Islamist groups, and which brought to fore memories of atrocities on UK soil, such as the 7/7 bombings in London.

Notably, the strategic appeal of the Leave campaign against Turkey's candidature for EU membership played into pre-existing Islamophobic sentiment and public fears about radical Islamist groups. The notorious 'Breaking Point' poster unveiled by Nigel Farage—showing predominantly non-white refugees making their way across Europe on the migration route from Turkey and Syria—played into racialised fears about an Islamic 'threat' to UK society (Browning, 2019; Stewart & Mason, 2016). Browning (2019: 234) explains that the anti-immigration message was underscored by social media and publicity events by the Leave Campaign centred around stoking public anxieties about free movement of people within EU borders. Meanwhile, Bello (2022: 1390) explains that the Leave campaign played upon a well-established 'trope' that 'far away' countries in the 'Global South' posed a security risk. In fact, this trope the very narrative that had been deployed by DfID and the FCO during the New Labour and Cameron administrations. Migration became constructed as a threat to the safety and integrity of the British way of life by presenting it as a means by which persons from 'fragile states' would bring insecurity and radicalism (ibid.). Nigel Farage and the Leave campaign built upon the discursive legacy of those Remain politicians—Blair and Cameron notably—who later decried his populist campaign to exit the EU. Without laying the earlier groundwork for UK public fears about migration, however, these Remain politicians would likely have had greater success in their efforts to keep the UK within the European supranational edifice.

Interestingly, elements of the UK media also laid much of the necessary groundwork in terms of pre-existing British public anxieties about migration, especially in terms of the 2015 'Migration Crisis'. While media images of a drowned Kurdish child momentarily awakened British sympathies towards the plight of refugees, a populist backlash against softening public attitudes was mounted by the influential Daily Mail newspaper. Gray and Franck (2019: 282) note here that:

> the Mail published pieces… that explicitly objected to the way many people had 'succumbed to a surge of emotion' around the refugee crisis… an article… scathingly mocked the 'idiocy' of the 'gormless Twitter generation' for showing compassion to in-comers, many of whom… were 'intent on

trying to murder us', to 'insist [that women do not] leave the house unless [they are] wearing a full burka', and to ban alcohol and pork.

The Daily Mail stoked a xenophobic English nationalism concerned about the Islamification of the UK via migration, and the supposed impact upon British cultural norms. Islamophobic narratives later found resonance in the Leave campaign's rhetoric in terms of the apparent 'dangers' of Turkish membership of the EU. The Leave campaign implied that British citizens were somehow in danger of a predominantly Muslim nation benefitting from freedom of movement. It also implied that Turkey—a transit country for refugees from Syria, Iraq and Afghanistan— would enable a higher flow of Muslim migrants into Europe and the UK. The Leave campaign's rhetoric also fed into public anxieties about African migrants from countries of origin with high proportions of Muslim citizens, including Nigeria, Somalia and Kenya. Abbas (2020: 498) explains that 'at the heart of much of Brexit lies the painful truth of xenophobia, anti-immigration hostility and, in particular, an emphasis on Muslim groups, whether existing or new, as confirming various threats to society'. An Islamophobic form of English nationalism that envisaged the 'nation' as somehow being under threat from an 'alien' Muslim influence gained traction within the 2016 referendum campaign.

The efforts of the Remain campaign—including then Home Secretary Theresa May—to instead emphasise the benefits of EU cross-border co-operation on migration and counter-terrorism failed to alter this trajectory. May warned about loss of EU-wide co-operation in terms of the European Arrest Warrant (EAW) and the Passenger Named Records Database (PNRD) (Wither, 2017). She challenged Leave narratives that freedom of movement left Britain vulnerable to security challenges in relation to 'fragile states':

> Now I know some people say the EU does not make us more secure because it does not allow us to control our border.... [but the] fact that we are not part of Schengen - the group of countries without border checks - means we have avoided the worst of the migration crisis that has hit continental Europe over the last year.

Even more ambitiously, May attempted to counter the Leave campaign's imperial romanticism. She instead made a case for 'maximising sovereignty' in an interdependent world, drawing historical parallels to the British Empire (and other imperial entities):

> the Roman Empire, Imperial China, the Ottomans, the British Empire, the Soviet Union, modern-day America, were never able to have everything their own way. At different points, military rivals, economic crises, diplomatic manoeuvring, competing philosophies and emerging technologies all played their part in inflicting defeats and hardships, and necessitated compromises even for states as powerful as these. (ibid.)

Nevertheless, the Leave campaign successfully overrode such Remain messaging about the necessity of EU collective action. The earlier securitisation of migration instead enabled the Leave campaign to capitalise upon racialised fears (Abbas, 2020: 498; Bhambra, 2017: 92). As the next section argues, this xenophobic fear not only underscored the success of the Leave campaign, but now influences UK elites' post-referendum approach to perceived 'security interests' in Africa.

BRITISH SECURITY INTERESTS IN AFRICA SINCE THE REFERENDUM

UK elites since the 2016 referendum have continued to make political capital from populist appeals to limiting migration and to enhancing Global Britains' border security. The securitisation of migration continues unabated (cf. Browning, 2019). Prime Minister Theresa May set the tone for this ongoing securitisation rhetoric as she opted for a 'Hard Brexit'. Leaving the single market, May assured the UK public, would mean that the UK would no longer be subject to freedom of movement. Moreover, in terms of securitised rhetoric, in November 2018, May's government published *EU Exit: Taking Back Control of Our Borders While Protecting Our Economy, Security and Union*, which promised to tackle 'illegal migration':

> managing illegal migration is a global challenge facilitated by organised crime and exploiting vulnerable migrants. So we will continue joint efforts to tackle this issue, ensuring no new incentives are created for people to make dangerous journeys to Europe, while providing support to the most vulnerable migrants. (UK Government, 2018a)

Interestingly, however, May refused to enact a points-based system for migration, as had been touted by Leave campaigners. This owed to her time in the Home Office where she had decided that such systems were open to manipulation (Heffer, 2019).

In the drive against migration, May focused upon security partnerships with, and aid delivery to, African countries deemed to be 'sending countries'. Notably, she announced a UK security partnership with Nigeria in 2018. The deal offered military training as well as assistance in 'countering terrorist propaganda' vis-à-vis Boko Haram (UK Government, 2018b). This consolidated military co-operation between the UK and Nigeria, with 350 British soldiers already being present in the country as of 2017, training up to 6,000 Nigerian troops (CAAT, 2020). May presented the partnership as a 'win-win', stating that 'we are determined to work side by side with Nigeria to help them fight terrorism, reduce conflict and lay the foundations for the future stability and prosperity that will benefit us all' (UK Government, 2018b). May's attempts to counter radical Islamist groups and to limit conflict-driven migration also included £13 million for education of up to 100,000 children within the conflict zone (Sabbagh, 2018). This aid delivery built upon existing DfID initiatives in the north-east of Nigeria to stem conflict. However, as Lazell and Petrikova (2021) explain, UK initiatives have been largely ineffectual. Often they have done more to override the Nigerian federal government's jurisdiction within the conflict zone (ibid.).

The UK-Nigeria security partnership has continued during the premierships of May's successors. In February 2022, the two states issued a joint communique expressing the need for continued co-operation (UK Government, 2022a). The communique highlighted British pledges to support civilian policing within Nigeria, especially in terms of post-conflict zones (ibid.). The UK has also continued to provide arms to the Nigerian state, with British arm sales totalling £43 million since 2015–2020 (CATT, 2020). This has included £19 million in relation to military vehicles and £1 million for small arms. It has also included 'body armour, military helmets and weapon sights' to be used in relation to 'law enforcement' (ibid.). However, this has been highly controversial. Namely, there are grave concerns that the UK empowered the Special Anti-Robbery Squad (SARS), whose alleged human rights abuses—including allegations of rape and murder—provoked widespread protests within Nigeria (Iroanusi, 2020). The UK's Minister for Africa belatedly admitted in 2020 that 'British officials had trained officers from the now-disbanded

Special Anti-Robbery Squad (SARS) between 2016 and 2020—having initially denied any ties' (Forest, 2020). In response, Amnesty International stated that 'it's alarming that UK government funds have apparently been used to train and equip the notorious SARS police unit that for years has been operating with systematic torture' (ibid.).

Moreover, human rights abuses allegedly committed by Nigerian police had long been known to UK authorities. Reuters in 2017 had documented Nigerian civilian concerns regarding SARS (Achirga, 2017). In 2014, Amnesty International (2014) had also published a lengthy report cataloguing the alleged abuses committed by Nigerian military and police personnel. Nevertheless, May's security partnership went ahead and has continued well into the Johnson-Truss-Sunak premierships. As noted, this has been justified by UK governments in terms of support for anti-terror operations against Boko Haram. However, Amnesty International (2017) has also documented the close historical connections between the Nigerian security apparatus and British oil interests, namely in terms of allegations relating to the operations of Anglo-Dutch firm, Shell. Amnesty International (2017) have accused Shell of complicity in historical human rights abuses including rape and torture allegedly committed by Nigerian security forces against civilians within the oil-rich Oganiland region (ibid.).

Shell has also been accused of funding armed militants to 'help protect its oil infrastructure' (Brock, 2011). For instance, Shell in 2010 allegedly transferred over USD $159,000 to militants to enhance its own security (ibid.). In this context, the UK's provision of arms to the Nigerian military and police must be understood not only in terms of British concerns about mass migration and terror groups emanating from conflict zones. It must also be assessed in terms of the historical presence of UK energy operators and their apparent connection to Nigerian security services. The UK government's desire for 'energy security', and the needs of British firms such as Shell to operate without disruption, are tied to the effectiveness of the Nigerian security apparatus to put down dissent. The security needs of UK energy operators have also opened up lucrative opportunities for British PMCs. UK firm, G4S, for instance, has operated in Nigeria to provide security to energy extractors, amid allegations of labour rights abuses (Hopkins, 2023). In this context, Global Britain's recent launch of a 'critical minerals strategy' is particularly worrying, especially with the historical militarisation of British firms' mineral extraction in African countries, as documented by the London Mining Network (2020).

The UK's post-referendum assistance to Nigeria's security services also has parallels in terms of Somalia. As noted, Prime Minister Cameron had placed a special emphasis on military support in the fight against Al Shabaab. This has continued in the Global Britain era, particularly in the context of the 2021 publication of *Global Britain in a Competitive Age: The Integrated Review of Security, Defence, Development and Foreign Policy* by the Boris Johnson government (UK Government, 2021). In a survey of British support to 'state-building' in Somalia, Jones (2023: 13) notes that assistance is now clothed in a Global Britain rhetoric in which the UK seeks to demonstrate its continued influence on the global stage. He explains that British efforts are understood in terms of benefits for the UK's security:

> the 2021 Integrated Review reflected similar themes to those shared across the UK Government Strategy – Somalia (including Somaliland) (2014–17), UK Somalia Strategy (2017–22), and an unpublished country action plan. In each case, security and development programming was nested within a wider state-building approach designed to "reduce the threat ... posed to UK national interests by building a more stable, peaceful, and prosperous Somalia" (ibid.)

Jones (2023: 42) also notes that the UK's state-building project in Somalia has parallels to Afghanistan. Namely, that the presence of UK support in the country has distorted local political bargaining and has therein jeopardised the long-term stability of the country, contrary to ostensible UK security objectives (ibid.).

Furthermore, the UK government in the Global Britain period has placed emphasis on Kenya as a regional base for countering apparent security threats emanating from Somalia and South Sudan. The 2021 Integrated Review highlighted the importance of Kenya, while the British army website emphasises the importance of UK-Kenyan military co-operation and training exercises (British Army, 2023; UK Government, 2021: 63). The British Army (2023) explains the role of the British Army Training Unit Kenya (BATUK) within the UK's security mission:

> BATUK is a permanent training support unit based mainly in Nanyuki, 200 km north of Nairobi, but with a small element in Nairobi. BATUK provides demanding training to exercising units preparing to deploy on operations or assume high-readiness tasks. BATUK consists of around

100 permanent staff and reinforcing short tour cohort of another 280 personnel.

The UK has similarly provided support to the Kenyan police force in the post-referendum period. With parallels to Nigeria, however, such support is highly problematic given allegations of human rights abuses committed by Kenyan police personnel. Human Rights Watch (2014) explains that Kenya's Anti-Terrorism Police Unit (ATPU) stands accused of 'a series of extrajudicial killings and enforced disappearances... [and] arbitrary arrests and mistreatment of terrorism suspects' (UK Government, 2022b). In 2016, the NGO detailed that there had been at least 34 forcible disappearances related to Kenyan counter-terrorism operations (Human Rights Watch, 2016). Despite these serious allegations, the UK government has continued to provide financial support to Kenyan antiterrorism policing. UK officials announced in 2022 that Kenyan shillings (KhS) 81 million had been made available for an 'ATPU Coast Regional Headquarters and Mombasa Police Station' (equivalent to approximately £444,000) (UK Government, 2022b).

This financing was soon followed by a 2023 announcement in which the UK Government (2023a) lauded a new UK-Kenya security compact in which the UK would provide £10 million a year over a three-year period for Kenya's counter-terrorism efforts, as well as broader policing support for 'community security, law enforcement and criminal justice' (ibid.). This builds upon previous compacts (and past financing arrangements) agreed in 2018 and 2021 between the two countries, as well as the 2020 Kenya-UK Strategic Partnership (Maina, 2023). There are fears therefore that the UK is financing, and enabling, a Kenyan police service that stands accused of serious human rights abuses, including alleged rapes and sexual violence. Note, for example, allegations of rape made against the regular Kenyan police by refugees in Nairobi, documented by Human Rights Watch (2013). As well as allegations of rape by Kenyan police officers during the 2017 presidential election won by Uhuru Kenyatta (Fick, 2017).

In terms of gender-based violence, there are also serious concerns surrounding the alleged behaviour of members of the UK army towards women and girls in Kenya (Amnesty International, 2021). Allegations of rape and sexual violence have arisen despite the UK government's commitment since 2005 to the UN Women, Peace and Security (WPS) agenda (Achilleos-Sarll, 2023; Wright et al., 2023).

Since the 2016 referendum, the May government had especially highlighted the UK's commitment to WPS by launching the UK National Action Plan on Women, Peace and Security, 2018–2022 (UK Government, 2018c). Under Prime Minister Rishi Sunak, the UK has since published an updated plan for 2023–2027 (UK Government, 2023c). The Sunak government's document includes UK commitments to eradicating 'gender based violence... supporting survivors to cope, recover, and seek justice' (ibid.: 3). Yet in the context of the permanent UK military training facility in Kenya, Amnesty International (2003) stated that it was:

> gravely concerned about serious allegations that members of the United Kingdom (UK) Army, posted to Kenya for training, raped hundreds of Kenyan women. To date about 650 rape allegations have been made…- More than half of the cases involve allegations of gang rape.

As of August 2023, Kenya's parliamentary defence committee has launched an enquiry into such allegations (Kamau, 2023). One murder victim—allegedly killed by a British soldier—whose maccabre death led to public outcry was Agnes Wanjiru, a hairdresser, who died aged 21 years old (Norris & Overton, 2022). The British newspaper, *The Guardian*, reports that she had been partying with British soldiers at the Lions Court Hotel in Nanyuki, where the UK has the BATUK garrison. The newspaper notes allegations that a 'British solider had confessed to killing Wanjiru and showed comrades where he had dumped her body in a septic tank behind the hotel' (Hall, 2021).

These allegations against British military personnel are compounded by serious concerns about the behaviour of British PMCs in Kenya. In 2020, security guards employed by UK firm G4S were accused of attacking a LGBT+ refugee as he sought help from the UN High Commissioner for Refugees (UNHCR) office in Nairobi, which they were guarding (Cakaric & Skrinjar, 2022). The refugee in question 'later, hanged himself on a nearby tree' (ibid.). Following this event, UNHCR Kenya stated that it was 'profoundly shocked and saddened by the tragic death and apparent suicide of a refugee today in Nairobi' (ibid.). In 2017, Kenyan media reported another concerning incident involving this UK PMC within Kenya. Namely that a Labour Relations Court had ordered the firm to pay a former employee 35 million Kenyan shillings (approximately £191,000) 'for wrongful dismissal after she refused her boss' sexual advances' (Kubwa, 2017). Whether the UK's pursuit of its perceived security interests and the commercial profitability of UK PMCs are compatible with the wellbeing of Kenyan citizens is highly contestable.

Moreover, UK elites as part of a Global Britain project have sought to provide support to security personnel within North African transit countries to counter migration. Notably, the UK has stepped up support to Tunisian and Algerian security services in terms of co-operation with the UK's National Crime Agency (NCA) (Dathan, 2023). The then British immigration minister, Robert Jenrick, undertook a visit to both countries in May 2023 where he promised that this security co-operation would help fulfil Prime Minister Sunak's populist 'stop the small boats' pledge (ibid.). The UK government has also provided support to Libyan authorities. Nevertheless, there are serious concerns about UK support to these North African states' security services. In Tunisia, UK support is being given in the context of the Tunisia President's populist articulation of a 'replacement theory' that has heightened local attacks against black Africans (Bresillon, 2023). UK support is also being given despite the recent forcible deportation of hundreds of refugees from Tunisia to the Libyan border (ibid.). Meanwhile, in terms of UK support to Libya, Ferstman (2020: 477) notes that UK and EU support to detention centres and to the Libyan coast guard has potentially severe ramifications in terms of enabling abuses of refugees. The UK's support for voluntary return schemes in which refugees are sent to Libyan detention centres is equally problematic on human rights grounds (ibid.). Regardless, the Sunak government is optimistic that such support—in combination with its Rwandan deportation plan discussed in Chapter 4—will mitigate migration (Dathan, 2023). Moreover, the Conservative Party appears to hope that it will gain political capital by satiating an xenophobic English nationalism that 'others' refugees, and which has roots in Blair's securitisation rhetoric post-9/11 (Abrahamsen, 2004).

Since Russia's 2022 illegal invasion of Ukraine, meanwhile, UK elites have highlighted the security risks posed by President Vladimir Putin and the Wagner group PMC to human rights in African countries, as well as to the security of the UK. By extending its sphere of influence, Russia and its proxy groups threaten to heighten instability in the continent. In fact, there are fears that Russian authorities may be seeking to deliberately exacerbate migration flows as part of its aggression towards Europe (Tony Blair Institute for Global Change, 2023). In this context, the UK government—and a recent British parliamentary report issued by the Foreign Affairs Committee—have convincingly pointed to alleged atrocities committed by Russian-affiliated mercenaries (UK Government, 2023d: UK Parliament, 2023). They have also rightly pointed to how such groups serve Russia's commercial interests in terms of access to lucrative mineral and energy supplies (UK Parliament, 2023). What is omitted from these UK government and parliamentary sources, however, are the unfortunate parallels between the behaviour of Russian PMCs in African countries and that of UK PMCs. Both Russia and 'Global Britain' appear to behave as predatory forces in Africa via mercenary proxies. And while Russia may utilise anti-Western rhetoric—as opposed to the UK's rhetoric of democratisation—to appeal to African officials, nevertheless, both states exacerbate ill-being and instability by undermining the sovereignty of African countries. Russia and the UK both divorce African governments and security services from the wellbeing of their own citizenries through the corrupting influence of 'aid' for ethically dubious security initiatives.

British Security Interventions and Neo-colonialism in Africa

The UK's pursuit of its perceived security interests in Africa can be usefully assessed in terms of neo-colonialism and global coloniality (Ndlovu-Gatsheni, 2015; Nkrumah, 1965). Nkrumah warned that foreign powers would seek to wield influence over African states that had recently won their juridical independence through military means. Nkrumah foresaw that external powers would seek to maintain military facilities in Africa, as is the case within the UK-Kenya strategic partnership. He foresaw foreign meddling within internal conflicts. Nkrumah had witnessed the downfall of his friend President Patrice Lumumba in the Democratic Republic of the Congo (DRC). Lumumba had sought to pursue an independent foreign policy in the Cold War and had been brought down by rebels in the mineral-rich Katanga province allied to Belgian corporate interests (Nkrumah cited in Obeng, 1979: 63). Nkrumah therefore warned that one of the tools of neo-colonialism was foreign exercise of military intervention and coercion (ibid.). External powers would denude the sovereignty of African states that attempted to exert genuine policy autonomy by installing 'puppet' governments or ensuring that internal conflicts gave local access to lucrative energy and raw material supplies (ibid.).

Nkrumah's warnings appear especially prescient in the context of the UK's tumultuous relationship with Libya. Under Blair, the UK had sought access to Libya's oil wealth through 'soft power' diplomacy, including the sale of arms to the Gaddafi state (Honeyman, 2017). This was accompanied by financial assistance from other EU members, notably Italy in terms of its 2008 migration deal with Gaddafi (Chothia, 2018). David Cameron's volte-face in 2011 can be understood through the lens of neo-colonialism (Dawson, 2022: 369). Namely, that the UK along with France and other allies engaged in a regime change strategy that facilitated longer-term access to energy wealth within Libya's borders. By assisting the rebels—and by enabling the murder of Gaddafi—Western forces augured in a period of lawlessness within Libya's borders. This is a period that has been highly conducive to the exploration and extraction of Libyan oil wealth by foreign companies. Note, for instance, the resumption of exploration by UK firm, BP, as well as the apparent imminent return of Anglo-Dutch firm, Shell (AFP, 2023; Bousso, 2021; Ghaddar & Bousso, 2018). UK PMCs have also profited from the instability within Libya, providing security for oil companies operating within what many commentators now refer to as a 'failed state' (see, for instance, Colombo & Varvelli, 2020). While profitable for the UK, this situation has led to a vast deterioration in the human rights situation (even compared to the time of the Gaddafi state), especially in terms of the abuse and enslavement of black African migrants. The UN Human Rights Council's (2023) Independent Fact-Finding Mission on Libya reported in March 2023 that:

> Allegations of violations and abuses have rightly warranted the attention of the Human Rights Council. Indeed, the Mission has found reasonable grounds to believe that since 2016 crimes against humanity have been committed against Libyans and migrants throughout Libya in the context of deprivation of liberty. Notably, the Mission documented and made findings on numerous cases of, inter alia, arbitrary detention, murder, torture, rape, enslavement and enforced disappearance, confirming their widespread practice in Libya.

The abuse of Libyans and migrants within the post-intervention Libyan state coincides with the warnings of Nkrumah (1965) about neo-colonialism. Namely that neo-colonialism means misery for civilians since it brings 'power without responsibility', as local elites pay more attention to the needs of their foreign benefactors, than to their own citizenries.

Moreover, the British state's funding of police forces within African countries, especially in terms of Kenya and Nigeria, can also be assessed through the lens of neo-colonialism. Discursively justified in terms of the fight against radical Islamist groups—as well as the desire to stem migration—the UK government has provided financial assistance and training to security personnel (Forest, 2020; UK Government, 2022b). However, the foreign funding of police services is inherently problematic in terms of divorcing the state apparatus from accountability to its own citizens. Rather than owing their operations to taxation revenues derived from the local population, certain 'anti-terror' police units are in large part funded by an external benefactor and act with a much greater degree of impunity than might otherwise be the case. Without UK funding and training, the capacity of units such as ATPU and SARS to inflict alleged human rights abuses would have likely been much reduced. Social tension and domestic protest would also have been reduced if the UK had desisted from financing police services accused of gross violations of human rights, including rape and sexual violence (Fick, 2017; Human Rights Watch, 2013; Iroanusi, 2020). The UK's financing of an ATPU headquarters in Mombasa is but one recent example of how African state sovereignty is denuded by the interference of the Global Britain (UK Government, 2022b). UK funding of ATPU enables the counter-terrorism unit to apparently act with a degree of impunity towards its own citizens—and migrants—within Kenya's borders. Nkrumah (1965) warned that African officials should beware foreign aid and finance since this would reduce their policy autonomy and make the state apparatus beholden to external interests. This appears to be the case in terms of the UK's financing of such police services (and indeed its support for military units too).

Furthermore, the presence of a permanent UK military training facility in Kenya aligns to Nkrumah's fears about neo-colonial influence within Africa. Clearly the presence of a foreign military facility is not compatible with Kenya's exercise of full sovereignty, making the country vulnerable to political and military interference from its former colonial power (see Kasau, 2023 for detailed historical coverage of Kenyan nationalist opposition to British military presence). Human rights abuses against women and girls allegedly committed by British troops would, if proven, also confirm Nkrumah's fears about the divorce between the 'development' rhetoric espoused by foreign benefactors and the material consequences of their interventions in Africa (Amnesty International, 2021). In this situation, the UK's benevolent language surrounding the UN's WPS agenda—including the UK's ostensible commitment to end gender-based violence—would appear wholly incompatible with the alleged actions of British forces within Kenya (cf. Wright et al., 2023). The murder of a 21-year-old hairdresser is but only one example of these alleged abuses (Norris & Overton, 2022).

Moreover, these allegations are compounded by concerns raised in several African countries about the behaviour of UK PMCs (whose staff often have army backgrounds). The death of a LGBT+ refugee near the UNHCR headquarters in Nairobi after apparently being beaten by security guards from a UK PMC is, again, only one example of alleged abuses (Cakaric & Skrinjar, 2022). British PMC's apparent arming of both sides in Sierra Leone's civil war during the Blair period also underscores the dangers of foreign mercenary activities in Africa. As in fact does Blair's apparent use of the 2000 intervention in Sierra Leone to distract from the domestic 'arms to Africa' scandal, to test his Chicago Doctrine, and to enhance the UK's international standing. The operation of British PMCs in protecting British energy and mining interests in countries including Libya and Nigeria further underscores how extraction in Africa has become divorced from the needs of local citizens. PMCs—alongside local police often funded by external actors—serve as a safeguard against possible civil society dissent that could interrupt profitable extraction. Nkrumah's warnings about the negative consequences of foreign interference in the internal affairs of African states for African citizenries appear to be borne out by the ethically dubious role of British PMCs.

Finally, Ndlovu-Gatsheni's (2013, 2014, 2015) critique of global coloniality offers further insights into the behaviour of UK actors. His articulation of the concept of the 'coloniality of knowledge' helps us to consider how Euro-American actors try to exert epistemological hegemony and control over African counterparts (Ndlovu-Gatsheni, 2014: 199). In the case of the UK's pursuit of perceived security interests in Africa, it helps us to consider how UK elites from Blair to Sunak have securitised the continent through strategic discourse. Moreover, the securitisation of migration—via language surrounding terrorism, drugs and sexual assaults—demonstrates how Euro-American actors construct forms of knowledge that disempower African actors (cf. Browning, 2019: 234; Grinan-Moutinho, 2022). By 'othering' African migrants as a source of risk, Euro-American actors legitimise interventions in the African continent, including their interference with internal policing systems, on the grounds of limiting conflict-driven migration. Furthermore, the concept of the 'coloniality of being' is helpful in the assessment of the UK's securitisation of African citizenries (Ndlovu-Gatsheni, 2013: 10). UK elites have engaged in a racialised 'othering' of African citizenries as potential sources of 'threat' to British citizens (Abbas, 2020: 498; Bhambra, 2017: 92). These British discourses draw upon colonial-era racial hierarchies and imaginaries, which cast predominantly black African citizenries as somehow threatening. The use of the 'Breaking Point' poster by Farage in the 2016 referendum did not arise in a vacuum. His campaign gained traction on the fertile ground laid since the 'war on terror' amid New Labour's racialised securitisation of the African continent (Abrahamsen, 2004).

Conclusion

UK elites have securitised the African continent, especially in the aftermath of 9/11 and the launch of the US-led 'global war on terror'. New Labour depicted the African continent as a 'scar upon the conscience of the world' that required debt relief and 'development' aid monies. However, it also utilised rhetoric that depicted African countries—and citizenries—as a source of risk in relation to radical Islamist groups in the post-9/11 environment. Migration from 'fragile states' especially became viewed in DfID and FCO policy documents as a risk to the UK. New Labour's inculcation of fear within the British public towards an alien 'other'—continued under Cameron—offered fertile ground to the Leave Campaign in 2016. Namely, proponents of Brexit were able to draw upon pre-existing UK public anxieties about migration from the 'Global South' and its presumed impact in terms of terrorism and cultural stability. The Leave campaign's targeting of Turkey's candidacy for EU membership, combined to sharp anti-migration rhetoric, drew upon the legacy of the securitised discourse of New Labour, and of David Cameron himself, in terms of their governments' approach to 'developing countries' in Africa, and beyond.

Not only did the UK's securitised approach to Africa open up opportunities for the Leave campaign, but it has led to serious consequences for African citizenries. The UK's collective destruction of the Gaddafi state alongside NATO partners has led to social deterioration and worsening human rights within Libya. The recent report from the UN Human Rights Council's (2023) Independent Fact-Finding Mission in Libya documents a litany of abuses committed in the post-intervention Libyan state. This situation of despair for ordinary Libyan citizens is despite that UK energy firms and PMCs are making substantial profits from the extraction of oil and gas reserves. Moreover, the UK's financing and training of police units within countries such as Kenya and Nigeria has brought about a situation in which counter-terrorism units appear to have gone 'rogue'. Namely that they have become divorced from respect for their own citizenries (and for migrants within their territories). They have thus allegedly engaged in gross violations of human rights, including sexual violence and rape. Paradoxically, these violations appear to occur despite the UK's ostensible commitments to the UN WPS agenda. Furthermore, they are mirrored in terms of the allegations levied against UK armed forces present within Kenya.

UK elites' post-referendum focus upon limiting inward migration also bodes ill for the future trajectory of UK security approaches vis-à-vis the African continent. There appears to be very little political space for an alternative to the securitised approach pursued by UK politicians. There in fact appears to now be a consensus between the current Conservative government and the New Labour opposition under Sir Keir Starmer about the possible 'threats' posed by predominantly non-white refugees to the UK. The two main UK political parties continue to engage in populist appeals against non-white migration, compared to their welcoming of migrants from predominantly white Ukraine. These UK parties' racialised 'othering' of African citizenries bodes ill for Global Britain's respect for human rights within African country contexts. Indeed, UK officials demonstrate an apparent lack of concern for the consequences of the UK's securitised interventions for the wellbeing of African citizenries. Note for example, continued financing of Kenya's ATPU unit despite well-known allegations of human rights abuses. As Nkrumah predicted, neo-colonial relations with external powers, such as the UK, are not conducive to social prosperity or human rights.

Bibliography

Abbas, T. (2020). Islamophobia as Racialised Biopolitics in the United Kingdom. *Philosophy and Social Criticism, 46*(5), 497–511.

Abrahamsen, R. (2004). A Breeding Ground for Terrorists? Africa & Britain's "War on terrorism." *Review of African Political Economy, 31*(102), 677–684.

Achilleos-Sarll, C. (2023). The (Dis)Appearance of Race in the United Kingdom's Institutionalization and Implementation of the Women, Peace and Security Agenda. *International Studies Quarterly, 67*(1), 1–12.

Achirga, A. (2017, December 6). *Nigerian Police Official Defends Unit Against Brutality Accusations*. Reuters. https://www.reuters.com/article/uk-nigeria-police-sars-idUKKBN1E028C. Accessed 27 July 2023.

AFP. (2023, August 4). *BP, Sonatrach and ENI Resume Operations in Libya*. AFP. https://www.theafricareport.com/317982/bp-sonatrach-and-eni-resume-operations-in-libya/. Accessed 28 August 2023.

Amnesty International. (2003). *United Kingdom—Decades of Impunity: Serious Allegations of Rape of Kenyan Women by UK Army Personnel*. Amnesty International. https://www.amnesty.org/en/documents/eur45/014/2003/en/. Accessed 10th June 2023.

Amnesty International. (2006). *The Call for Tough Arms Control: Voices from Sierra Leone*. Amnesty International.

Amnesty International. (2014). *Welcome to Hellfire: Torture and Other Ill Treatment in Nigeria*. Amnesty International.

Amnesty International. (2017). *Investigate Shell for Complicity in Murder, Rape and Torture*. https://www.amnesty.org/en/latest/press-release/2017/11/investigate-shell-for-complicity-in-murder-rape-and-torture/. Accessed 10th June 2023.

AOAV. (2023). *UK Arms Exports to Libya (2012–2022)*. AOAV.

Apuuli, K. (2019). The UK and Africa Relations: Construction of the African Union's Peace and Security Structures. In D. Beswick, J. Fisher, & S. Hurt (Eds.), *Britain and Africa in the Twenty-First Century: Between Ambition and Pragmatism* (pp. 54–72). Manchester University Press.

Bello, V. (2022). 'The Spiralling of the Securitisation of Migration in the EU: From the Management of a 'Crisis' to a Governance of Human Mobility? *Journal of Ethnic and Migration Studies, 48*(6), 1327–1344.

Bhambra, G. (2017). Locating Brexit in the Pragmatics of Race, Citizenship and Empire. In W. Outhwaite (Ed.), *Brexit: Sociological Responses* (pp. 91–100). Anthem Press.

Bousso, R. (2021, November 30). *Shell Eyes Return to Libya with Oil, Gas, Solar Investments*. Reuters. https://www.reuters.com/markets/commodities/exclusive-shell-eyes-return-libya-with-oil-gas-solar-investments-2021-11-30/. Accessed 27 July 2023.

Bresillon, T. (2023, August 7). *Sub-Saharans Are No Longer Welcome in Tunisia*. Le Monde Diplomatique. https://mondediplo.com/2023/05/04tunisia. Accessed 26 August 2023.

British Army. (2023). *Deployments Africa—The British Army in Africa*. British Army. https://www.army.mod.uk/deployments/africa/. Accessed 27 August 2023.

Brock, J. (2011, October 3). *Shell Fuelled Human Rights Abuses in Nigeria—NGO*. Reuters. https://www.reuters.com/article/nigeria-shell-idUSL5E7L33Q720111003. Accessed 27 July 2023.

Browning, C. (2019). Brexit Populism and Fantasies of Fulfilment. *Cambridge Review of International Affairs, 32*(3), 222–244.

Burkhalter, H. (1994, August 9). *US Might Have Avoided Rwandan Tragedy*. The Christian Science Monitor. https://www.csmonitor.com/1994/0809/09191.html. Accessed 26 July 2023.

CAAT. (2000). *UK in Sierra Leone Mercenary Scandal*. CATT. https://caat.org.uk/news/2000-09-07-2/. Accessed 26 July 2023.

CAAT (2020) *Country Profiles—Nigeria*. CATT. https://caat.org.uk/data/countries/nigeria/. Accessed 26 July 2023.

Cakaric and Skrinjar. (2022, July 15). The Human Cost on G4S' Watch. *Ostro*. https://www.ostro.si/en/stories/the-human-cost-of-g4s-watch. Accessed 27 August 2023.

Colombo, M., & Varvelli, A. (2020). Libya: A Failed State in the Middle of the Mediterranean. In *IED Mediterranean Yearbook 2020*. European Institute of the Mediterranean.

Canadian Government. (2018). *International Military Assistance and Training Team (IMATT)*. Canadian Government. https://www.canada.ca/en/department-national-defence/services/military-history/history-heritage/past-operations/africa/sculpture.html. Accessed 25 August 2023.

Chothia, F. (2018, July 7). *How Libya Holds the Key to Solving Europe's Migration Crisis*. BBC News . https://www.bbc.com/news/world-africa-44709974. Accessed 27 July 2023.

Dathan, M. (2023, May 29). British Police Try to Stop Migrants Leaving Africa. *The Times*. https://www.thetimes.co.uk/article/british-police-try-to-stop-migrants-leaving-africa-dh0mk7p9p. Accessed 25 July 2023.

Davidson, J. (2013). France, Britain and the Intervention in Libya: An Integrated Analysis. *Cambridge Review of International Affairs, 26*(2), 310–329.

Dawson, G. (2022). "No Future for Libya with Gaddafi": Classical Realism, Status and Revenge in the UK Intervention in Libya. *Cambridge Review of International Affairs, 35*(3), 357–374.

Donati, R. (2011, May 12). *Libyan Rebels Seal New Deal with Vitol: Traders*. Reuters. https://www.reuters.com/article/us-libya-vitol-idUSTRE74B5KF20110512. Accessed 28 July 2023.

Dorman, A. (2009). *Blair's Successful War: British Military Intervention in Sierra Leone*. Routledge.

Enayaba, I. N. (2021). United Kingdom's Counterterrorism and Counterinsurgency Policy in Africa. In U. A. Tar (Ed.), *Routledge Handbook of Counterterrorism and Counterinsurgency in Africa* (pp. 246–264). Routledge.

Ero, C. (2001). A Critical Assessment of Britain's Africa Policy. *Conflict, Security and Development, 1*(2), 51–71.

Ferstman, C. (2020). Human Rights Due Diligence Policies Applied to Extraterritorial Cooperation to Prevent "Irregular" Migration: European Union and United Kingdom Support to Libya. *German Law Journal, 21*(3), 459–486.

Fick, M. (2017, December 14). *Kenyan Police Assaulted and Raped Women During Election: Rights Group*. Reuters. https://www.reuters.com/article/us-kenya-police-idUSKBN1E818P. Accessed 27 August 2023

Fisher, J., & Anderson, D. (2015). Authoritarianism and the Securitisation of Development in Africa. *International Affairs, 91*(1), 131–151.

Forest, A. (2020, October 30). End SARS Protests: UK Government Admits It Did Train and Supply Equipment to Nigeria's "Brutal" Police Unit. *The Independent*. https://www.independent.co.uk/news/uk/politics/sars-nigeria-police-protests-uk-government-training-equipment-b1424447.html. Accessed 28 August 2023.

Ghaddar, A., & Bousso, R. (2018, October 8). *Eni to Acquire Half of BP's Libya Oil and Gas Assets*. Reuters. https://www.reuters.com/article/us-oil-libya-bp-eni-idUSKCN1MI1RP. Accessed 28 August 2023.

Gegout, C. (2018). *Why Europe Intervenes in Africa: Security Prestige and the Legacy of Colonialism*. Oxford University Press.

Gower, M., Butchard, P., & McKinney, C. J. (2022, December 20). *The UK-Rwanda Migration and Economic Development Partnership*. House of Commons Library Research Briefing. https://commonslibrary.parliament.uk/research-briefings/cbp-9568/. Accessed 29 May 2023.

Gray, H., & Franck, A. (2019). Refugees as/at Risk: The Gendered and Racialized Underpinnings of Securitization in British Media Narratives. *Security Dialogue, 50*(3), 275–291.

Grinan-Moutinho, H. (2022). *An Analysis of the Anti-Immigration Discourse During the Official 2016 Brexit Referendum Campaign*. Observatoire De La Societe Britannique, No, 29, online. https://journals.openedition.org/osb/5821. Accessed 23 July 2023.

Haines, S. (2016). "A World Full of Terror to the British Mind": The Blair Doctrine and British Defence Policy. In D. Brown (Ed.), *The Development of British Defence Policy: Blair, Brown and Beyond* (pp. 63–80). Routledge.

Hall, R. (2021, November 10). Family of Kenyan Woman Allegedly Murdered by UK Solider to Sue MOD. *The Guardian*. https://www.theguardian.com/uk-news/2021/nov/10/family-of-kenyan-woman-allegedly-murdered-by-uk-soldier-to-sue-mod-agnes-wanjiru. Accessed 10 September 2023.

Hansen, S., & Marsh, N. (2015). Normative Power and Organized Hypocrisy: European Union Member States' Arms Export to Libya. *European Security, 24*(2), 264–286.

Harris, R. (2001). Blair's "Ethical" Policy. *The National Interest, 63*, 25–36.

Heffer, G. (2019, October 16). *Theresa May Criticises Boris Johnson's "Points Based" Immigration Plan*. Sky News. https://news.sky.com/story/theresa-may-criticises-boris-johnsons-points-based-immigration-plan-11837108. Accessed 27 July 2023.

Honeyman, V. (2017). From Liberal Interventionism to Liberal Conservatism: The Short Road in Foreign Policy from Blair to Cameron. *British Politics, 12*(1), 42–62.

Hopkins, R. (2023, May 18). G4S Has a Problematic History Across Africa. *The Mail & Guardian*. https://mg.co.za/africa/2023-05-18-g4s-has-a-problematic-history-across-africa/. Accessed 27 June 2023.

Human Rights Watch. (2013, May 29). *You Are All Terrorists: Kenyan Police Abuse of Refugees in Nairobi*. Human Rights Watch. https://www.hrw.org/report/2013/05/29/you-are-all-terrorists/kenyan-police-abuse-refugees-nairobi. Accessed 27 August 2023.

Human Rights Watch. (2014, August 8). *Kenya: Killings, Disappearances by Anti-Terror Police*. Human Rights Watch. https://www.hrw.org/news/2014/08/18/kenya-killings-disappearances-anti-terror-police. Accessed 27 July 2023.

Human Rights Watch. (2016, July 20). *Deaths and Disappearances: Abuses in Counterterrorism Operations in Nairobi and in Northeastern Kenya*. Human Rights Watch. https://www.hrw.org/report/2016/07/21/deaths-and-disappearances/abuses-counterterrorism-operations-nairobi-and. Accessed 27 August 2023.

Iroanusi, Q. E. (2020, September 29). *Senate to Investigate Alleged Rape, Murder of Woman by SARS*. Premium Times. https://www.premiumtimesng.com/news/more-news/417512-senate-to-investigate-alleged-rape-murder-of-woman-by-sars.html. Accessed 27 August 2023.

Jakobsen, P. (2012). Reinterpreting Libya's WMD Turnaround—Bridging the Carrot-Coercion Divide. *Journal of Strategic Studies, 35*(4), 489–512.

Jones, M. (2023). *Mired in Mogadishu: An Appraisal of UK Engagement in Somalia* (RUSI Occasional Paper Policy Brief, June 2023). RUSI, London.

Kamau, J. (2023, July 4). *UK-Kenya Colonial War Games and Fresh Bid by Parliament to Dig Up Long Secretive History*. https://nation.africa/kenya/weekly-review/uk-kenya-colonial-war-games-and-fresh-bid-by-parliament-to-dig-up-long-secretive-history--4291538. Accessed 10th August 2023.

Kasau, J. (2023, July 4). UK-Kenya Colonial War Games and Fresh Bid by Parliament to Dig Up Long, Secretive History. *The Daily Nation.* https://nation.africa/kenya/weekly-review/uk-kenya-colonial-war-games-and-fresh-bid-by-parliament-to-dig-up-long-secretive-history--4291538. Accessed 27 August 2023.

Kubwa, C. (2017). Kenya: Court Orders G4S to Compensate Former Employee for Wrongful Dismissal After She Complained of Sexual Harassment at Workplace. *The Star (Kenya).* https://www.business-humanrights.org/en/latest-news/kenya-court-orders-g4s-to-compensate-former-employee-for-wrongful-dismissal-after-she-complained-of-sexual-harassment-at-workplace/. Accessed 27 August 2023.

Lazell, M., & Petrikova, I. (2021). UK Securitisation of Aid Projects in Africa: Review of Evidence from Kenya, South Sudan, Mali, and Senegal. *Development Policy Review, 40*(1), 1–42.

London Mining Network. (2020). *Martial Mining: Resisting Extractivism and War Together.* London Mining Network.

Maina, N. (2023, May 10). *Kenya, UK Sign Security Pact to Counter Transnational Organised Crimes.* The Informer. https://theinformer.co.ke/62886/kenya-uk-sign-security-pact-to-counter-transnational-organised-crimes/. Accessed 27 August 2023.

Marsden, C. (1999, May 14). *British Labour Government Accused of Helping Organise Counter-Coup in Sierra Leone.* World Socialist Web Site. https://www.wsws.org/en/articles/1998/05/sier-m14.html. Accessed 28 June 2023.

Mcalister, T. (2009, August 30). Secret Documents Uncover UK's Interest in Libyan Oil. *The Guardian.* https://www.theguardian.com/world/2009/aug/30/libya-oil-shell-megrahi?CMP=Share_AndroidApp_Other. Accessed 27 July 2023.

Ndlovu-Gatsheni, S. J. (2013). *Coloniality of Power in Post-Colonial Africa.* CODESRIA.

Ndlovu-Gatsheni, S. J. (2014). Global Coloniality and the Challenges of Creating African Futures. *Strategic Review for Southern Africa, 36*(2), 181–202.

Ndlovu-Gatsheni, S. J. (2015). *Empire, Global Coloniality and African Subjectivity.* Berghahn Books.

Nkrumah, K. (1965). *Neo-Colonialism: The Last Stage of Imperialism.* Panaf Press.

Norris, S., & Overton, I. (2022, November 28). *Ongoing Concerns of Sexual Violence in the British Military: A Review.* AOAV. https://aoav.org.uk/2022/ongoing-concerns-of-sexual-violence-in-the-british-military-a-review/. Accessed 27 August 2023.

Obeng, S. (1979). *Selected Speeches of Kwame Nkrumah,* (Vol. 1). Afram Publishers.

Oliver, M. (2004, March 25). Blair Meets Gadfy. *The Guardian.* https://www.theguardian.com/world/2004/mar/25/libya.politics. Accessed 26 July 2023.

Olutokunbo, A., Suandi, T., Cephas, O. R., & Abu-Samah, I. H. (2015). Bring Back Our Girls, Social Mobilization: Implications for Cross-Cultural Research. *Journal of Education and Practice, 6*(6), 64–75.

Porteous, T. (2005). British Government Policy in Sub-Saharan Africa under New Labour. *International Affairs, 81*(2), 281–297.

Pradella, L., & Rad, S. T. (2017). Libya and Europe: Imperialism, Crisis and Migration. *Third World Quarterly, 38*(11), 2411–2427.

Reuters. (2007, May 30). *Factbox: Britain's Military Mission in Sierra Leone.* Reuters. https://www.reuters.com/article/us-britain-africa-leone-idUSL3070034720070530. Accessed 26 July 2023.

Reuters. (2011, March 18). *UN Okays Military Action on Libya: Gaddafi Warns.* https://www.reuters.com/article/libya-idUSLDE72G0UF20110318/. Accessed 10th June 2023.

Sabbagh, D. (2018, August 29). Theresa May Signs Security Partnership with Nigeria's President. *The Guardian.* https://www.theguardian.com/politics/2018/aug/29/theresa-may-signs-security-partnership-nigeria-president-military-training-fight-boko-haram. Accessed 26 July 2023.

Sloboda, J., & Abbot, C. (2004). *The 'Blair Doctrine' and After: Five Years of Humanitarian Intervention.* Open Democracy.

Stavrianakis, A. (2016). Legitimising Liberal Militarism: Politics, Law and War in the Arms Trade Treaty. *Third World Quarterly, 37*(5), 840–865.

Stewart, H., & Mason, R. (2016, June 16). Nigel Farage's Anti-Migrant Poster Reported to Police. *The Guardian.* https://www.theguardian.com/politics/2016/jun/16/nigel-farage-defends-ukip-breaking-point-poster-queue-of-migrants. Accessed 23 July 2023.

Taylor, I. (2012). Spinderella on Safari: British Policies Toward Africa Under New Labour. *Global Governance, 18*(4), 449–460.

Tony Blair Institute for Global Change. (2023). *Security, Soft Power and Regime Support: Spheres of Russian Influence in Africa.* Tony Blair Institute for Global Change.

Tyler, P. E. (2004, September 16). Annan Says Iraq War Was "Illegal". *The New York Times.* https://www.nytimes.com/2004/09/16/international/annan-says-iraq-war-was-illegal.html. Accessed 26 July 2023.

UK Government. (2014). *Our Approach to the Threat Posed by Isil: Article by David Cameron.* UK Government. https://www.gov.uk/government/speeches/our-approach-to-the-threat-posed-by-isil-article-by-david-cameron. Accessed 27 July 2023.

UK Government. (2015). *PM Pledges UK Troops to Support Stability in Somalia and South Sudan.* UK Government.

UK Government. (2018a). *EU Exit: Taking Back Control of Our Borders While Protecting Our Economy, Security and Union*. UK Government.
UK Government. (2018b). *UK and Nigeria Step Up Cooperation to End Boko Haram Threat*. UK Government.
UK Government. (2018c). *UK National Action Plan on Women, Peace and Security, 2018 to 2022*. UK Government.
UK Government. (2021). *Global Britain in a Competitive Age: The Integrated Review of Security, Defence, Development and Foreign Policy*. UK Government.
UK Government. (2022a). *UK-Nigeria Security and Defence Partnership Inaugural Dialogue Communique*. UK Government.
UK Government. (2022b). *First UK Funded Anti-Terrorism Police Unit Headquarters Opened in Kenya*. UK Government.
UK Government. (2023a). *Security Minister Travels to Kenya to Agree New Partnership*. UK Government.
UK Government. (2023b). *UK Women, Peace and Security National Action Plan, 2023 to 2027*. UK Government.
UK Government. (2023c). *UK Sanctions Wagner Group Leaders and Front Companies Responsible for Violence and Instability Across Africa*. UK Government.
UK Government (2023d, July 26). *Guns for Gold: the Wagner Network Exposed*. https://committees.parliament.uk/committee/78/foreign-affairs-committee/news/196695/guns-for-gold-the-wagner-network-exposed/. Accessed 10th August 2023.
UK National Archives. (2010). *Doctrine of the International Community [24/4/1999]*. UK National Archives. https://webarchive.nationalarchives.gov.uk/ukgwa/+/www.number10.gov.uk/Page1297. Accessed 25 July 2023.
Parliament, U. K. (1999). *Select Committee on Foreign Affairs Second Report (1999)—Sierra Leone*. UK Parliament.
Parliament, U. K. (2023). *Guns for Gold: The Wagner Group Exposed: Seventh Report of Session 2022–23 of the Foreign Affairs Committee*. UK Parliament.
UN Human Rights Council. (2023). *Report of the Independent Fact-Finding Mission on Libya*. UN Human Rights Council.
Vellichor Risk. (2020, January 28). *"Working Harder" in Libya*. Facebook. https://www.facebook.com/VellichorRisk/. Accessed 28 August 2023.
Vellichor Risk. (2021, March 14). *UK Ambassador Hosts Business Breakfast*. Facebook. https://www.facebook.com/VellichorRisk/. Accessed 28 August 2023.
War on Want. (2016). *Mercenaries Unleashed: The Brave New World of Private Military and Security Companies*. War on Want.
Watt, N., & Norton-Taylor, R. (1999, February 11). Blair Challenged on Arms Supplies for African Rebels. *The Guardian*. https://www.theguardian.com/politics/1999/feb/11/politicalnews.foreignpolicy. Accessed 26 July 2023.

Wither, J. (2017). *A Secure Brexit? UK Security and Defence and the Decision to Leave the European Union*. Marshall Centre.

Wright, K., Haastrup, T., & Guerrina, R. (2023). *Domestication: A Critical Analysis of the 5th UK National Action Plan on Women, Peace and Security*. Newlines Institute.

Zack-Williams, T. (2016, August 4). *The Road to Iraq: Tony Blair's Intervention in Sierra Leone*. Review of African Political Economy Blog. https://roape.net/2016/08/04/road-iraq-tony-blairs-intervention-sierra-leone/. Accessed 26 July 2023.

Zenko, M. (2016, March 22). *The Big Lie About the Libyan War*. Foreign Policy. https://foreignpolicy.com/2016/03/22/libya-and-the-myth-of-humanitarian-intervention/. Accessed 27 July 2023.

CHAPTER 8

Contesting Global Britain: Considering African Agency

Introduction

UK elites' pursuit of a Global Britain project in the wake of the 2016 referendum has aimed at demonstrating the UK's continued relevance on the global stage. Politicians from Theresa May to Rishi Sunak have spoken of the need for the UK to engage African 'old friends' to assist 'development', to stem migration and to bring about 'win-win' prosperity (UK Government, 2017, 2022a; Worley, 2022). Building upon the legacies of Empire, UK elites seek to enhance their own ontological security by demonstrating Global Britain's ongoing influence within the African continent (cf Haastrup et al., 2021). They also aim to fulfil promises made to the UK electorate during the referendum, notably in terms of mitigating migration, and to bring about the improved Africa-UK partnership which many Brexiteers spoke of during the campaign to leave the EU (Leave, 2016; Namusoke, 2016; Vote Dathan, 2016).

As the previous chapters have illustrated, however, Global Britain's claims to be a genuine partner and benefactor for Africa countries is highly contestable. UK elites continue to express an imperial 'mission civilisatrice' in their paternalistic approach to 'development' in the continent (cf. Połońska-Kimunguyi & Kimunguyi, 2017: 327, 343). The Foreign, Commonwealth and Development Office (FCDO)—like the Department for International Development (DfID) which it subsumed—continues to talk of the ways in which UK aid, trade and investment can 'solve' the

© The Author(s), under exclusive license to Springer Nature Switzerland AG 2023
M. Langan, *Global Britain and Neo-colonialism in Africa*,
https://doi.org/10.1007/978-3-031-42482-3_8

problem of persistent poverty and inequality in African contexts (UK Government, 2021, 2022b). In doing so, British officials fail to recognise how in fact UK aid, trade, migration and security policies work to 'lock in' many African countries into a neo-colonial relationship with their former colonise (cf. Nunn & Price, 2004).

Moreover, they fail to account for how UK energy and mining firms, private military companies (PMCs) and the FCDO-owned British International Investment (BII) group create conditions of poverty and ill-being through exploitative practices in the continent (see for example, Cakaric & Skrinjar, 2022; RIAO-RDC et al., 2021; War on Want, 2016a). Instead, they construct a benevolent 'development' discourse that casts Global Britain as a fair-minded partner for mutual prosperity, which they contrast with the nefarious behaviours of rival powers amid a 'new scramble' for African resources (cf. Carmody, 2016). As the last chapter's focus on PMCs made clear, however, there are worrying parallels between the predatory behaviour of UK actors and their counterparts in Russia (and indeed China, for instance, in terms of creating local health hazards from extractive processes). It appears that Global Britain's policies are primarily geared towards extraction, profit and political leverage in African contexts, not towards supposed objectives related to democratisation, human rights or poverty reduction.

In this context, the final chapter now concludes the book by considering the scope for African agency to resist the Global Britain project. The first section recaps the imperial impulse of Brexit and the problematic nature of UK trade, aid, investment and security policies. It underscores how a regressive English nationalism and UK elites' ontological security drives forward problematic policy agendas in the African continent (cf. Calhoun, 2017; Wellings, 2021). The second section then considers material forms of power, and how African officials may utilise new initiatives such as the African Union's African Continental Free Trade Agreement (AfCFTA) to counter UK influence. Namely, in that context, to offer African countries an alternative to premature trade opening with the UK (and the EU). This would fulfil Nkrumah's vision of pan-African alternatives to free trade deals with former colonisers (cited in Obeng, 1979: 52). Moreover, the section assesses how African civil society organisation and African officials already campaign for material reparations from the British state in the aftermath of slavery and human rights abuses committed during the era of formal Empire (see, for example, Ackah, 2020; Bhambra, 2022; McKeown, 2021). Rather than accept British 'aid' with conditionalities attached (for example, the Rwandan government's acquiescence to the deportation scheme amid the externalisation of migration and cuts to Official Development Assistance), African actors already rightly demand untied reparations payments. The section also explores debates surrounding corporate crimes and the potential role therein of the Rome Statute and the International Criminal Court (ICC) (Lambridis, 2021).

The chapter then turns to ideational sources of African resistance to the Global Britain project. It considers opportunities for African academics, civil society and officialdom to invert the disempowering 'development' language of the UK and its key agencies, including the FCDO. It especially considers how African actors might fruitfully co-opt the 'fragile states' discourse to point to the weaknesses of the UK. While the 'fragile states' rhetoric of UK donors usually implies the need for external intervention to improve governance within African countries, an African co-optation of this discourse might instead highlight the fragility of 'Global Britain' on the international stage (cf. Fanon, 2021 [1961]). African actors seeking to contest UK political interference and economic exploitation could usefully point, for example, to the constitutional, economic and societal crises currently facing the UK state (cf. Smith, 2022). By highlighting the UK's territorial fragility, British political corruption, UK security services abuses of British civilians and ongoing economic disruption post-Brexit, African actors can reply to the disempowering narratives which UK officials use to justify neo-colonial interventions within the continent. This ideational manoeuvre—if combined to other forms of discursive co-optation—might empower African academics, civil society groups and officials to question why 'Fragile Britain' is interfering within their societies and countries. It would also highlight that the UK is not a desirable model for African countries to emulate, especially in terms of democratic deficits, racial discrimination and economic turbulence within the UK (cf. Fanon, 2021 [1961]).

Finally, the chapter concludes by reflecting on the decolonial approach and the continued relevance of Nkrumah's (1965) work—in conjunction with more recent scholars such as Ndlovu-Gatsheni (2013, 2014)—for analysing the behaviour of Global Britain and other Euro-American polities. It reflects on the need for a decolonial approach to not merely decentre research by focusing on the perspectives of those within the 'Global South', but to actively confront global coloniality in its material, ideational and racialised expressions (Ndlovu-Gatsheni, 2014, 2015;

Orbie et al., 2023; Sondarjee & Andrews, 2023). Highlighting the need for decolonial research into UK trade policy, in particular, it calls for grounded engagement with business communities and labourers in African contexts who are impacted Brexit trade deals. In this vein, the chapter—and the book—concludes by calling for further decolonial scholarship on the Global Britain project. It expresses the hope that such scholars can meaningfully challenge the UK state as a neo-colonial actor.

Global Britain as an Expression of UK Elites' Ontological (In)Security

The 2016 referendum result was fuelled by a regressive English nationalism that denigrated minorities at home, as well as non-white refugees fleeing persecution from countries and regions destabilised by the US-led 'war on terror' (cf. Abbas, 2020; Wellings, 2021). Brexiteer campaigners promised that leaving EU institutions would enable the UK to regain its lost sovereignty and to rebuild relationships with Commonwealth countries. In the context of African former colonies, Brexiteer politicians attacked EU trade policies for their protectionist elements and promised that an independent UK trade policy would offer fairer opportunities for African exporters (see, for example, Hannan, 2016; Lilley, 2016). In addition, Brexiteer politicians promised that the UK's focus upon newly emerging economies—rather than upon intra-European trade—would bring about renewed prosperity for British citizens. Brexit trade deals with countries such as Nigeria and South Africa would therein enable the UK to move away from dependence upon the continental European market (Johnson, 2016).

Moreover, even prior to the referendum, UK elites had regularly focused upon foreign policy and 'development' narratives surrounding British engagement with African countries. As noted in Chapter 2, the Blair government especially highlighted Africa as a 'scar upon the conscience of the world' (Porteous, 2005: 289). As such, Blair promised that the UK would play a leading role within international forums such as the G8 to bring about fairer conditions for African economies, notably in terms of debt relief. Politicians from both of the main UK political parties, meanwhile, found renewed enthusiasm for the Commonwealth after the release of Nelson Mandela and the end of apartheid (that had poisoned the UK's relationship with African countries, especially in the context of

Prime Minister Thatcher's recalcitrant attitude towards the need for sanctions upon the white supremacist apartheid regime) (Beswick, 2019: 129; Murphy, 2011: 273–274).

However, UK elites' focus upon African countries—and citizenries—has also involved discourses that have 'securitised' the continent. Blair in the aftermath of 9/11, and his endorsement of the US-led 'war on terror', depicted African 'fragile states' as potential centres of instability and danger for UK citizenries (Abrahamsen, 2005). This securitised discourse continued into the era of David Cameron's coalition government where UK efforts against Boko Haram in Nigeria and Al Shabaab in Somalia especially came to the fore as part of government 'stabilisation' narratives (Apuuli, 2019). Under the New Labour and Cameron governments, UK 'development' policy became increasingly aligned to perceived security interests in the continent, especially in terms of efforts to enhance local security structures and to tackle poverty in conflict-affected zones (Petrikova & Lazell, 2019). Significantly in terms of the 2016 referendum, UK elites' securitisation of non-white migration in the aftermath of 9/11 laid fertile ground for the Leave campaign (Bello, 2022). The 'Breaking Point' poster and Brexiteers' appeals to English anxieties towards migration—and Islamophobia—gained traction in large part due to the earlier securitisation discourse of New Labour and of Cameron.

Since the referendum UK elites have sought to project Global Britain's power and influence onto the international stage, especially in terms of 'reclaiming' a sphere of influence among 'old friends' (UK Government, 2017). This is what alarmed UK civil servants dubbed project 'Empire 2.0' (Leroux, 2017). This attempted power projection is inherently tied up with UK elites' own ontological security, in the sense of a stable sense of self-identity that orientates foreign policy behaviour (cf. Haastrup et al., 2021). UK policy-makers have long perceived the UK as an important and influential global actor on the basis of the legacy of Empire (Namusoke, 2016). Narratives surrounding the 'Commonwealth' have particularly been central to UK elites' historical ontological security. Today, narratives surrounding Global Britain's remaining relevance in promoting security and 'development' within African countries holds together UK elites' sense of Britain's importance on the world stage, and their own importance in the sense of pursuing a 'mission civilisatrice' (cf. Połońska-Kimunguyi & Kimunguyi, 2017: 327, 343). As part of this attempted power projection, UK elites—and key agencies such as the FCDO—utilise legitimising narratives about pro-poor trade deals, the benevolent delivery of aid monies, democratisation and human rights, and 'win-win' co-operation that generates profits for UK businesses while disincentivising outward migration from African countries.

However, as the previous chapters have illustrated, Global Britain's pro-poor pledges are regularly contradicted by the material consequences of the interventions of UK actors in the continent. In terms of trade policy, the pursuit of 'cut and paste' Economic Partnership Agreements (EPAs) with African countries by UK ministers and trade officials runs contrary to developmental strategies necessary for diversification away from colonial patterns of production and exchange. Ghana, in particular, has been compelled to acquiesce to a free trade deal after a period in which the UK had defaulted its exporters to the less generous Generalised System of Preferences (GSP) (Merrick, 2020). The open rhetoric from UK ministers that aid monies will be tied to trade agreements also places pressures upon governments, such as that of Ghana, to acquiesce to disadvantageous free trade deals that exacerbate import flooding—for fear that aid may be cut if they do not sign. This allegedly occurred in the situation of Ghana-EU trade negotiations where EU budget support to the country was apparently leveraged as part of tactics to ensure Ghanaian implementation (Langan, 2023). Brexit trade deals do not therefore offer the progressive alternative to EU policies that certain Leave campaigners promised during the 2016 referendum.

In terms of Global Britain's aid agenda, meanwhile, the increasing allocations of monies towards 'Aid for Trade' programmes complement the UK's pursuit of Brexit EPAs. Aid for Trade monies ostensibly allow free trade deals to become 'win-win' for the UK and for African partners by allocating funds towards enhancing private sector competitiveness in the latter (cf. Langan & Scott, 2011). Through the giving of aid towards improving ports, roads and electricity supplies—as well as some support to priority export sectors through financing resources such as cold storage facilities—Aid for Trade will nominally enable African businesses to take advantage of free trade conditions (ibid.). However, the de facto tying of Aid for Trade to the signing of Brexit trade deals—as well as the use of such monies to improve infrastructural assets conducive to foreign corporations' exploitation of African energy and mineral supplies—does not bode well for African 'development' trajectories. Additionally, the use of UK aid monies for the externalisation of migration via the Rwanda deportation scheme (although apparently not counted as official 'ODA') is itself highly problematic. Not only does this jeopardise the human rights of the deportees, but it entrenches a neo-colonial form of relations between the UK and African countries, in this case Rwanda (Worley, 2022). The support of 'Global Britain' for the regime of Prime Minister Abiy Ahmed in Ethiopia—while other donors including the EU withdrew support—in the context of the Tigray war is extremely worrying in terms of the ongoing trajectory of UK aid spending (Rynn, 2023). The winning of a joint bid by UK firm, Vodafone, alongside international partners within the privatised Ethiopian telecommunications sector is of little comfort for civilians in Tigray abused by Ethiopian troops (ibid.).

At the same time, the pursuit of UK commercial interests via UK development finance instrument, British International Investment (BII), also bodes ill for Global Britain's nominal commitment to poverty reduction in African contexts. The BII group—formerly the Commonwealth Development Corporation (CDC)—has a chequered history, notably in terms of its financing of palm oil plantations in the Democratic Republic of the Congo (DRC) which operate on contested lands (RIAO-RDC et al., 2021). The involvement of CDC/BII in Zambian agribusiness operations is also highly questionable in terms of historical exit strategies, as well as the wellbeing of workers employed on farms financed by UK taxpayers' monies (Mujenja & Wolani, 2012). The role of UK firms in energy and mineral extraction in the continent further brings into question Global Britain's image. Alleged environmental and health hazards caused by UK firms such as Glencore UK in their operations are extremely worrying in terms of the wellbeing of workers and host communities in countries such as Chad (RAID, 2020). Alleged land grabs associated with agribusiness operations related to UK firms such as Associated British Foods (ABF) are equally problematic for Global Britain's image in the African continent (Bae, 2019). Moreover, the Serious Fraud Office (SFO, 2022)'s recent penalties against Glencore UK for corruption in its dealings in countries such as Nigeria and South Sudan—as well as the seeming use of the penalties to enrich the British state rather than to compensate African governments—is a further blow to the reputation of UK actors and their 'development' rhetoric (Bunyan, 2023).

Additionally, UK elites' pursuit of their perceived security interests in African contexts is another hazard for Global Britain's image in terms of nominal norms of fair-dealing and respect for human rights. UK governments' failure to properly scrutinise and hold accountable UK private military companies (PMCs) is highly problematic, not least in terms of historical allegations levied at British PMCs in countries such as Sierra Leone, as well as their more recent entry into post-Gaddafi Libya (CAAT, 2000; War on Want, 2016b). Allegations levied at British troops in Kenya, as well as UK financial and training support for police in countries such as Nigeria and Kenya that stand accused of human rights violations, are also a threat to Global Britain's attempts to present itself as a benevolent actor committed to democratisation and respect for citizens' rights in African contexts (Amnesty International, 2014, 2021; Forest, 2020). UK companies' apparent historical financing of militias—both in Nigeria and Libya with respect to the protection of oil extraction objectives—is equally problematic in terms of the 'security' agenda of UK actors within the African continent (Brock, 2011; Donati, 2011). UK elites' recent critique of Russia as a security threat to African states—while certainly justified in terms of the Wagner group PMC—sits uneasily with an apparent strategic silence regarding the record of UK PMCs and other British commercial operators.

Unfortunately, these worrying trends appear likely to continue even if there is a shift in UK government in 2024. New Labour under Blair adopted discourse that securitised the African continent as a potential 'threat', enthusiastically supported UK arms sales, failed to properly regulate British PMCs and utilised aid monies in the pursuit of unjust free trade deals (see, for example, Taylor, 2012). New Labour in opposition under Keir Starmer has wholly adopted the 'Third Way' rhetoric and outlook of Blair. Starmer had even apparently hesitated on previous pledges to restore DfID as a separate department independent from the FCDO (Stacey, 2023). More recently, Starmer abolished the Shadow Minister for Peace and Disarmament in a Shadow Cabinet reshuffle, bringing into doubt his leadership campaign pledge to regulate the British arms industry (Labour CND 2023). UK-Africa relations under Starmer would likely therefore mirror existing trends under Prime Minister Rishi Sunak. For instance, New Labour under Starmer—given its own anti-migrant rhetoric—would likely continue 'externalisation of migration' policies (cf. Mitchell, 2023). Albeit perhaps via initiatives more nuanced than the Rwandan deportation plan. Altogether, UK relations with African countries remains central to UK elites' ontological security and finds expression within the post-referendum Global Britain project. Without supposed influence in African contexts, UK elites—whether New Labour or Conservative—would perceive the British state as a 'declining power'—witness, for example, Cameron's readiness to bring about regime change in Libya to demonstrate Britain's international clout (Dawson, 2022). UK elites' fixation on dealing with 'old friends' in the Commonwealth in Africa—as well as with Francophone African states in the aftermath of Brexit—bodes ill for the continent's attempts to wrest itself from foreign influence and domination. The next section, however, considers material power and potential strategies of African actors to contest the Global Britain project.

Contesting Global Britain: Material and Ideational Forms of Resistance

African actors' agency to contest the Global Britain project has much to gain from ongoing engagement with the work of Nkrumah (1965) on neo-colonialism. Nkrumah's pan-African solutions to economic exploitation and political manipulation by external entities have resonance for a twenty-first-century contestation of British interventions in the continent. Moreover, the work of Ndlovu-Gatsheni (2013, 2014) on global coloniality also yields potential dividends in terms of strategies of resistance. In terms of pan-Africanism and the African Union (AU), the recently established African Continental Free Trade Area (AfCFTA) is one key example of how pan-African solidarity may establish alternatives to neo-colonial formations. The AfCFTA seeks to build economies of scale through market-opening among its African members. Liberalisation of trade between African states themselves is viewed as central to the establishment of regional value chains within non-traditional sectors conducive to industrialisation and a shift away from colonial patterns of trade with European countries, including the UK (Hurt, 2022). The AfCFTA—if successful—will bring about increased trade between its members and enable them to diversify their economies.

However, Brexit trade deals—as well as EU EPAs—pose a threat to the integrity and developmental logic of this AU initiative (ibid.). Namely, premature trade liberalisation between a country such as Ghana and the EU or the UK imperils developmental strategies as pursued by neighbours such as Nigeria. Smuggling of cheap European commodities from a country with a free trade deal with the UK or EU, means that neighbouring countries' industries and jobs are also threatened by import flooding. For example, in terms of Nigeria's poultry industry—which despite high tariffs and import bans—suffers from the smuggling of chicken meat across its borders from countries such as Ghana and Benin.

This has heightened political tensions in the region, as well as undermined integration in terms of the Economic Community of West African States (ECOWAS) (cf. Rudloff & Schmieg, 2016). If the AfCFTA, on the other hand, can provide sufficient economic prosperity for countries such as Ghana that have implemented European free trade deals, then it opens up the possibility of a wholesale renunciation of free trade terms with the UK and the EU. The AfCFTA if pursued in a fashion that enables developmental states within the continent—based upon open borders among African countries but combined to strict tariffs against cheap imports from Europe (that would collapse nascent industries)—can provide a material alternative to disadvantageous UK or EU deals.

The ability of countries such as Ghana to resist free trade—and predatory forms of corporate investment—vis-à-vis the UK, however, necessitates overcoming reliance on foreign aid. As articulated within Global Britain's own rhetoric, UK aid monies will be increasingly tied to British interests whether in the sense of economic access to African markets under free trade deals—or potentially to controversial political schemes equivalent to the Rwandan deportation initiative (Amnesty International, 2022; Harris, 2016). African officials' ability to resist the 'coloniality of power' in the form of UK (and EU) aid lies in establishing economic prosperity within the AfCFTA conducive to taxation revenues derived from thriving businesses and local taxpayers. However, in the context of existing campaigns for reparations for colonial crimes, former British colonies such as Ghana also may seek restitution for the historical atrocities committed by the British Empire (Ackah, 2020; Bhambra, 2022; McKeown, 2021). Reparations payments—if removed from British oversight and control—could act as a short-term substitute for 'aid' monies while countries such as Ghana enhance their economic performance and competitiveness via the medium of the AfCFTA. The successful receipt of UK reparations would also prove a moral victory in the sense of forcing contemporary UK officials to face the historical realities of British colonial criminality. This would do much to puncture the regressive imperial romanticism currently deployed by UK politicians in their appeals to a xenophobic form of English nationalism (cf. Wellings, 2021).

With regard to human rights abuses against African citizenries allegedly committed by the UK army, British corporations, as well as UK private military companies (PMCs), African actors could also build upon existing proposals to strengthen the International Criminal Court (ICC) (Lambridis, 2021). There are already proposals to extend the remit of the

ICC to include corporate criminality (ibid.). While the ICC, to date, has predominantly focused upon alleged military and political culprits from African countries, a reformulated ICC could work to hold accountable Euro-American elites where they are found guilty of abuses in terms of the corporate poisoning of water supplies, the egregious abuse of workers, the employment of militia groups for 'security' purposes and so forth. Rather than rely upon 'Global Britain' to police its own corporate entities through mechanisms such as the OECD's National Contact Point (NCP) for Guidelines on Multi-National Enterprises, a reimagined ICC—or another global governance equivalent—could play a useful role in disciplining UK commercial actors accused of gross crimes within the continent. Similarly, a reformed ICC might usefully investigate the crimes allegedly committed by British forces in Kenya against women and girls (Amnesty International, 2021). A reformed ICC might provide a useful tool for African countries to seek meaningful redress from Global Britain for crimes committed by British citizens and enterprises.

African actors might also usefully co-opt the discourses of UK elites, especially as deployed as part of Global Britain's justification of its neocolonial interventions in Africa. As noted in this chapter's introduction, African academics and civil society groups might usefully dissect 'state fragility' in terms of the UK in its post-Brexit phase. The concept of state fragility has been used in Western development circles to depict African governance as 'weak' and in need of 'development' interventions from countries such as the UK. A paper published on the UK government website proposes three main 'failures' that help to define 'state fragility' (Stewart & Brown, 2009). These are i) authority failures where the state cannot protect its citizens from violence and where central state authority does not always stretch to all parts of the state's territory, ii) service failures where life necessities are not provided to citizens and poverty remains unaddressed, and iii) legitimacy failures where democratic deficits and a lack of political space for opposition and protest undermine effective governance (ibid.). The paper therein offers this definition:

> Fragile states are thus to be defined as states that are failing, or at risk of failing, with respect to authority, comprehensive service entitlements or legitimacy. We should note that both DfID and OECD particularly emphasise failure to deliver services to the poor. However, almost by definition any failure will be a failure towards the poor, as poverty consists in and results from failure to deliver services comprehensively (defined to include

a failure to reduce monetary poverty as well as a failure to provide public services). (ibid.: 3)

Given the multiple crises affecting the UK state today, it is not difficult to imagine how a reworked conceptualisation—and co-optation—of the language of 'state fragility' might be usefully deployed to counter-act Global Britain's public diplomacy in Africa. Puncturing the reputation of the UK among African citizenries would empower them to more robustly contest UK policy initiatives—and British actors' alleged crimes—in the continent. With regard to state authority, the UK's loosening grip on colonial possessions such as the Malvinas Islands and Gibraltar, for instance, might be usefully explored in terms of the concept of state fragility (cf. Canessa, 2023). The collapse of devolved government in Northern Ireland under the weight of Brexit turmoil might also be usefully assessed in these terms (cf. Ridley-Castle, 2022). Additionally, the recent energy crisis facing UK households under a privatised energy infrastructure, the pollution of UK beaches with human waste, air pollution leading to infant mortalities and the entrenched problems of an underfunded National Health Service (NHS) might usefully be explored by African actors in terms of UK 'state fragility' (cf. Smith, 2022). Finally, legitimacy failures might be fruitfully explored in terms of the Westminster parliament's increasingly frequent corruption scandals (see, for example, Bienkov, 2023). The concept of 'fragility' might also be usefully explored in terms of Scottish independence, Irish unity and the likely break-up of the UK as a state in the next decades (McTague, 2022).

Through the co-optation of the disempowering rhetoric frequently employed in British elites' discussion of African countries, African actors could delegitimise the Global Britain project by pointing to the domestic weaknesses of the UK state itself. This in combination with material strategies such as the pursuit of economic diversification via the AfCFTA, the pursuit of untied reparations payments from the British state (and implicated institutions such as the British Monarchy), as well as a reformed ICC are all possible strategies that might be pursued in opposition to the Global Britain project. This is of course in addition to existing strategies pursued by African officials, civil society and actors. Indeed, the allegations explored in the previous chapters are only known to us via the existing work and campaigns provided by African actors, as well as the bravery of those who have brought to the fore their allegations against British companies, British PMCs and the British army. Moreover, it is due to the existing trade justice and reparations campaigns of African civil society groups that such possibilities to further challenge the Global Britain project exist.

Nkrumah, Neo-colonialism and the Decolonial School

The preceding chapters' discussion of the Global Britain project has emphasised the relevance of Nkrumah's work for assessing Euro-American elites' policies towards African countries. Nkrumah (1963, 1965) warned that pan-African unity would be necessary to ensure that newly won juridical independence in the 1950s and 1960s was translated into genuine and sustainable forms of African sovereignty. Namely that without pan-African co-operation, individual African countries would be subjected to forms of neo-colonialism in which external powers would continue to enjoy economic dominance (in terms of corporate ownership of key resources, as well as aid-giving) and hence also enjoy political dominance over African governments. African officials under the sway of neo-colonialism would be compelled to acquiesce to the demands of their foreign benefactors, or else lose aid monies and investment necessary for the maintenance of the state apparatus or, worse, face overthrow in a foreign-sponsored coup d'etat. Nkrumah's downfall in 1966, coupled to earlier setbacks such as the assassination of Patrice Lumumba by Belgian-backed forces in the Democratic Republic of the Congo (DRC), demonstrate the violence which Western powers were prepared to condone in the pursuit of continued sway over African territories (Williams, 2021).

Unfortunately, an overview of recent UK policies since the Blair government to the post-referendum launch of 'Empire 2.0' under the Global Britain brand, illustrates that Nkrumah's fears remain well founded. UK elites now openly talk of how aid monies will be made subordinate to British security and economic interests (Price, 2018, 2019). The Rwandan deportation scheme—with UK authorities seeking to send refugees to Rwandan facilities—is one clear example here (Worley, 2022). Namely, the Rwandan government has consented to this degrading initiative (both in terms of degrading refugees and the international reputation of Rwanda) on the basis that the UK has promised aid delivery (cf. Chime, 2022; Tasamba, 2022). Nkrumah's (1965) analysis here points to how governments—in this case, that of Paul Kagame—may acquiesce to Western demands in the hopes of securing revenues. The fact that Rwanda requires such revenues, meanwhile, is inherently linked to the skewed economic and trade relationships that continue to exist between African countries and European states, including the UK.

Nkrumah's call for greater economic unity—and hence prosperity—for African countries is one solution to aid dependency. A more prosperous Rwanda—for instance, as part of a flourishing AfCFTA—would not be as reliant upon UK aid-giving and could more readily inform UK counterparts that they do not wish to be part of legally dubious and morally indefensible deportation plans aimed against predominantly non-white refugees. They could also explain to UK partners that a sovereign Rwanda would not wish to partake in the UK's 'externalisation of migration' strategies and perhaps suggest to their UK peers that they ought to improve their human rights record vis-à-vis vulnerable migrants in Britain itself (cf. Amnesty International, 2023). Nkrumah's pan-African vision, if realised via the AfCFTA, combined to greater political solidarity within the AU, would empower officials in Rwanda (and beyond) to resist the UK's anti-immigration agenda and to reject conditional forms of aid.

Moreover, a stronger, unified AU could take bolder leadership on preserving the territorial sovereignty of its members vis-à-vis foreign mercenaries, including UK PMCs. As Nkrumah (1965) predicted, former colonial powers such as the UK have wished to maintain a military presence in African contexts. For the UK, this has meant the establishment of a permanent training facility on Kenyan soil. In the post-referendum Integrated Review, the importance of this British presence in Kenya has been re-emphasised with a view to positioning UK forces to potentially intervene in conflict-affected states within the region, notably in terms of South Sudan and Somalia (UK Government, 2021). As Nkrumah predicted, however, the presence of foreign troops not only has a deleterious impact in terms of the 'sovereignty' of the host nation, but also has alleged negative implications for citizens. Nkrumah here would not be surprised by the allegations levied at British troops in Kenya in terms of alleged rapes of women and girls (Amnesty International, 2021). He would also not be surprised by the allegations made against British PMCs in countries including Sierra Leone, Libya and Nigeria (see, for example, CAAT, 2000; War on Want, 2016b). Nkrumah understood that neo-colonialism entailed the perpetuation of racialised violence upon African citizenries by foreign entities. In the case of Libya, his analysis underscores why Western governments pursue regime change—namely in terms of securing longer-term access to key resources under pliable 'puppet' governments.

Likewise, a stronger AU could push for reform of the ICC to include the prosecution of alleged corporate crimes in the continent (cf. Lambridis, 2021). Nkrumah predicted that foreign corporations would continue to seek access to Africa's raw material and energy supplies. He understood that without proper oversight from a federal African executive that such foreign companies would be able to continue colonial-era practices, including the abuse of poorly remunerated workers (and the abuse of the natural environment with its attendant health consequences for local communities). A stronger AU could also seek to preserve the 'sovereignty' of its members with regard to law enforcement and policing. Namely, through the collective allocation and sharing of wealth within the AU, African states such as Kenya and Nigeria would be less reliant upon British funding of police units, including highly controversial counter-terrorism forces accused of gross human rights violations against civilians and refugees (see, for example, Human Rights Watch, 2013, 2014, 2016). Policing units, if funded by their own governments in conjunction with the AU, would become more accountable to their own citizenries and be less beholden to the demands of foreign benefactors vis-à-vis external security agendas.

Given the prescience of Nkrumah's analysis and the ongoing relevance of his conceptualisation of 'neo-colonialism', it is surprising that relatively few scholars—with notable exceptions such as Ndlovu-Gatsheni (2014, 2015)—systematically explore his work in tandem with a modern critique of global coloniality. The decolonial school has much to gain from a more pronounced and explicit engagement with the work of Nkrumah. As the first chapter made clear, this not only includes his written work, but also may usefully extend to his political speeches. His oral critique of neo-colonialism remains a powerful resource for African officials, civil society groups and academics seeking to confront the policies of 'Global Britain'. Nkrumah's critique of the strategies of former colonisers—as well as his articulation of the necessary responses from African governments—sits neatly with the decolonial critique of the three forms of global coloniality—the 'coloniality of power', the 'coloniality of knowledge' and the 'coloniality of being' (Ndlovu-Gatsheni, 2014, 2015). Nkrumah understood the material power of foreign aid and trade arrangements. He understood how 'development' discourse might be strategically utilised by donors in a fashion which undermines the sovereignty of recipient states in Africa. And he understood the racialised hierarchies that Western states sought to perpetuate in their 'othering' of African citizenries, disempowering them in the process. A fuller engagement with Nkrumah within the decolonial school is warranted.

Furthermore, there is clearly a need for ongoing decolonial scholarship and grounded forms of research in terms of the implications of the Global Britain project for African citizenries. On the question of UK trade policies, for example, there is a need for grounded engagement with the business enterprises and workers negatively impacted by premature trade liberalisation, as in countries such as Ghana and Kenya. By engaging the sectors impacted by the inflow of British commodities (for example, by the flow of frozen chicken meat), decolonial researchers can challenge the legitimising 'development' discourse of the UK Department for Business and Trade (cf. Langan, 2023). Moreover, they can point to how UK elites' persistent focus on limiting migration is undermined by trade deals that may lead to job losses and economic turbulence in states such as Ghana (cf. Langan & Price, 2021). By engaging the views and lived experiences of those African business managers and workers facing the material consequences of unjust UK (and EU) trade policies, researchers within the decolonial school can apply concepts such as the 'coloniality of power' and the 'coloniality of knowledge' to investigate how the UK causes social dislocation and distress in the African continent.

Conclusion

This book has sought to explore the implications of Brexit in terms of the launch of 'Empire 2.0' and the Global Britain project vis-à-vis African countries. It has focused upon the competing analyses of the Brexit referendum and the importance of imperial nostalgia therein; the historical centrality of Africa-UK ties to UK elites' ontological security since 'decolonisation'; as well as the impact of UK trade, aid, corporate activities, development finance and security agendas upon African citizenries. In this discussion, it has sought to draw a distinction between the legitimising 'development' rhetoric of UK elites embedded within key agencies such as the FCDO (and formerly, DfID) and the material consequences of UK actors' behaviour for African citizens. In this process, it has pointed to a number of alleged abuses of African workers, citizens and communities in relation to UK actors' pursuit of commercial profits and 'security' agendas. It has also pointed to the UK's strategic use of its economic weight (downgrading Ghanaian exporters to the GSP to pressurise their government, for example), its aid policies, as well as its military capabilities (note Libya) in the pursuit of perceived British interests in the African continent.

Moreover, it has pointed to the relevance of the concepts of neo-colonialism and global coloniality for making sense of—and challenging—the Global Britain project. Namely, it has pointed to how UK elites perpetuate the economic exploitation of African resources as part of a 'new scramble' (cf. Carmody, 2016). It has pointed to the use of military power, PMCs and funding of internal police to serve perceived UK security objectives. It has highlighted the use of development finance to prolong colonial-era forms of exploitation, notably in terms of palm oil operations in the DRC upon contested land taken from local communities during the Belgian colonial era (see RIAO-RDC et al., 2021). It has highlighted, also, the need for pan-African solutions to the problems caused by 'Global Britain', in keeping with Nkrumah's (1965) prescient analysis of neo-colonialism. It has also engaged Ndlovu-Gatsheni's (2013, 2014) work—particularly in terms of the concepts of the 'coloniality of knowledge' and the 'coloniality of being'—to demonstrate how a more recent decolonial analysis is wholly compatible with (and augments) the work of Nkrumah on neo-colonialism. It has also highlighted the continued importance of Nkrumah's political speeches for a contemporary assessment of neo-colonialism, not least in terms of confronting the Global Britain project.

Finally, this concluding chapter has pointed to the 'fragility' of the Global Britain project in terms of the multiple domestic crises facing the UK in the post-Brexit period. In terms of state authority, the provision of life necessities, and the legitimacy of Westminster authorities, the UK is clearly failing its own citizens. Moreover, the UK appears destined for constitutional collapse amid Scottish independence and Irish unity within the coming decades. Utilising the language of 'state fragility' to confront—and to deflate—the Global Britain project would be an interesting strategy for African scholars and activists to adopt in their resistance to UK demands in the continent. This would align to the decolonial school itself in terms of challenging the 'coloniality of knowledge'—in this case, in terms of Western 'development' discourse and its preoccupation with interventions within so-called 'fragile states' in Africa. Furthermore,

African actors could usefully here hasten the demise of the UK as a constitutional entity. Voicing support for Scottish independence, Irish unity and the fragmentation of 'Global Britain' would be a forceful strategy aimed at blunting the strategic reach of UK elites.

Bibliography

Abbas, T. (2020). Islamophobia as Racialised Biopolitics in the United Kingdom. *Philosophy and Social Criticism, 46*(5), 497–511.
Abrahamsen, R. (2005). Blair's Africa: The Politics of Securitization and Fear. *Alternatives: Global, Local, Political, 30*(1), 55–80.
Ackah, W. (2020). The Politics of Pan-Africanism. In R. Rabaka (Ed.), *Routledge Handbook of Pan-Africanism* (pp. 48–56). Routledge.
Amnesty International. (2014). *Welcome to Hellfire: Torture and Other Ill Treatment in Nigeria.* Amnesty International.
Amnesty International. (2021). *United Kingdom—Decades of Impunity: Serious Allegations of Rape of Kenyan Women by UK Army Personnel.* Amnesty International.
Amnesty International. (2022b, June 17). *Rwanda: Commonwealth Leaders Must Oppose UK's Racist Asylum Seeker Deal.* Amnesty International News. https://www.amnesty.org/en/latest/news/2022/06/rwanda-commonwealth-leaders-must-oppose-uks-racist-asylum-seeker-deal/. Accessed 29 May 2023.
Amnesty International. (2023, April 5). *UK Plan to House People Seeking Asylum on a Barge Is "Ministerial Cruelty".* Amnesty International Press Releases. https://www.amnesty.org.uk/press-releases/uk-plan-house-people-seeking-asylum-barge-ministerial-cruelty. Accessed 10 September 2023.
Apuuli, K. (2019). The UK and Africa Relations: Construction of the African Union's Peace and Security Structures. In D. Beswick, J. Fisher, & S. Hurt (Eds.), *Britain and Africa in the Twenty-First Century: Between Ambition and Pragmatism* (pp. 54–72). Manchester University Press.
Bae, Y. J. (2019). A Displaced Community's Perspective on Land-Grabbing in Africa: The Case of the Kalimkhola Community in Dwangwa, Malawi. *Land, 8*(187), 1–16.
Bello, V. (2022). The Spiralling of the Securitisation of Migration in the EU: From the Management of a 'Crisis' to a Governance of Human Mobility? *Journal of Ethnic and Migration Studies, 48*(6), 1327–1344.
Beswick, D. (2019). Rehabilitating the "Nasty Party"? The Conservative Party and Africa from Opposition to Government. In D. Beswick, J. Fisher, & S. Hurt (Eds.), *Britain and Africa in the Twenty-First Century: Between Ambition and Pragmatism* (pp. 121–138). Manchester University Press.

Bhambra, G. K. (2022). A Decolonial Project for Europe. *Journal of Common Market Studies, 60*(2), 229–244.

Bienkov, A. (2023, September 1). *Rishi Sunak's Government Is "Institutionally Corrrupt" Says Voters*. Byline Times. https://bylinetimes.com/2023/09/01/rishi-sunak-government-institutionally-corrupt-poll-voters/. Accessed 10 September 2023.

Brock, J. (2011, October 3). *Shell Fuelled Human Rights Abuses in Nigeria—NGO*. Reuters. https://www.reuters.com/article/nigeria-shell-idUSL5E7L33Q720111003 Accessed 27 July 2023.

Bunyan, A. (2023, February 22). *Oiling the Wheels*. 2 Hare Court Blog. https://www.2harecourt.com/training-knowledge/oiling-the-wheels/. Accessed 22 July 2023.

CAAT. (2000). *UK in Sierra Leone Mercenary Scandal*. CATT. https://caat.org.uk/news/2000-09-07-2/. Accessed 26 July 2023.

Cakaric and Skrinjar. (2022, July 15). *The Human Cost on G4S' Watch*. Ostro. https://www.ostro.si/en/stories/the-human-cost-of-g4s-watch. Accessed 27 August 2023.

Calhoun, C. (2017). Populism, Nationalism and Brexit. In W. Outhwaite (Ed.), *Brexit: Sociological Responses* (pp. 57–76). Anthem Press.

Canessa, A. (2023, July 28). Borders, Boots and Brexit: What's Behind the Gibraltar and Spain Impasse? In *UK in Changing Europe Commentary*. UKICE. https://ukandeu.ac.uk/borders-boots-and-brexit/. Accessed 10 September 2023.

Carmody, P. (2016). *The New Scramble for Africa*. Polity Press.

Chime, V. (2022, April 22). *"We're Not Trading Human Beings"—Kagame Explains UK-Rwanda Deal on Asylum Seekers*. The Cable. https://www.thecable.ng/were-not-trading-humans-kagame-explains-uk-rwanda-deal-on-asylum-seekers. Accessed 10 September 2023.

Dathan. (2016, June 8). *More Black People Will Be Allowed into Britain If We Leave the EU and Immigration Will Become a "Non-Issue" Says Nigel Farage*. The Daily Mail. https://www.dailymail.co.uk/news/article-3630847/More-black-people-allowed-Britain-leave-EU-immigration-non-issue-says-Nigel-Farage.html. Accessed 6 March 2023.

Dawson, G. (2022). "No Future for Libya with Gaddafi": Classical Realism, Status and Revenge in the UK Intervention in Libya. *Cambridge Review of International Affairs, 35*(3), 357–374.

Donati, R. (2011, May 12). *Libyan Rebels Seal New Deal with Vitol: Traders*. Reuters. https://www.reuters.com/article/us-libya-vitol-idUSTRE74B5KF20110512. Accessed 28 July 2023.

Fanon, F. (2021 [1961]). *The Wretched of the Earth*. Grove Press

Forest, A. (2020, October 30). End SARS Protests: UK Government Admits It Did Train and Supply Equipment to Nigeria's "Brutal" Police Unit. *The Independent*. https://www.independent.co.uk/news/uk/politics/sars-nigeria-police-protests-uk-government-training-equipment-b1424447.html. Accessed 28 August 2023.

Haastrup, T., Duggan, N., & Mah, L. (2021). Navigating Ontological (In)Security in EU–Africa Relations. *Global Affairs, 7*(4), 541–557.

Hannan, D. (2016, June 21). Free Britain to Trade with the World. *The Financial Times*. https://www.ft.com/content/6d4a444a-36f5-11e6-a780-b48ed7b6126f Accessed 6 March 2023.

Harris, A. (2016). *Post-Brexit Aid Policy: What Is Aid for Trade? And What Is It Not?* Bond.

Human Rights Watch. (2013, May 29). *You Are All Terrorists: Kenyan Police Abuse of Refugees in Nairobi*. Human Rights Watch. https://www.hrw.org/report/2013/05/29/you-are-all-terrorists/kenyan-police-abuse-refugees-nairobi. Accessed 27 August 2023.

Human Rights Watch. (2014, August 18). *Kenya: Killings, Disappearances by Anti-Terror Police*. Human Rights Watch. https://www.hrw.org/news/2014/08/18/kenya-killings-disappearances-anti-terror-police. Accessed 27 July 2023.

Human Rights Watch. (2016, July 20). *Deaths and Disappearances: Abuses in Counterterrorism Operations in Nairobi and in Northeastern Kenya*. Human Rights Watch. https://www.hrw.org/report/2016/07/21/deaths-and-disappearances/abuses-counterterrorism-operations-nairobi-and. Accessed 27 August 2023.

Hurt, S. (2022). Written Evidence from Dr Stephen Hurt (Oxford Brookes University). In *International Trade Committee (ITC) Written Evidence: UK Trade Approach Towards Developing Countries*. UK Parliament. https://committees.parliament.uk/work/1700/uk-trade-approach-towards-developing-countries/publications/written-evidence/. Accessed 14 April 2023.

Johnson, B. (2016, May 9). *The Liberal Cosmopolitan Case to Vote Leave*. Vote Leave. http://www.voteleavetakecontrol.org/boris_johnson_the_liberal_cosmopolitan_case_to_vote_leave.html. Accessed 6 March 2023.

Labour CND. (2023, September 8). *Starmer Removes Peace and Disarmament Role from Shadow Cabinet*. Labour CND. https://www.labourcnd.org.uk/2023/09/starmer-removes-peace-and-disarmament-role-from-shadow-team/. Accessed 10 September 2023.

Lambridis, P. (2021). Corporate Accountability: Prosecuting Corporations for the Commission of International Crimes of Atrocity. *International Law and Politics, 53*, 144–151.

Langan, M. (2023). 'The Double Movement in Africa: A Nkrumah-Polanyi Analysis of Free Market Fatigue in Ghana's Private Sector. *Review of International Political Economy, 30*(2), 463–486.

Langan, M., & Price, S. (2021). Migration, Development and EU Free Trade Deals: The Paradox of Economic Partnership Agreements as a Push Factor for Migration. *Global Affairs, 7*(4), 505–521.

Langan, M., & Scott, J. (2011). *The False Promise of Aid for Trade* (Brooks World Poverty Institute Working Paper, No. 160). Manchester: University of Manchester.

Leroux, M. (2017, March 6). Ministers Aim to Build "Empire 2.0" with African Commonwealth. *The Times.* https://www.thetimes.co.uk/article/ministers-aim-to-build-empire-2-0-with-african-commonwealth-after-brexit-v9bs6f6z9. Accessed 24 June 2023.

Lilley, P. (2016, May 26). The Truth About Britain's Trade Outside the European Union. *The Telegraph.* https://www.telegraph.co.uk/politics/2016/05/26/the-truth-about-britains-trade-outside-the-european-union/. Accessed 6 March 2023.

McKeown, M. (2021). Backward-Looking Reparations and Structural Injustice. *Contemporary Political Theory, 20,* 771–794.

McTague, T. (2022, January 5). How Britain Falls Apart. *The Atlantic.* https://www.theatlantic.com/international/archive/2022/01/will-britain-survive/621095/. Accessed 10 September 2023.

Merrick, R. (2020, December 20). Brexit: Final Bid to Prevent Huge Tariffs Ruining African Farmers Amid Allegations of UK "Bullying". *The Independent.* https://www.independent.co.uk/news/uk/politics/brexit-tariffs-africa-ghana-farmers-b1766278.html. Accessed 6 March 2023.

Mitchell, A. (2023, September 10). Keir Starmer Launches Illegal Migration Crackdown to Woo Tory Voters. *The Independent.* https://www.independent.co.uk/news/uk/politics/keir-starmer-labour-small-boats-rishi-sunak-b2408713.html. Accessed 10 September 2023.

Mujenja, F., & Wolani, C. (2012). *Long-Term Outcomes of Agricultural Investments: Lessons from Zambia.* International Institute for Environment and Development.

Murphy, P. (2011). Britain and the Commonwealth: Confronting the Past—Imagining the Future. *The round Table, 100*(414), 267–283.

Namusoke, E. (2016). A Divided Family: Race, the Commonwealth and Brexit. *The round Table, 105*(5), 463–476.

Ndlovu-Gatsheni, S. J. (2013). *Coloniality of Power in Post-Colonial Africa.* CODESRIA.

Ndlovu-Gatsheni, S. J. (2014). Global Coloniality and the Challenges of Creating African Futures. *Strategic Review for Southern Africa, 36*(2), 181–202.

Ndlovu-Gatsheni, S. J. (2015). *Empire, Global Coloniality and African Subjectivity*. Berghahn Books.

Nkrumah, K. (1963). *Africa Must Unite*. Panaf Press.

Nkrumah, K. (1965). *Neo-Colonialism: The Last Stage of Imperialism*. Panaf Press.

Nunn, A., & Price, S. (2004). Managing Development: EU and African Relations Through the Evolution of the Lomé and Cotonou Agreements. *Historical Materialism, 12*(4), 203–230.

Obeng, S. (1979). *Selected Speeches of Kwame Nkrumah*, (Vol. 1). Afram Publishers.

Orbie, J., Alcazar, A. S. M., III., Bougrea, A., Nagy, S., Oleart, A., Paz, J. C., & Wodzka, I. (2023). Editorial: Decolonizing Rather Than Decentring "Europe." *European Foreign Affairs Review, 28*(1), 1–8.

Petrikova, I., & Lazell, M. (2019). The Securitisation of UK and DfID Programmes in Africa: A Comparative Case Study of Cameroon, Central African Republic, Ethiopia, Kenya and Uganda. In D. Beswick, J. Fisher, & S. Hurt (Eds.), *Britain and Africa in the Twenty-First Century: Between Ambition and Pragmatism* (pp. 73–98). Manchester University Press.

Połońska-Kimunguyi, E., & Kimunguyi, P. (2017). "Gunboats of Soft Power": Boris on Africa and Post-Brexit "Global Britain." *Cambridge Review of International Affairs, 30*(4), 325–349.

Porteous, T. (2005). British Government Policy in Sub-Saharan Africa Under New Labour. *International Affairs, 81*(2), 281–297.

Price, S. (2018). Brexit and the UK-Africa Caribbean and Pacific Aid Relationship. *Global Policy, 9*, 420–428.

Price, S. (2019). The Impact of Brexit on EU Development Policy. *Politics and Governance, 7*(3), 72–82.

RAID. (2020). *Glencore's Oil Operations in Chad: Local Residents Injured and Ignored*. RAID. https://www.raid-uk.org/sites/default/files/raid_report_glencore_chad.pdf. Accessed 22 July 2023.

RIAO-RDC, FIAN Belgium, Entraide et Fraternité, CCFD-Terre Solidaire, FIAN Germany, urgewald, Milieudefensie, The Corner House, Global Justice Now, World Rainforest Movement and GRAIN. (2021). *Development Finance as Agro-Colonialism: European Development Bank Funding of Feronia-PHC Oil Palm Plantations in the Democratic Republic of the Congo*. RIAO-RDC. https://www.cidse.org/wp-content/uploads/2021/02/EN-Development_Finance_as_Agro_Colonialism_Feronia_PHC.pdf. Accessed 29 May 2023.

Ridley-Castle, T. (2022). *Why Does the Northern Ireland Assembly Keep Collapsing?* Electoral Reform Society. https://www.electoral-reform.org.uk/why-does-the-northern-ireland-assembly-keep-collapsing/. Accessed 10 September 2023.

Rudloff, B., & Schmieg, E. (2016). More Bones to Pick with the EU? Controversial Poultry Exports to Africa: Sustainable Trade Policy as a Task for the G20. In *SWP Comment*, 57/2016. Stiftung Wissenschaft und Politik -SWPDeutsches Institut für Internationale Politik und Sicherheit.

Rynn, S. (2023, February). *On Shifting Ground: An Appraisal of UK Engagement in Ethiopia* (RUSI Occasional Paper). RUSI, London.

SFO. (2022, November 3). *Glencore to Pay £280 Million for "Highly Corrosive" and "Endemic" Corruption*. News Releases. https://www.sfo.gov.uk/2022/11/03/glencore-energy-uk-ltd-will-pay-280965092-95-million-over-400-million-usd-after-an-sfo-investigation-revealed-it-paid-us-29-million-in-bribes-to-gain-preferential-access-to-oil-in-africa/. Accessed 22 July 2023.

Smith, M. (2022). *The Rise of the Chaotic State: Decline, Decadence and Failure in British Government*. Leverhulme Trust. https://www.leverhulme.ac.uk/major-research-fellowships/rise-chaotic-state-decline-decadence-and-failure-british-government. Accessed 10 September 2023.

Sondarjee, M., & Andrews, N. (2023). Decolonizing International Relations and Development Studies: What's in a Buzzword? *International Journal*, early view edition, pp. 1–21.

Stacey, K. (2023, June 28). Keir Starmer Considers Ditching Labour Pledge to Reinstate DfID. *The Guardian*. https://www.theguardian.com/politics/2023/jun/28/keir-starmer-considers-ditching-labour-pledge-to-reinstate-dfid-international-development. Accessed 10 September 2023.

Stewart, F., & Brown, G. (2009). *Fragile States*. CRISE. https://assets.publishing.service.gov.uk/media/57a08b62e5274a27b2000af7/wp51.pdf. Accessed 10 September 2023.

Tasamba, J. (2022, April 28). *Rwanda's Decision to Take in Migrants Not Surprising: Analysts*. Anadolu Ajansi. https://www.aa.com.tr/en/africa/rwanda-s-decision-to-take-in-migrants-not-surprising-analysts/2575001. Accessed 11 September 2023.

Taylor, I. (2012). Spinderella on Safari: British Policies Toward Africa Under New Labour. *Global Governance, 18*(4), 449–460.

UK Government. (2017, January 17). *The Government's Negotiating Objectives for Exiting the EU: PM Speech*. UK Government Online. https://www.gov.uk/government/speeches/the-governments-negotiating-objectives-for-exiting-the-eu-pm-speech. Accessed 14 April 2027.

UK Government. (2021). *Global Britain in a Competitive Age: The Integrated Review of Security, Defence, Development and Foreign Policy*. HM Stationery Office.

UK Government. (2022a, July 6). *A UK-Africa Trading Partnership for the 21st Century*. UK Government Online. https://www.gov.uk/government/speeches/a-uk-africa-trading-partnership-for-the-21st-century. Accessed 14 April 2023.

UK Government. (2022b). *Strategy for International Development*. HM Stationery Office.

Vote Leave. (2016, April 27). *Speech by James Cleverly MP: "How the EU's Common Agricultural Policy Is Making Africans Poorer"*. Vote Leave. http://www.voteleavetakecontrol.org/speech_by_james_cleverly_mp.html. Accessed 6 March 2023.

War on Want. (2016a). *The New Colonialism: Britain's Scramble for Africa's Energy and Mineral Resources*. War on Want.

War on Want. (2016b). *Mercenaries Unleashed: The Brave New World of Private Military and Security Companies*. War on Want.

Wellings, B. (2021). Brexit, Nationalism and Disintegration in the European Union and the United Kingdom. *Journal of Contemporary European Studies, 29*(3), 322–334.

Williams, S. (2021). *White Malice: The CIA and the Covert Recolonization of Africa*. Public Affairs.

Worley, W. (2022, April 26). *UK-Rwanda Project Called "Uglier Version of Development Diplomacy"*. Devex. https://www.devex.com/news/uk-rwanda-project-called-uglier-vision-of-development-diplomacy-103083. Accessed 30 June.

Index

0–9
32nd Brigade, 195
7/7 bombings, 200
9/11 attack, 98, 115, 191, 213, 227

A
Academics, 8, 10, 24, 25, 72, 109, 114, 225, 233, 237
Accra, 49
Afghanistan, 41, 191, 192, 201, 205
Africa Adaptation Acceleration Programme (AAAP), 176
African, Caribbean and Pacific (ACP), 31, 36, 45, 62, 93
African Continental Free Trade Area (AfCFTA), 19, 20, 49, 62, 80, 82, 83, 146, 161, 224, 231, 232, 234, 236
African Development Bank's (AfDB), 159, 176, 181
African Growth and Opportunity Act (AGOA), 72
African Marshall Plan, 8
African National Congress (ANC), 174, 178, 181
African Union, 21, 49, 62, 194, 231
Afro-Asian Solidarity Conference, 18
Agribusiness, 81, 125, 129, 133, 139, 144, 146, 156, 163, 164, 174, 176, 181, 229
Agriculture, 13, 46, 51, 64, 75, 130, 141, 146, 160, 175
Ahmed, Abiy, 108, 229
Aid, 4, 11, 12, 13, 19, 20, 23, 25, 32, 36, 42, 43, 45, 52, 79, 81, 84, 94–115, 124, 125, 127–131, 135, 136, 141, 143, 144, 146–148, 158, 175, 178, 179, 189, 198, 203, 209, 211, 223, 224, 228, 229, 230, 232, 235–239
Aid for Trade (AfT), 4, 65, 71, 94, 97, 98, 99, 102, 104, 106, 107, 108, 112, 113, 115, 158, 228
Algeria, 190, 198
Al Shabab, 199, 205, 227
America, 13, 18, 22, 44, 157, 202

Anglo-American, 159, 160
Anglosphere, 33, 35, 43, 44, 52
Annan, Kofi, 193
Anti-immigration, 2, 6, 200, 201, 236
Anti-terror campaign, 98
Anti-Terrorism Police Unit (ATPU), 206
Apartheid, 37, 38, 42, 226, 227
Armaments, 190, 230
Arms, 5
Arm sales, 96, 203
Arms to Africa, 5, 192, 193, 198, 212
Arms Trade Treaty (ATT), 190, 197
Asia, 12, 13, 22, 32, 24, 34, 53, 126, 130, 157
Associated British Foods (ABF), 156, 163, 174, 176, 229
Association, 1, 6, 12, 19–21, 23, 33, 36, 37, 39, 43, 44, 49, 63, 178, 194
Austerity, 5, 6, 42, 100, 126, 127, 158, 169, 195
Australasia, 44
Australia, 32, 33, 35, 43, 44, 46, 76

B
Badenoch, Kemi, 77
Balfour Declaration, 33
Balkanization, 21
Balkans, 191
Banks, 126, 127, 140, 167
Barroso, Jose Manuel, 66
Belgium, 1, 21
Belt and Road Initiative (BRI), 4, 111, 127, 129, 141
Benghazi, 196
Benin, 142, 163, 231
Benn, Tony, 38
Bermuda, 173
Biafra, 170
Blair, Tony, 2, 3, 7, 8, 10, 24, 32, 38–41, 47, 49, 51–53, 66, 94, 96–100, 104, 106, 112, 114, 115, 139, 155, 157–159, 161, 190–195, 197–200, 208, 210, 212, 226, 227, 230, 235
Boko Haram, 198, 199, 203, 204, 227
Bono, 97
Borrell, Josep, 8, 9, 32, 114
Braverman, Suella, 9, 10
Breaking Point, 46, 47, 189, 200, 213, 227
Bretton Woods institutions, 13
Brexit, 1–6, 8–10, 24, 31–33, 38, 43–48, 50, 53, 54, 61, 66, 69, 71, 77, 78, 80, 94–96, 99, 100, 102, 104–108, 111, 113, 115, 116, 129, 137, 145, 155, 156, 160, 161, 180, 189, 190, 199, 224, 226, 228, 231, 234, 238
Brexiteer politicians, 2, 7, 9, 10, 24, 31, 43, 46, 52, 54, 68, 82, 94, 95, 102, 106, 112, 115, 189, 226
Bribery, 164, 165, 166, 172, 173, 178, 180
Bring Back Our Girls, 199
British army, 205, 234
British Army Training Unit Kenya (BATUK), 205
British Empire, 2, 3, 5, 14, 33, 47, 202, 232
British International Investment (BII), 4, 108, 111, 123, 136, 224, 229
British Petroleum (BP), 196
Brown, Gordon, 2, 7, 39, 96, 97, 104
Brussels, 5, 31, 45, 67
Budget support, 98, 127, 228
Buhari, Muhummadu, 64

C

Cameron, David, 8, 24, 41, 42, 47, 51, 70, 94, 96, 97, 103, 125, 160, 195, 210, 213, 227
Cameroon, 73, 142, 162, 164
Campaign Against the Arms Trade (CAAT), 194
Canada, 32–34, 37, 43
Canadian government, 191
CANZUK (Canada, Australia, New Zealand, UK), 33, 43, 44, 46
Cape Town, 47, 161
Capitalist, 12
Cargill, 175
Caribbean, 63, 66, 103, 191
Caribbean Forum (CARIFORUM), 64
Casablanca Group, 21
Cement factories, 142
Central Africa, 63
Césaire, Aimé, 15, 19
Chad, 165, 179, 180, 229
Chamberlain, Joseph, 44, 100
Chibok kidnapping, 198, 199
Chicago Doctrine, 191, 212
Child labour, 79
China, 1, 4, 45, 49, 70, 93, 111, 127, 129, 135, 148, 202, 224
Chirac, Jacques, 7
Churchill, Winston, 33, 34
City of London, 49, 136
Civilisation, 13, 14, 19
Civil servants, 1, 5, 192, 227
Civil society, 5, 64, 67, 68, 71, 72, 74, 80, 82, 97, 103, 105, 107, 108, 110, 137–139, 141, 142, 156, 158, 161, 163, 212, 224, 225, 233, 234, 235, 237
Civil war, 42, 112, 115, 191, 195, 212
Class, 6, 22
Clegg, Nick, 41
Cleverly, James, 45, 46, 50, 51, 54
Climate change, 142, 163, 177
Clinton, Bill, 155, 158, 192
Cocoa, 65, 73, 79, 81
Cold War, 11, 21, 32, 34, 37–39, 42, 53, 125, 126, 129, 131, 209
Collective colonialism, 1, 2, 6, 8, 12, 20, 145
Colonial Development Corporation (CDC), 125, 130
Colonialism, 1, 6, 8, 12, 14, 15, 16, 19, 20, 23, 145
Coloniality of being, 14, 18, 32, 96, 113, 114, 179–181, 213, 237, 239
Coloniality of knowledge, 13, 15, 18, 52, 81, 83, 96, 113, 145, 179, 181, 212, 237–239
Coloniality of power, 13, 14, 18, 23, 81, 84, 95, 113–115, 146, 232, 237, 238
Common Agricultural Policy (CAP), 45, 46, 64
Common sense, 14, 81, 82, 113, 146, 179
Commonwealth, 1, 4, 5, 9, 10, 24, 25, 31–54, 61, 68, 69, 72, 74, 82, 94, 97, 103, 131, 226
Commonwealth Business Council (CBC), 39
Commonwealth Business Forum, 49
Commonwealth Development Corporation (CDC), 4, 108, 111, 124–126, 130, 147, 229
Commonwealth Heads of Government Meetings (CHOGM), 39
Communism, 34
Comparative advantages, 69, 71, 78, 81, 124
Competitiveness, 65, 67, 83, 97, 106, 228, 232

Conditionalities, 77, 79, 113, 158, 225
Conflict, 35, 109, 112, 114, 124, 132, 170, 191–194, 196, 198, 203, 204, 209, 213, 227, 236
Conservative Party, 6, 9, 10, 34, 40, 42, 52, 53, 71, 95, 97, 177, 208
Conservatives, 9, 42, 162, 195
Consumer, 51, 61, 63, 65, 66, 70, 74, 77, 156, 158, 166
Contamination, 130, 143, 168
Contracts, 108, 131, 161, 162, 169, 180, 196
Cook, Robin, 39, 41, 53, 192
Cool Britannia, 96
Corbyn, Jeremy, 40, 138
Corporate citizens, 158
Corporate social responsibility (CSR), 142, 156
Corrupt, 43, 115, 140, 165, 178, 209, 225, 229, 234
Cosmopolitan, 71, 95, 96, 100–104, 112, 115
Cote d'Ivoire, 66, 73, 160, 162, 164
Cotonou Partnership Agreement, 45
Counter-movements, 25
Coup d'etat, 11, 18, 235
Cox, Robert, 14
Credit crunch, 127
Crisis, 127, 128, 135, 157, 175, 191, 194, 200, 234
Critical minerals, 173, 176, 204
Critical minerals strategy, 176, 204
Cultures, 13, 15, 18
Cumulation, 77

D

Daily Express, The, 73
Daily Mail, 42, 200, 201
Darfur, 42
Darfur crisis, 194

Davis, David, 102
Debt, 97, 126, 127, 134, 141, 213, 226
Debt diplomacy, 135, 141, 144, 148
Decolonial scholarship, 3, 4, 12, 15, 16, 18, 23–25, 226, 238
Decolonisation, 2, 4, 14, 16, 18, 23, 25, 32, 35, 53, 126, 130, 238
Deep and Comprehensive Free Trade Agreement (DCFTAs), 63
de Gaulle, Charles, 12, 21
Democracy, 38, 39, 44, 52, 71, 93, 147, 191, 192
Democratic Republic of the Congo (DRC), 21, 132, 134, 137–141, 198, 209, 229, 235, 239
Department for Business and Trade (DBT), 61, 156, 162, 166, 238
Department for International Development (DfID), 4, 40, 94, 125, 155, 189, 223
Dependency, 12, 67, 72, 79, 145, 236
De-radicalisation, 41
De-risking, 128, 131, 162, 163
Detention centres, 208
Developing Countries Trading Scheme (DCTS), 62
Developmental state, 114, 124, 126, 129, 144–146, 178, 232
Development Assistance Committee (DAC), 110
Development finance, 4, 111, 116, 123–125, 130, 144, 145, 229, 238, 239
Diageo, 175
Diplomacy, 14, 38, 103, 125, 135, 136, 210, 234
Directorate General (DG), 62, 66
Displacement, 167, 168, 172, 174, 176, 179, 180
Dividends, 48, 82, 113, 155, 231

Doha Development Round (DDA), 94
Domestic violence, 172
Domination, 13, 15, 19, 20, 35, 231
Dominion, 33–36, 43
Drugs, 189, 191, 212
Duty free and quota free (DFQF), 65, 73, 74, 77, 79

E
East African Community (EAC), 66, 78
East Asia, 126
East Asian Financial Crisis, 127, 157
Eastern Africa, 12, 63
Eastern and Southern Africa (ESA), 73
Economic Community of West African States (ECOWAS), 66, 232
Economic diversification, 19, 64, 126, 129, 143, 144, 234
Economic Partnership Agreements (EPAs), 4, 7, 20, 47, 48, 62, 76, 96, 98, 228
Economic, Social and Governance (ESG), 142
Edinburgh, 39
Ed Miliband, 138
Education, 64, 127, 142, 160, 203
Egypt, 73, 162
Empire, 2
Empire 2.0, 1, 5, 32, 227, 235, 238
Enabling environment, 126, 155, 157–159
End of history, 192
Energy, 114, 128, 133, 140, 141, 156, 160–162, 165, 173, 177, 179, 186, 196, 204, 209, 210, 212, 214, 224, 228, 229, 234, 237
England, 2, 7, 70, 100

Environment, 48, 64, 76, 82, 103, 138, 146, 159, 160, 165, 166, 176, 179, 213, 237
Environmental abuses, 128, 139
Environmental Impact Assessments (EIAs), 142, 167
Epistemic, 12, 13, 15, 24
Equatorial Guinea, 164
Equity, 128, 131, 134, 135, 139, 142, 143, 147, 148
Ethical foreign policy, 41, 96, 192, 193, 198
Ethiopia, 45, 94, 103, 107, 108, 109, 112, 113, 115, 123, 229
EU Commission, 2, 3, 7, 129
EU Commissioner for Trade, 3, 7
EU member states, 3, 6, 8, 46, 64, 80, 101, 128, 145
Eurafrican, 20
Eurocentrism, 13, 15
Euro-Mediterranean Free Trade Area (EMFTA), 63
European Arrest Warrant (EAW), 201
European Central Bank (ECB), 128
European Commission, 62–66, 75, 80, 83, 102, 104, 109, 111, 113
European Development Fund (EDF), 19, 65, 93, 98
European Economic Community (EEC), 1, 35, 44, 63
European Neighbourhood Policy (ENP), 63
European Parliament, 45, 64, 67, 102, 175
European Single Market, 180
European Union (EU), 1, 10, 50
Eurosceptic, 40, 41
Everything But Arms (EBA), 60, 62, 65
Exceptionalism, 2, 3, 6, 24, 93
Exploitation, 11, 13, 18, 20, 146, 181, 225, 228, 231, 239

Externalisation, 63, 67, 110, 115, 190, 225, 228
Extractive industries, 129, 144, 163

F
Failed state, 210
False consciousness, 15
Fanon, Frantz, 15, 19, 225
Farage, Nigel, 43, 46, 54, 99, 189, 200
Farlam Commission, 173
Farmers, 46, 109, 139, 163, 166
Federalism, 21
Federal Republic of Nigeria (FRN), 165
Feronia Inc., 132, 134, 135, 137–140, 145
Finance, 32, 49, 123, 124, 126–130, 134, 135, 139, 143–145, 147, 162, 177, 178, 181, 211, 229, 238, 239
Financialisation, 124, 125, 127, 129, 136, 145, 147
Financial Times, 45
Fishers, 172
Fishing, 172, 174
Florence speech, 101
Flowers, 72, 78, 81, 107
Food, 46, 130, 168, 171, 174
Food crops, 133
Food security, 132, 139, 175, 176
Foreign Affairs Committee, 39, 209
Foreign and Commonwealth Office (FCO), 40, 94, 96, 97, 103, 136, 160, 199, 200, 213
Foreign direct investment (FDI), 70, 107, 114, 157, 158
Foreign investment, 12, 129, 143, 144, 155, 178, 181
Foreign investors, 22, 107, 126, 143, 144

Foreign policy, 7, 24, 34, 40, 41, 43, 47, 51, 101, 141, 192–194, 209, 226, 227
Foreign Secretary, 50, 51, 102, 172, 179, 192, 197
Fortress Europe, 31
Foucault, Michel, 15
Fox, Liam, 43, 48, 51, 52, 61, 69, 81, 102
Fragile states, 41, 100, 112, 128, 189, 199–201, 213, 225, 227, 233, 239
Fragility, 5, 225, 234, 239
France, 1, 7, 175, 195, 200, 210
Francophone African, 37, 231
Freedom of movement, 189, 201, 202
Free trade agreements (FTAs), 64, 102, 112
Free trade deals, 3, 4, 7, 19, 47, 63–67, 70, 74, 76, 78, 80, 81, 83, 98, 99, 106, 115, 224, 228, 230–232
Fund managers, 128, 131

G
G4S, 196, 204, 207
G7, 40, 50, 136, 137
G8, 40, 97, 160, 175, 226
G8 Gleneagles Summit, 97
Gabon, 163
Gaddafi, 42, 196, 197, 198, 210, 213
Gaddafi, Khamis, 195
Gaddafi, Muammar, 194
Gas flaring, 171
Geldof, Bob, 97
Gender, 100, 112
Gender-based violence, 206, 207, 212
General Agreement on Tariffs and Trade (GATT), 35
Generalised Scheme of Preferences (GSP), 62, 65
Geneva, 106

Genocide, 110, 192
Geoeconomic, 113
Geopolitical, 3, 17, 21, 49, 51, 94, 98, 99, 104, 111, 113, 144
Germany, 191
Ghana, 1, 17, 19, 32, 33, 36, 37, 49, 62, 66, 73–75, 77, 78, 81, 83, 125, 131, 144, 160, 162, 167, 173, 175, 228, 231, 232, 238
Glencore, 156, 164–167, 173, 176, 178–180, 229
Global Britain, 1–5, 7, 10, 17, 20, 24, 25, 32, 33, 45, 47–51, 54, 61, 62, 69, 79, 93–95, 97, 101, 103, 105, 107, 109, 111, 113–116, 123–125, 129, 136, 139, 141, 147, 155, 176–181, 189, 205, 208, 209, 211, 223–226, 230, 231, 233, 235, 237–240
Global coloniality, 3–5, 11–16, 18, 24, 25, 52, 54, 63, 94, 111–113, 125, 143, 145, 147, 156, 177, 179, 181, 190, 209, 212, 225, 231, 237, 239
Global Financial Crisis (GFC), 127, 135
Global food crisis, 175
Global Gateway, 4, 111, 129, 145
Globalisation, 2, 13, 67, 69, 71, 155, 191
Global North, 16, 25, 70, 77, 131
Global South, 5, 10, 12–14, 25, 45, 50, 53, 67, 71, 72, 77, 79, 82, 95, 99–101, 106, 110, 128, 130, 134, 157, 189, 190, 199, 200, 213, 225
Gold, 173, 174
Good governance, 127
Gove, Michael, 43
Government-to-government (G2G), 127
Gramsci, Antonio, 14

Greening, Justine, 43, 135
Greenpeace, 177
Gross Domestic Product (GDP), 48–50
Gross National Income (GNI), 42, 95
Guarantees, 111, 128, 135, 162, 176, 180

H
Hague, William, 172, 179, 197, 198
Hamburg Summit, 102
Hannan, Daniel, 43, 45, 54, 61, 226
Harare, 39
Hard Brexit, 202
Hard power, 194
Health, 23, 64, 127, 133, 134, 147, 163, 164, 165, 171, 173, 176, 179, 237
Hegemony, 13, 14, 15
High Level Prosperity Partnerships (HLPPs), 160
Highly Indebted Poor Countries Initiative (HIPC), 127
Home, Lord, 34
Home Office, 103, 203
House of Commons, 70, 77, 79, 107
Howard, Michael, 40, 41
Humanitarian, 32, 42, 53, 96, 99, 109, 110, 112, 115, 125, 127, 128, 131, 191, 198, 199
Human rights, 5, 65, 76, 79, 95, 97, 99, 108–110, 112–115, 127, 138, 156, 166, 176, 179, 180, 190–195, 197, 203, 204, 206, 208, 210, 211, 214, 224, 228–230, 232, 236, 237

I
Ibori, James, 140
Ideas, 14
Ideologies, 13, 38, 71

Ilmenite, 174
Ilovo, 174, 175, 176
Imperial China, 202
Imperialism, 11, 18, 19, 22, 193
Imperial nostalgia, 1, 2, 6, 24, 25, 32, 44, 54, 238
Imperial preferences, 35, 44
Imperial romanticism, 2, 3, 31, 32, 46, 52, 54, 103, 201, 232
Independent Commission for Aid Impact (ICAI), 106, 136
India, 33, 34, 36, 45, 46, 100, 130, 131
Industrialisation, 12, 20, 36, 68, 82, 83, 124, 126, 143, 144, 231
Industrial parks, 108
Inequalities, 12, 18, 46, 146
Infrastructure, 71, 107, 111, 123, 125, 127–129, 131, 141, 145, 160–162, 169, 180, 204, 234
International Criminal Court (ICC), 225, 232
International development, 39, 41, 42, 62, 101, 105, 108, 115, 130, 135, 138
International Development Committee (IDC), 107, 132, 134, 136
International Finance Corporation (IFC), 127, 167
International Monetary Fund (IMF), 13, 126, 158
International Oil Companies (IOCs), 170
International Relations and Defence Committee (IRDC), 76
International trade, 45, 67, 82
International Trade Committee (ITC), 70
Investment, 32, 39, 42, 48, 52, 70, 82, 94, 107, 114, 126, 129, 132, 133, 135, 138, 140, 141, 143–145, 155, 159, 161, 162, 169, 177, 180, 181, 224, 232, 235
Investment climate, 159, 161
Investment Climate Facility (ICF), 159
Iraq, 3, 7, 24, 41, 191, 193, 194, 201
Irish Free State, 33
Irish unity, 234, 239, 240
Islamophobic, 200, 201

J
Jenrick, Robert, 208
Job creation, 65, 70, 78, 82, 97, 123, 129, 130, 134, 145, 147
Johnson, Boris, 6, 9, 44, 47–49, 52, 61, 73, 99, 102, 103, 105, 112, 115, 137, 161, 163, 176, 205, 226
Jonathan, Goodluck, 141
Joyce, Eric, 40
Jubilee oilfield, 172
Juridical, 2, 4, 14, 16, 18, 23, 25, 33, 125, 126, 130, 177, 209, 235

K
Kabbah, Ahmed Tejan, 192–194
Kagame, Paul, 236
Katanga, 21, 209
Kenya, 47, 62, 66, 72–74, 76, 102, 126, 131, 142, 160, 161, 167, 169, 170, 173, 181, 197, 198, 201, 205–207, 209, 211, 212, 214, 230, 233, 236–238
Kenyan Petroleum Department, 170
Kenyatta, Uhuru, 170, 206
Kidnappings, 172
Kosovo, 41, 98, 191, 192
Kurdish, 200

L
Labour Party, 10, 40, 138, 196
Labour standards, 76, 77, 79
Laissez-faire approach, 126, 146, 159
Lancaster House speech, 68, 101
Land, 4, 109, 124, 138, 139, 145, 156, 167, 168, 171, 174, 175, 181, 239
Land grabs, 138, 163, 175, 229
Language, 5, 9, 10, 15, 24, 38, 48, 70, 80, 97, 103–105, 135, 138, 155, 156, 161, 163, 212, 225, 234, 239
Latin American, 12, 18
Leave campaign, 4, 31, 100, 189–191, 200–202, 213, 227
Legitimacy, 130, 233, 234, 239
Liberal Democrats, 41, 193
Libreville Declaration, 63–64
Libya, 8, 42, 190, 194–198, 208, 210, 212, 214, 230, 231, 236, 237, 239
Lilley, Peter, 61, 226
Liquid natural gas (LNG), 176
Livestock, 166, 168, 169
Loans, 111, 128, 131, 132, 134, 135, 162, 176, 180
Lockerbie bomber, 195
Lockerbie bombing, 195
Lokichar, 169
Lomé Conventions, 36, 37, 63, 65
Lomenen, James, 170
Lonmin, 173, 174, 176, 178
Lumumba, Patrice, 17, 209, 235

M
MacMillan, Harold, 37
Macron, Emmanuel, 8, 163
Major, John, 39
Make Poverty History, 97, 115
Malawi, 175, 176, 181
Malaysia, 33, 96
Mali, 175
Mandela, Nelson, 38, 42, 226
Mandelson, Peter, 3, 52, 62, 66, 78, 115, 139
Manufacturing industries, 129
Marikana, 174, 176, 178, 179, 181
Marikana platinum, 173
May, Theresa, 9, 47, 51, 68, 93, 95, 101, 136, 160, 201, 202, 223
MDC, 133, 139
Member of the European Parliament (MEP), 45
Migrants, 6, 10, 46, 99, 100, 110, 112, 114, 180, 191, 201, 202, 210–212, 214, 236
Migration, 4, 5, 9, 10, 43, 46, 47, 99, 100, 110, 112, 115, 129, 146, 180, 189, 190, 196, 199–204, 208, 210, 211, 213, 214, 223–225, 227, 228, 230, 236, 238
Migration compacts, 96
Migration Crisis, 200, 201
Military, 11, 15, 23, 25, 191–195, 199, 202–205, 207, 209, 211, 233, 236, 239
Millennium Development Goals (MDGs), 39, 65, 96, 127, 155
Minerals, 4, 127, 145, 156, 163, 164, 173, 181
Mining, 13, 111, 142, 156, 159, 160, 174, 176, 212, 224
Miscarriages, 171, 172
Mission civilisatrice, 32, 93, 114, 126, 131, 147, 223, 227
Mitchell, Andrew, 42, 135, 136, 138, 230
Modernity, 13, 15, 16
Mogadishu, 199
Mombasa, 206, 211
Monarchy, 14, 234

Monrovia Group, 21
Monsanto, 175
Mordaunt, Penny, 71, 81
Morocco, 63, 73, 162, 198
Mozambique, 66, 73, 160, 176
Mugabe, Robert, 39, 79
Multinational corporations (MNCs), 156
Museveni, Yoweri, 79, 172
Muslim, 9, 41, 53, 201

N
Nairobi, 205–207, 212
Nanyuki, 205, 207
National Audit Office (NAO), 134, 143
National Contact Point (NCP), 166, 233
National Crime Agency (NCA), 190, 208
National Health Service (NHS), 43, 234
Nationalism, 2, 7, 10
National Rally, 8
National Transitional Council (NTC), 196
Ndlovu-Gatsheni, S.J., 3, 4, 13–15, 18, 24, 25, 32, 52, 63, 81, 82, 94, 95, 111, 113, 125, 145–147, 156, 177, 179, 209, 212, 225, 237, 239
Neighbourhood Development and International Cooperation (NDICI), 102
Neo-colonialism, 1, 3–5, 10, 11, 15–18, 23–25, 54, 63, 84, 94, 111–113, 125, 143, 144, 147, 156, 177, 178, 190, 209–211, 213, 231, 235, 237, 239
(Neo)liberalism, 13
New Alliance for Food Security and Nutrition (NAFSN), 175
Newfoundland, 33
New International Economic Order (NIEO), 64
New Labour, 2–4, 7, 8, 10, 39–41, 51, 52, 62, 66, 68, 71, 94–97, 99, 103, 112, 113, 115, 131, 133, 138, 139, 156, 158, 191–198, 200, 213, 214, 227, 230
New Partnership for African Development (NEPAD), 82
New scramble, 1, 3, 17, 33, 51, 54, 94, 104, 111, 124, 135, 141, 145, 160, 162, 176, 224, 239
New Zealand, 32, 33, 35, 43, 44, 76
Nigeria, 42, 47, 64, 66, 68, 76, 78, 123, 126, 140–142, 160, 164, 165, 170, 175, 198, 201, 203, 206, 211, 212, 214, 226, 227, 229–231, 236, 237
Nkrumah, Kwame, 1, 3, 11, 12, 36, 37, 80, 83, 94, 113, 125, 144, 146, 147, 156, 177, 178, 209–211, 231, 235, 236
No-fly zone, 195
North Africa, 63, 198
North America, 44
North Atlantic Free Trade Agreement (NAFTA), 70
North Atlantic Treaty Organisation (NATO), 8, 40, 195
Nyerere, 2

O
Obama, Barack, 47
Obama, Michelle, 199
Official Development Assistance (ODA), 95, 110, 125, 225
Oganiland, 204
Oil, 4, 140–142, 156, 163–168, 170–173, 176, 178–181, 194, 196, 204, 210, 214, 230

Oilfields, 165
Old Dominions, 35, 43
Ontological security, 4, 32, 34, 35, 40, 42, 46, 51–54, 69, 72, 93, 223, 224, 227, 230, 238
Organisation for Economic Co-operation and Development's (OECD), 110, 125, 155
Orientalism, 15
Osborne, George, 100
Ottomans, 202
Outgrower, 176
Overseas development assistance (ODA)., 42
Oxfam, 103, 142, 163, 167, 174, 175

P
Pakistan, 33, 131
Palm oil, 132, 134, 137, 138, 144, 145, 147, 229, 239
Pan-African, 12, 82, 224, 231, 235, 236, 239
Paris, 200
Paris Agreement, 177
Partition, 33
Passenger Named Records Database (PNRD), 201
Patel, Priti, 9, 43, 102, 106, 107, 111, 136
Paternalistic, 32, 51, 52, 96, 193, 223
Patriotic Front (PF), 140
Pax Americana, 14
Pax Britannica, 14
Pergau Dam, 96
Plantation, 125, 127, 132, 133, 137, 138, 144–146, 175, 229
Planning, 126
Police, 15, 138, 173, 174, 190, 195, 204, 206, 211, 212, 214, 230, 233, 237, 239
Policy space, 69, 71, 75, 76, 80, 83, 124, 129, 145, 147, 148

Pollution, 164, 168, 174, 234
Populism, 2, 3, 5, 6, 129
Postcolonialsim, 15
Post-Washington Consensus, 39, 62, 71, 99, 113, 127, 155
Poverty, 19, 20, 67, 69, 70, 97, 106, 108, 130, 170, 189, 191, 224, 227, 233, 234
Poverty reduction, 8, 39, 40, 41, 53, 62, 65, 67, 69–71, 80–82, 84, 94–101, 106, 108, 111, 113, 116, 123–125, 127, 129, 134, 137, 143, 157–159, 163, 177, 178, 224, 229
Primary exports, 81
Private equity funds, 128, 131, 134, 135, 139, 143, 147, 148
Private military companies (PMCs), 190, 224, 229, 232
Private sector, 39, 71, 78, 82, 99, 113, 126, 127, 134, 135, 155, 157–159, 161, 169, 228
Private sector development (PSD), 5, 71, 125, 135, 147, 155, 157
Privatisation, 107–109, 113, 115, 131
Production Sharing Agreement (PSA), 170
Profit, 124, 161, 175, 177, 197, 224
Prosperity Party (PP), 108
Protectionist, 31, 44, 45, 51, 61, 79, 82, 226
Psychological hierarchy, 23
Public Interest Law Centre (PILC), 166
Putin, Vladimir, 208

R
Raab, Dominic, 105
Race, 6, 22
Racialisation, 14
Racism, 8, 22
Radicalisation, 41, 98

Ramaphosa, Cyril, 173, 174, 178
Rape, 109, 113, 203, 204, 206, 207, 210, 211, 214
Raw materials, 35, 79, 107, 127, 145, 147, 162, 178
Realist, 40–42, 94–96, 99, 100, 102–104, 110–112, 114, 115
Rebel militia, 191
Redundancies, 140, 174
Reeves, Rachel, 138
Refugees, 10, 189, 191, 200, 201, 206, 208, 214, 226, 235–237
Regime change, 8, 195, 196, 210, 231, 237
Regional Economic Communities (RECs), 62
Regionalisms, 12
Regional value chains, 77, 80, 231
Regulations, 155, 158
Remain politicians, 2, 200
Reparations, 224, 225, 232, 234, 235
Reputation, 24, 96, 98, 113, 131, 137, 176, 192–194, 229, 234, 235
Resource curse, 170, 179
Respiratory diseases, 143, 171
Rhodesia, 37–39, 53
Rights and Accountability in Development (RAID), 165
Right-wing, 5, 6, 42, 99, 129
Rio Tinto, 174
Roman Empire, 202
Rule of law, 44, 52, 93, 161, 191, 192
Rules of origin, 77
Russia, 1, 17, 49, 208, 209, 224, 230
Rwanda, 10, 42, 48, 94, 105, 110–112, 114, 228, 229, 235, 236

S
Sadiq Khan, 139
Safeguard measures, 69
Sandline International, 192
Sarah Champion, 107
Scandals, 96, 103, 139, 174, 193, 234
Scandal, Windrush, 9, 103
Scholarships, 172
School, 15, 16, 20, 133, 235, 237–239
Scotland, 7, 167
Scottish independence, 234, 239, 240
Scottish nationalism, 7
Secessionism, 170
Secrecy jurisdictions, 128, 134, 143, 147, 148
Securitisation, 5, 49, 95, 115, 137, 189, 190, 199, 202, 208, 212, 213, 227
Security, 4, 5, 15, 25, 32, 34, 35, 40–42, 46, 48, 50–54, 69, 72, 93, 96, 98, 104, 112, 113, 115, 132, 138, 139, 189–191, 197–212, 223–227, 230, 233, 235, 237–239
Security partnerships, 203
Senegal, 64
Sensitive goods basket, 65
Serious Fraud Office (SFO), 164, 176, 229
Seven Energy, 140, 141
Sexual assaults, 189, 212
Sexual violence, 206, 211, 214
Shadow Cabinet, 10, 138, 230
Shell, 194, 196, 204, 210
Short, Clare, 40, 96, 198
Sierra Leone, 41, 46, 98, 190–194, 198, 199, 212, 230, 236
Smallholders, 176
Smith, Adam, 52
Social clauses, 77, 79
Socialist, 23

INDEX 259

Social prosperity, 65, 78, 82, 93, 113, 214
Social services, 42, 100, 168
Soft power, 4, 93, 102, 125, 194, 210
Somalia, 42, 194, 199, 201, 205, 227, 236
South Africa, 21, 33, 37, 38, 42, 47, 53, 73, 75, 160, 173, 174, 198, 226
Southern Africa, 38, 63, 81
Southern African Customs Union plus Mozambique (SACUM), 73
Southern African Customs Union (SACU), 66
Southern Agricultural Growth Corridor (SAGCOT), 175
South Sudan, 42, 164, 199, 205, 229, 236
Sovereignty, 2, 11, 13, 16, 23, 48, 52, 54, 81, 95, 113, 144, 148, 178, 190, 202, 209, 211, 226, 235–238
Soviet Union, 53, 202
Special Anti-Robbery Squad (SARS), 203, 204
Sphere of influence, 11, 208, 227
Sri Lanka, 33, 36
Starmer, Keir, 10, 52, 138, 139, 177, 214, 230
State-building, 205
Stephenson, Andrew, 70
Stiglitz, Joseph, 71, 155, 157
Strike, 173
Structural adjustment programmes (SAPs), 126, 158
Sugar, 174–176
Suicide, 207
Sunak, Rishi, 9, 45, 47, 50, 79, 105, 110, 115, 177, 207, 223, 230
Sustainable development, 65, 70, 175
Sweatshop labour, 156
Switzerland, 164

Syria, 200, 201

T
Taliban, 192
Tanzania, 2, 66, 78, 159, 160, 175, 198
Tariff, 12, 35–37, 63–66, 68, 71, 74, 75, 77, 80, 81, 83, 84, 106
Taxation, 134, 143, 148, 157, 159, 166, 178, 180, 211, 232
Tax havens, 134
Technology, 49, 166
Telecoms industry, 108
Telegraph, The, 48, 172
Thatcher, Margaret, 7, 38, 39, 42, 96, 195
Third Way, the, 39, 68, 94, 97, 155, 157, 164, 180, 230
Tigray People's Liberation Front (TPLF), 108
Tigray War, 108, 229
Times, The, 49
Titanium, 174
Tobruk, 196
Togo, 163
Tourism, 171
Trade, 4, 11, 12, 19, 20, 23, 24, 25, 31, 32, 36, 37, 38, 39, 42, 44–49, 51, 52, 61–84, 93–98, 102–104, 106–108, 111–115, 160, 161, 197, 223, 224, 226, 228, 230–232, 235–238
Trade liberalisation, 24, 36, 63, 64, 67, 76, 80, 81, 106, 231, 238
Trade Partnership Agreement (TPA), 74
Trade unions, 24
Training, 172, 190, 194, 199, 203, 205, 207, 211, 214, 230, 236
Transition organisation, 34
Trevelyan, Anne-Marie, 71, 73
Trickle-down, 78, 82

Tripoli, 195–197
Truman, 130
Trump, Donald, 70, 112
Truss, Liz, 47, 49–51, 73, 141, 163
Tullow Oil, 114, 167–170, 173, 177, 179, 181
Tunisia, 63, 162, 190, 208
Turkana, 167, 169–171, 179
Turkey, 200, 201

U
UK-Africa Investment Summit, 49
UK Department for International Trade (DIT), 61, 69, 197
UK Export Finance (UKEF), 5, 156
UK Global Tariff (UKGT), 74
UK Independence Party (UKIP), 46
UK media, 42, 200
Ukraine, 107, 208, 214
UK Supreme Court, 177
UN General Secretary, 193
UN High Commissioner for Refugees (UNHCR), 207
Unilateral Declaration of Independence (UDI), 38
Unilever, 132, 156, 163, 175, 180
Union of African States, 18, 144
Unipolar, 192
United Africa, 12, 17
United Nations Global Compact (UNGC), 70
United Nations (UN), 18, 39, 49, 95, 100, 106, 127, 158, 192
United Party for National Development (UPND), 140
United States of America (USA), 11, 35
United States (US), 7, 50, 70, 132, 192
US Marshall Plan, 130

V
Vodafone, 108, 113, 114, 229
Volta Dam, 125

W
Wade, Abdoulaye, 64
Wagner group, 208, 230
Wales, 100
Wall Street Consensus, 125, 128, 129, 145–147, 163
Wanjiru, Agnes, 207
War on terror, 98, 113, 198, 213, 226, 227
War on terrorism, 41
Waste, 168, 234
Water, 127, 133, 134, 143, 162, 166, 168, 169, 175, 180, 233
Weapons of Mass Destruction (WMD), 194
Welfare state, 130, 131
West Africa Trade and Investment Forum, 163
Western Africa, 63
Westminster, 3, 5, 7, 39, 234, 239
West, the, 13, 16, 21, 129, 144, 145, 158, 191
White Dominions, 32, 33, 53
Whitehall, 42, 52
White Man's Burden, 32
White settler, 33, 36, 44
White supremacism, 10, 14
Windrush Scandal, 9, 103
Women, Peace and Security (WPS), 206, 207
Workers, 111, 124, 128, 132–135, 138–141, 145–147, 163, 164, 173, 174, 180, 181, 198, 229, 233, 237, 238
Working-class, 2, 7, 10
World Trade Organisation (WTO), 13, 63, 94
World War Two (WW2), 2, 32, 130

WTO Hong Kong Summit, 97
WTO Singapore Ministerial
  Conference, 79

Y
Yaoundé Conventions, 37

Youth, 70, 123, 146, 172, 192

Z
Zambeef, 133, 139–141, 144
Zenawi, Meles, 108
Zimbabwe, 39, 73, 79, 98

MIX
Papier aus verantwortungsvollen Quellen
Paper from responsible sources
FSC® C105338

If you have any concerns about our products,
you can contact us on
ProductSafety@springernature.com

In case Publisher is established outside the EU,
the EU authorized representative is:
**Springer Nature Customer Service Center GmbH
Europaplatz 3, 69115 Heidelberg, Germany**

Printed by Libri Plureos GmbH
in Hamburg, Germany